AQUANAUT

AQUANAUT

A Life Beneath the Surface:
The Inside Story of the Thai Cave Rescue

RICK STANTON
with Karen Dealy

PEGASUS BOOKS
NEW YORK LONDON

AQUANAUT

Pegasus Books, Ltd.
148 West 37th Street, 13th Floor
New York, NY 10018

Copyright © 2022 by Rick Stanton

First Pegasus Books cloth edition January 2022

ISBN: 978-1-64313-919-7

10 9 8 7 6 5 4 3 2 1

Printed in the United States of America
Distributed by Simon & Schuster
www.pegasusbooks.com

My first example of courage, dignity, strength and
humanity came from a woman whose diminutive stature and quiet
nature did not prevent her from having a profound impact on the
lives around her.
Mum.

With one comment made, one night in front
of the television, you set my life on its course.
I owe this book, and the stories it contains, to you. I was called to
Tham Luang when I was fifty-seven, which was
your age when you departed. I wish you could have
seen your impact on the person I've become.
Thank you.

Contents

PART 4

Perform

Prologue
The End of the Line

Monday, 2 July 2018, Thailand

What could possibly go wrong?

I pulled myself through a tunnel of rock, blindly fighting against an underground river that was flowing deep inside a mountain. The current pushed against me so forcefully that it felt like the water – or maybe the mountain itself – was trying to keep me out. Thirteen young men had been the last to travel this path before me, and I had gone there to save them.

Although millions around the world were waiting and watching, hoping to hear news of the boys' safe discovery, many had already given up hope. (*They can't possibly still be alive in there.*) In the week since I had flown to Thailand to take part in this search, I had been plagued with thoughts about what I would be finding. I too assumed that the boys were dead, but that was unimportant to me. I stayed there, searching, pushing myself through the cave, because I had to see it through to the end. I had to see for myself.

Maybe I was just looking for an answer so that I could put an end to the searching.

This wasn't the first time I'd been sent into a cave to bring out a body, but this was the first time that the ones I was searching for were a group of children. That made a difference – that made a better story for the press – and the throngs of journalists camped on the mountain just outside served as an unmistakable sign that the world wanted to be given a happy ending.

More important to me than the media, though, were the mothers and families who had not left their posts on that mountain for over a week. I could walk past the cameras and microphones without a glance, but even I couldn't ignore the much smaller huddle of women, whispering prayers and watching us as we walked into the cave that held their sons. I avoided the women, but I knew they were there, and they acted as constant reminders of why I was there.

As the sun shone high in the midday sky on a fateful Saturday in late June, thirteen young men – all members of the Wild Boars football team – had walked into Tham Luang Nang Non cave, whose opening is on the side of a mountain in the Doi Nang Non range. The team had taken the same path that I am on now, but the way for them had been largely dry and clear. When they had taken this journey, they had moved forward by walking, scrambling and crawling. They had likely been talking and laughing as they went along, perhaps discussing Night's upcoming birthday party, or a recent school exam; perhaps Coach Ek had been reviewing some football moves he had taught them earlier that day in practice. I imagined the sounds of their voices and laughter echoing through the empty chambers, fading into the blackness that surrounded their feeble lights. The solid feeling of sediment beneath their hands and feet would have been reassuring to them as they moved along and encouraged each other onward, scrambling over boulders and crawling on their bellies through the low sections. The journey would have been physical and demanding, an exercise in spirit and solidarity for the team.

Not only were they not afraid, they didn't realize that they should be.

While they were scurrying their way forwards through the cave, with the lighthearted goal of etching their names into the mud at the far end, rain had started falling onto the mountain above them. The boys were nestled within the silence of the cave, protected from the elements and unaware of the danger approaching them, as rain seeped through the layers of rock. The open cave passage provided a clear funnel for the water to flow through, as it had done so many times before, and the cave began to fill. When the team finally turned to make their way out, they found that their playground had drastically changed.

With their exit blocked, the team made an unusual decision. Instead of staying where they were and waiting for rescue, the group turned back into the mountain and moved deeper into the cave. This time they weren't chasing an adventure; now they were hoping for survival. By the time the moon had risen above, they were trapped inside with a kilometre of rock above them and 2,300 metres of flooding cave passage behind them.

They were utterly alone inside the mountain, isolated from the rest of the world by the elements that were surrounding them and the rain that continued to fall outside. They might as well have been on another planet.

Ten days later, John and I were there, following the boys' path into the cave through a passage that was now largely underwater. Our way forward was made not by scrambling and scurrying, but by finning and feeling. I reached out ahead of me, using my fingers to guide me. I was prepared at any moment to feel my hand collide with something soft and fleshy: a floating corpse that would have decayed rapidly after being submerged in warm water for more than a week. The discovery wouldn't be pleasant.

'But that is why you're here,' I reminded myself.

The water was so thick with silt that I could barely see my hand in front of my face. I had high-powered lights attached to my helmet, but they were ineffective in this murk. I only had one turned on, and that was at its lowest setting; it produced a dim glow in the brown water, which I found comforting. I listened to the reassuring mechanical sounds of my breath moving through the regulator between my lips. I breathed in air that had a familiar metallic tang. As I exhaled, bubbles escaped through my regulator and were released into the water, where they rose up until they broke and dispersed against the ceiling above our heads. When diving in a cave – especially a cave with poor visibility – you learn to rely on your senses in different ways than you do above ground. This was all so familiar to me.

People who are not cave divers often describe cave diving as the most dangerous sport in the world, while caves are seen by many as hostile and frightening places to be avoided at all costs. Hollywood films use caves as the setting for horrors imagined by our subconscious and appearing in our nightmares. Not all of us turn away, though. Some of us are beckoned into caves by the mystery of the unexplored. We take comfort in the very things that bring fear to others. Caves are where we belong.

I was eighteen when I entered my first cave, and in some ways I've never left.

$$\oplus \quad \oplus \quad \oplus$$

The change in pressure inside my ears indicated that I was rising, while a change of note in the exhaled bubbles suggested they were now reaching an air surface. I moved upwards very slowly, mindful of the stalactites hanging from the ceiling. The weight of my helmet returned as I lifted my head above the surface, and I watched the brown water slowly recede down my mask like a falling tide. We found ourselves in an underground canal – a gloomy passage about 6 metres wide, its walls arching up to a ceiling that peaked 4 metres above our heads.

The water here was just shallow enough to let us balance on the tips of our fins with our heads and shoulders above the surface. When we reached these canal passages, we'd raise our heads out of the water to take a quick rest and discuss next steps.

'How far have we travelled?' . . . 'Shall we continue?' . . . 'How much line is left?'

Much like Ariadne's thread, given to Theseus before he entered the labyrinth of the Minotaur, cave divers use a line to mark their way to the exit as they proceed through a cave. John indicated that his reel was very nearly empty, with about 20 metres left before he'd reach the end of the line. It was time to turn around.

As we were several hours into this journey, I'd started to feel a bit hungry. After a moment of rest, I remembered that I still had to lift my mask as I had done before, so I could smell for signs of life. Thinking about the Snickers bar I had tucked in my wetsuit pocket, I reached for my mask, lifting it away from my face and breaking the seal to expose my nose to the surrounding atmosphere.

In that moment, everything changed.

I was immediately struck by the pungent air, so thick it was suffocating as it entered my nostrils and mouth. The stench of decay was overpowering, unmistakable, and not unfamiliar. I'd smelled this before – in other caves and at other times – and my stomach churned as I recognized what it meant. *They must be dead. We've found their bodies.* This thought was followed almost immediately with a consolation. *At least we've finally found something.*

'John, they're here,' I said to him. 'Smell for yourself.'

I watched him as he lifted his mask, then he looked at me and nodded in agreement. We'd certainly found something. John and I were still looking at each other, our thoughts racing, when we received our next shock: voices. One teenaged male voice, and then another. Thoughts and questions raced between us silently. *The boys! They're alive!? How many?*

I knew that we were considering the same possibilities, and my mind quickly settled on the option that seemed like the worst but most likely. We'd be finding some boys alive, with the others dead or dying. I realized with horror that we had been so focused on the search that the reality of finding them had never been fully thought through. Nobody had prepared for this. From this moment on, I knew that we would be flying blind.

'The two of you wanted to be calling the shots . . .' a voice in my head taunted.

Knowing that we would have to move the deceased away from the boys who were still alive, John and I began discussing where we could take the corpses. Our planning stopped when we saw the faint glow of a weak electric torch, coming from around a bend and several metres above us, accompanied by the muffled shuffling sounds of people moving closer. With a few quick words and gestures, we began taking off our equipment, leaving it on a sand bank. Partially de-kitted, we moved through the water towards the voices. I saw John fumbling with something and I realized he'd had the foresight to set up and switch on the waterproof camera that had been given to him that morning by the Royal Thai Navy SEALs.

I raised my eyes towards the voices and received the third surprise in what felt like a lifetime, but which had only been a few short minutes. The lights mounted on our helmets shone upwards to a muddy slope that was holding a group of young men. The focused beams illuminated the Wild Boars – still alive and still dressed in their football clothes – as they descended towards us, gingerly easing themselves down the ramp on their haunches. Within a moment they'd all gathered before us, taking centre-stage beneath our roaming spotlights. Although they were skinny and appeared frail, their very presence was a testament to their strength. Their grins lit up the passage, and their eyes gleamed brightly as they looked at the two strangers who had just arrived, as if from another world.

I quickly began scanning the bodies and counting. *One, two three . . . eight, nine . . .* We had come in looking for thirteen. As I counted, I heard John's voice call out clearly, resonating in the hollow chamber.

'How many of you?'

I finished my quick headcount at thirteen. Unbelievable.

'They're all alive,' I said, incredulously, just as one of the voices answered John's question: 'Thirteen.'

'Thirteen?' John echoed, in disbelief. 'Brilliant.'

The surprise and relief heard in our voices during that exchange revealed what John and I had been expecting to find in the cave that day.

This scene that John captured has been shown around the world and seen by millions. When I look back and watch this video, as I still do occasionally, I am struck by several things.

How remarkable was the strength and spirit of the boys, who had been able to remain calm and clear-headed during their time in the darkness and even during their unexpected visit from two strange men clad in black neoprene, one of whom was wearing an inflated inner tube on his back.[1]

How fortunate that John had been given the camera on that day, with the sole intention of recording features in the cave for the Thai SEALs who were waiting on the surface. Instead, it had been used to record a moment whose global impact could – and likely will – never be replicated.

Finally, I can't help but recognize the personal significance of that moment. I had spent my life building a very specific and refined set of skills and experiences, all of which had led me to that place at that time. In many ways it seems that I had spent my life preparing to find – and then ultimately rescue – those boys. Yet I'd be lying if I said I was expecting any of this to happen as it did.

PART ONE
Plan

I.

Water Flowing Underground

'Rick Stanton is not the most domesticated of men.'
Amanda Mitchison, *Sunday Telegraph*

In the centre of England is a city called Coventry, which is best known for a number of unique reasons. One thousand years ago, Lady Godiva rode through the market centre, naked on horseback, while being spied upon by the original Peeping Tom. Nine hundred years later, Britain's first car was built in the then-industrial city. During the Second World War, the city was famously bombed in the 'Coventry Blitz', during which its sprawling cathedral was demolished. The city has had a long and varied history, and somewhere along the way – most likely due to its containment of prisoners during the Civil War – an English idiom was born. 'Being sent to Coventry' has come to mean being effectively erased, ostracized, treated as though you don't exist. Nothing could be worse than being sent to Coventry, according to the phrase, yet this is where I live.

Near the centre of Coventry, there is a modest residential street that is lined with semi-detached homes and comfortable cars. One house on this street stands out a bit from the others: its loose fascia and guttering need to be replaced; the paint flaking off the cracked rendering signals a long-overdue renovation; the tall grass, withered rosebushes and visible weeds in front of the house reveal a distinct lack of interest in gardening. The inside of this house is even less welcoming, with diving equipment strewn throughout the living and dining rooms, a lathe and milling machine standing where the dining table used to be found, and kayaks spanning the floor. The walls have unrepaired holes; the thin carpeting has been worn through in places; and a kitchen wall bears the scar of a cupboard that I tore down one day when I was struck with the urge to renovate the kitchen, before quickly losing interest.

This is my home, though it is not very homey.

When the reporter arrives at my front door, accompanied by a cameraman, I lead them quickly through the ground floor of the house, through the sliding glass door at the back and onto the paved garden. I've placed two garden chairs in an empty space, and as the cameraman sets up his tripod, I see the reporter looking around. Is this what he was expecting to find? Instead of keeping a green garden behind the house, I've laid down block paving to create a place where I can work. Clothing and diving gear are hanging to dry on the washing line, industrial gas storage cylinders are standing against the house, and a bare Land Rover chassis is parked outside the towering garage.

I had the garage built after I moved in, and it covers an area of land more than half that of my house. I know that some neighbours may consider it to be an oversized eyesore, but it is as essential to me as the house itself. Inside live my Land Rover and an unbuilt off-road buggy. My kayaks take up any remaining walking space on the floor and hang overhead from the exposed wooden beams of the ceiling joists. The shelving on the side walls is packed with diving cylinders, equipment, tools, loose hardware – all of which had been overflowing from inside my house before I gave them a new home.

When the builders had completed the garage structure, the front and rear door openings were left unfinished. Years have passed, but

I still haven't got around to properly installing doors; instead, I use two large sheet-metal doors – leaning against the rear wall and braced by spare tyres – to secure my gear from the entry behind it.

As the reporter speaks with the cameraman, I sit down and look over at the opening of the garage. I do need to take care of those doors, particularly because the items held in the garage are the things which are most valuable to me. Still, I can't be arsed. I have endless and constantly evolving lists of things to do running through my head all the time, and fitting garage doors never rises to the top in terms of urgency.

Dismissing the idea of ever having a properly completed garage, I'm suddenly reminded of the feedback I'd received from teachers in school. They'd all been pretty consistent: pointing out my lack of effort in class, too much time spent daydreaming, never showing interest in the things I was supposed to. Most of them were the typical 'He shows potential, but . . .' comments, but I've always remembered a report given to me just prior to O-level exams:[1] 'Richard continues to do just enough to get by satisfactorily without putting himself out. He must shake off his usual comatose condition if luck is not to play the most important part in his O-level results. Of course, I realize that such action is out of character and highly unlikely.'

As my form teacher, Mr D. A. Boreham had come to know me quite well over the course of several years. He'd made regular reports of my progress during that time, and his reports had all shared this common theme: generalized apathy. The criticism was fair. I'd passed all of my exams easily, but nothing ever held my interest or motivated me to extend my effort beyond the requirements in most of my classes. In his final report, Mr Boreham had gone on to write something like: 'Richard is showing us an economy of effort. It's a dangerous game, and I hope it works out for him.'

An economy of effort. I'd found that thoroughly amusing and have held onto that report for all of these years – it lives in a filing cabinet in my office, crammed in between newspaper clippings and old logbooks. When I presented this report to my parents, though, they hadn't been quite as happy with it as I would come to be.

'I didn't raise you to be lazy,' my father said, and he was correct. I was never lazy, but I have always been very selective with the things that I choose to spend energy on; it just so happened that none of those things occurred in school. Displaying this economy of effort was not valued in the home where I was raised, unfortunately. My parents displayed their own sense of economy for material possessions, but they placed high value on the effort that a person puts into their actions.

'Mind what you're doing,' was my father's oft-repeated mantra. Plan for what you're going to do, he was telling us, and then be mindful of everything while doing it. Act with purpose. I agreed very much with his motto, while also displaying an economy of effort. I was always very mindful of what I was doing when I was doing something important; I just found fewer things important than most people.

I grew up in Buckhurst Hill, a small Essex town on the north-eastern outskirts of London, with two supportive parents and a younger sister. Jane and I never wanted for anything and yet – like many restless children – I was content but not completely satisfied, and I had no idea why. It's hard to explain the feeling of missing something you have never known, of longing for a place you have never been, but that's kind of how I felt. I passed through most of my childhood and adolescence in a dream state, without really connecting to anything or anybody. I spent a lot of time alone, and it was rare that anything held my interest for very long.

The first thing that had sparked any excitement or curiosity was fishing, which I had taken up as a hobby. I'd just been looking for something to do to fill the time on weekends, but it soon began taking up all of my conscious thought as I began daydreaming and analysing every nuance of the activity. These endless thoughts became a sort of escapism, and I began disappearing for hours into the nearby Epping Forest with my rods and reels.

As members of the Christian Church of the Brethren,[2] my parents – and by extension my sister and I – lived a simple life. My father William and mother Josephine were pragmatic and level-headed, traits which have been passed onto both Jane and myself. My dad was an accounts manager in the Bank of China and appeared always to be working. When I was growing up, banks were open on Saturdays, and he worked six-day weeks. He'd often get home late from work, and by then he'd be tired. He was also a lay preacher, visiting different churches on Sundays,[3] so we really didn't see much of him. I never thought of him as being either happy or unhappy; I'd have just said he was very content. It was a content house.

I was forty when Dad passed away from congestive heart failure, and when I went to see him just before he died, he came out with that classic line: 'I wish I'd spent more time with you when you were growing up.' I know that a lot of parents say that, but I guess it had an impact. His words made me think: *While I haven't got any children and I never will . . . there's no point in sacrificing your life and not doing what you want to do, and then regretting it when you die.* The truth is, I'd already been living my life in that way – uncommitted, free to do what I wanted – but I guess his words confirmed the choices I'd been making.

Mum, on the other hand, was more engaged with family life. I would describe her as being quietly charismatic. She was always taking Jane and me on excursions that held some educational value; whether to help us learn about culture or facets of the countryside, her efforts were all geared towards giving us a broader education to foster our independence. (My cousin Sallie later reflected that Mum had brought me up to be independent, but she may have gone too far.) Those outings stand out among my earliest childhood memories, particularly the ones when my mum acted in some way that caught me by surprise.

She once took us to an agricultural market, where we stood watching an auctioneer leading the crowd in rounds of mad bidding for various livestock. The energy from the crowd was as real as the smell of manure permeating the air. Soon after we arrived, the next item up for bid was presented: a massive breeding sow, so big that it looked almost comical. I stared at the pig in awe until I suddenly noticed the auctioneer was nodding towards my mother as he called out the prices, as if she was the one placing the bids. In one fleeting exchange – which might have cleared up my confusion, if I'd seen it – the auctioneer had met my mother's eye and, with a quick wink, their game had begun. It was a game only he and she were a part of, with the other bidders fixated on their potential purchase. Having missed their silent interchange, I was perplexed. *Is she bidding on that thing? What on earth are we going to do with it?*

When the auction ended, as confused bidders approached her with questions, Mum just laughed and took my hand as we left the crowd. I'm not sure why she and the auctioneer had been so keen to play along; I suppose some people like to be invited in on other people's games.

Another time when I was quite young, the three of us were on the tube to London, probably heading for Oxford Street to go shopping. This was a favourite Saturday excursion of mine and Jane's, because we'd always end the day in Hamleys toy store.[4] This time, we changed trains at a tube station – I believe it was Chancery Lane – just as there was a riotous clash between football fans going on. It was the late 1960s, when football hooliganism was rife. Two teams had got off the same train and there was utter chaos. The stations aren't very wide, maybe 5 metres across; people were jostling each other and coming to blows.

I looked up at Mum for guidance. *What should we do?* There's no reason why they would attack a mother and her children, but I expected Mum to hesitate, to play it safe and hold back until she could see a way to avoid the intimidating crowd, as I was seeing other mothers do with their children on the sides of the station. Mum calmly took our hands and led us through the pandemonium fearlessly. She walked straight into the crowd and out the other side. She was a tiny lady – standing only 5'2" – but she hadn't hesitated.

That's how she was. Small in stature, but large in presence. On the surface she was a mild-mannered housewife, a mother who had dedicated her life to raising her family. She lived happily, taking pride in her home and her children, and the security she'd provided allowed us to develop into confident and independent adults. Still, I remember those stories, the glimpses of her character, and they tell me that there was more to Josephine Stanton than was easily seen with the eye. What was lying underneath that calm surface? Unfortunately, I never learned the answer to that question. I was twenty-five when she passed away, too consumed with my own life to be a part of hers.

While I was growing up, our conversations were never intensely personal nor particularly revealing; emotions were never discussed in our home. Therefore, I appreciate the insight shown one evening when I was seventeen years old. I was sitting in the living room, watching a programme on television, when she suddenly called to me from the kitchen.

'Richard . . . I think you might be interested in watching this.' Intrigued, I switched to the channel she'd indicated.

On the dark television screen, pins of light suddenly appeared, growing larger as they approached the camera. As a diving mask became visible, the lights revealed themselves to be torches mounted to the diver's helmet. The words 'Once in a Lifetime' floated in script across the screen, followed by the show's paradoxical title: *The Underground Eiger*.[5] As the diver moved through the frame and my living room filled with the mechanical sound of underwater breathing, I sat back, entranced. The camera panned across the peaks of the Yorkshire Dales and then began heading downward, alluding to the cavities formed by the 'disappearing rivers' that cut vertical shafts into and through the landscape, to create a hidden world. The narrator mentioned those who have spent – or sacrificed – their lives in an attempt to answer two questions.

'What was down there?' and 'Where does all that water go to?'

I was transfixed as I watched the story of Oliver 'Bear' Statham and Geoff Yeadon, mates who were considered two of the most skilled cave divers in Britain. First we see Geoff, waking up from his makeshift bed in the back of his vehicle, a Morris Traveller that has to be push-started from its place on the side of a road. After driving to meet Oliver, who lives in a shabby but comfortable flat with his partner Anne, they go to work in a pottery barn in the Yorkshire Dales, where they sell pots and mugs to fund their passion of cave diving. They live modestly but are happy and doing what they love. They are free.

I didn't know people lived like that, and everything about their lives immediately resonated with me. I hung on every word as they calmly recounted the story of their first dive together, which had nearly ended with Oliver's death. They discussed what had gone wrong during the dive, how they had responded to make sure they both got out alive, and what the dive had taught them. More than friends, they were two parts of one team, with complete trust in each other. The bond between them was apparent.

The film shows a pre-emptive celebration being held for them on the night before their dive, 'just in case'.[6] I watched as the group of cavers and friends spent the night laughing, dancing, and drinking at the Old Hill Inn.

Early the next morning, the men are seen donning the 'accoutrement of complex equipment' needed for their dive. Rubber flippers and neoprene suits. A harness made of nylon webbing around their waist. Diving cylinders hanging from the harness, one on each side. A helmet with four mounted torches. As I watched, I realized I was making mental notes, recording every detail. To me, it looked otherworldly.

With everything in place and burdened by the weight of their equipment, they need to be helped to their feet and to the water's edge. Once submerged, however, they become buoyant and graceful, hovering just below the surface as they test their equipment before descending out of sight. I wanted to know what that felt like.

While the divers are in the cave, Anne is alone on the surface. She stands on the ground above them and uses underground communication devices to follow their progress. 'They're just approaching Dead Man's Handshake,' she says. 'This will be the worst part.' When asked how she would feel if something went wrong, she takes a breath. 'Well, I can't really say how I would feel. Cave diving is such an all-or-nothing sport, really. If anything went wrong, they would die.' She looks at the filmmaker and says calmly, 'It's not something that you can be rescued from.' I was enticed by what she called the 'worst part' – the restriction known as Dead Man's Handshake – and I wondered how I would fare passing through the narrow squeeze.

Geoff and Oliver would become the first to follow the route of the underground river from West Kingsdale Master Cave to where it later re-emerges at Keld Head. They had been working for years to make this connection, creeping closer with each dive – 'Seeing the limb of the Kingsdale Master Cave creeping towards the limit of our Keld Head explorations was intoxicating,' Geoff has said[7] – and the film shows them finally making the full traverse. The pay-off dive.

As I sat in my living room, their path through the cave – a record-breaking 1,800-metre dive – was displayed on the television screen. I studied the diagram and for the first time I considered how water flows underground. I tried to imagine myself inside a mountain, breathing underwater, searching for the way forward, following a river as it snakes through layers of earth.

I knew immediately. *I could do this. This is what I want to do.*

I already knew of the caves that lie underground in England, and I was vaguely interested in caving. I'd read Jacques Cousteau's books, and I knew enough about scuba diving to think that I'd like to try it. But something had been missing that had kept it from grabbing my imagination or motivating me to do anything. Watching *The Underground Eiger* revealed the missing element: exploration. Being the first to find the way on, discovering new places, extending maps, making connections – that's what made it significant. And it could be done right here in the UK. Those hills I'd walked on had unexplored caves underneath them. I found that idea thrilling, and I couldn't turn away.

At seventeen years old, I was in my final year of school with plans to continue my studies by going to university in the autumn. Without any burning passions calling me towards a particular career path, I had halfheartedly selected Transport and Urban Planning as my course of study. Truthfully, I hadn't been excited about any of it. But now . . .

I'll join the university's caving club. And the diving club.

Which caving areas will be most easily accessible? What will I need to learn?

Instead of sleeping that night, I lay in bed with my heart racing as I mentally replayed every scene of the documentary I had watched earlier. I had finally found direction. I knew what I wanted to do, and I knew that nothing would stop me. It was 21 February 1979. The day had begun like many others, but before it ended the course of my life had been changed.

Eight months after watching the film, I experienced my first venture into a cave, and the regular underground trips quickly became the main focus of my life. ('Richard traded one obsession for another,' Jane later pointed out, reflecting on how my intense focus had switched from fishing to cave diving.) Over the years, I've thought about that viewing of *The Underground Eiger* many times, particularly when I found myself seeming to re-enact the experiences of Geoff and Oliver.

I've had more than my share of nights spent sleeping on the side of a road in the back of my own vehicle (usually a Land Rover Defender). The 'specialized diving equipment' has expanded over the past forty years, as I've learned to carefully select, modify and then build my own equipment to take me where I need to go. Testing the equipment prior to a dive, talking through a dive plan, spending years on a chosen project – these have all become routine to me, as have the numerous nights spent in pubs surrounded by caving friends. Some of those nights were even spent at the Old Hill Inn, the same one visited by Geoff and Bear.

When I was seventeen years old, that party scene in the documentary had made as much of an impression on me as the underwater scenes had done. I was very shy in school and had only a few close friends; seeing the camaraderie among the group of cavers had made me yearn to experience that for myself.

With the wisdom afforded by the personal experience I have gained over the years, I can also watch the documentary now and understand the things that had not been shown.

I understand what Oliver was thinking as he recounted that he and Geoff had had 'no rapport' on their disastrous first dive. That rapport – involving trust, non-verbal communication, the ability to stay calm and think two moves ahead – has meant the difference between life and death for my diving partners, and for me, on several occasions.

I value the importance of meticulous preparation. I know the countless hours, days, weeks and months that are required in planning every step of a dive, playing out all scenarios and contingencies, imagining and accounting for every risk. Just as important as the planning is the practice: building up to a final dive with scores of practice dives, adding one new element to each dive, making tiny steps forward in a plan as muscle memory is built. Every step in the preparation is critical for success, and the process is painstakingly time-consuming.

Life-consuming.

I have felt the excitement of finding a next big project, tempered with the knowledge that I would have to see it through to its conclusion, whatever that meant. When something is important to me, I can't leave it unfinished, and this trait has been a curse in my life as much as it has been a blessing. I've spent years visiting the same cave, going back until a conclusive terminus is reached and closure has been achieved.

I know what it means to leave someone waiting alone on the surface, not knowing what's happening underground. I've learned what it does to a person to watch their partner disappear, determined to reach a destination from which they might not return.

For most of my life, that had been my life.

⊕   ⊕   ⊕

After four decades, the grip of the caves began to weaken as I found myself spending less time underground and more time on the water's surface. I was pleased that many of my caving friends showed interest in joining me on kayaking trips, even if it meant I was often blamed for their growing boat collections. One of these friends is Jonathan Sims, a UK-born caver who had heeded my advice to take up kayaking. Jonathan spends most of his time in China, so I was surprised when he rang me from England one day in the spring of 2018 to invite me out for a day of paddling with himself and a friend.

'Her name is Amp,' Jonathan told me. 'She works as a dementia care specialist for my parents in Thailand, and they adore her; she's like part of our family. She's here visiting for a couple of weeks and she's keen to go on a kayak trip. Would you come with us? It'll be great to see you and catch up.' I knew that Jonathan was probably inviting me because he wanted me to do the work of organizing the trip, but I didn't mind. I was always looking for a chance to paddle, so I immediately agreed and started to plan the day.

She's a tourist, I thought, *so she'll like something scenic and iconic.* The royal wedding of Meghan and Harry had been held in Windsor Castle earlier that week, viewed by millions around the world, and it gave me an idea. I began checking maps for spots to put in on the River Thames upstream of Windsor. Before long, I had planned a full day, with a paddle through town and lunch at a pub.

When the day arrived, I rode to Windsor by train and quickly realized that there was an unexpected adventure to be had. I was surprised to find myself quite taken with Amp, a Thai woman whose full name is Siriporn Bangngoen. As Jonathan had described, she was both lovely and keen on paddling. I was immediately impressed with how well she and I worked together while inflating the boat by the side of the river and then paddling together through the idyllic town. Although it was her first time in a kayak, she more than held her own with Jonathan and me, keeping up with us in both paddling and in good conversation.

Eventually, talk had turned to the subject of my involvement with cave rescues, one of which had involved Jonathan directly. 'How many people have you rescued from caves, Rick?' Amp asked me.

I did a quick count. 'Ten now. There were the six in Mexico, and then four others.' I hesitated. 'I'm not sure I should count those last four. Sure, they would have died if I hadn't been there . . . but if I hadn't been there, they would never have been in the cave in the first place.'

Jonathan laughed. 'I think you can count them.'

Amp continued with more questions about my cave rescues. 'I'd like to see something like that,' she said wistfully, after I'd described some of the more exciting moments.

When Jonathan dropped me at the train station, Amp and I vowed to keep in touch with each other, which we began doing immediately. Within a few days, she surprised me by offering to abandon her remaining holiday plans so that she could spend more time with me in Coventry. I'd painted a horrendous picture of my house, and this woman who had never been to the UK before was willing to give up her time in London to come here?

I was impressed by her enthusiasm and spent a few days acting as her tour guide, showing her the more appealing areas of Coventry[8] and nearby Warwick Castle. Before we knew it, her holiday was ending, and it was time for her to return to Thailand. 'I really enjoy your life,' she told me before boarding her bus for London. 'No pressure. Calm and exciting.'

She flew home to Thailand on a Saturday, while I spent the weekend with old friends for a reunion and a paddling trip down the River Tryweryn. Then, on Monday morning, I received an urgent message from her: 'Please call me the moment you wake up . . . I've got a feeling that you're coming to Chiang Rai.' Intrigued, I dialled Amp's number.

'Have you heard about the football team stuck in a cave near me?' she asked in greeting. Being completely uninterested in team sports, all I heard was 'football team', and my initial reaction was dismissive. 'Why would I care about football?' I scoffed. She patiently explained to me that this wasn't a sports story, but the plight of a group of boys trapped in a cave.

'People get lost in caves all the time,' I told her, still unconcerned. 'I'm sure they'll find their way out eventually.'

The news had not yet broken far outside the province in northern Thailand where the drama was unfolding, so Amp had to fill me in. A football team had gone into a nearby cave after their Saturday practice. Heavy rains had begun to fall, and their exit had been flooded with water. Thailand's rainy season typically extends from July until November, so there was no chance of the cave emptying any time soon. The boys had no way of getting out.

'They're only kids, and they've already been missing for forty-eight hours,' she said. I could hear the urgency in her voice. 'I think it's serious.'

I first heard of the boys in the cave in Thailand on Monday morning, 25 June 2018. I had no way of knowing what was about to happen in the next few weeks, but I knew one person who I wanted to share this information with. I ended the call with Amp and dialled John Volanthen.

'Something's happening in Thailand,' I said as soon as he answered, then relayed the information Amp had shared. 'Do you think we should get involved?'

'I think we should make attempts,' was his immediate reply. 'We have to act.'

And that is how two unlikely men from Britain – one a pensioner, the other a computer geek – became involved in what would become one of the greatest rescue missions on record.

'Please call me the moment you wake up . . . I've got a feeling that you're coming to Chiang Rai.'

Saturday, 23 June 2018, Thailand
The Search Phase

The Wild Boars meet for their weekly practice on Saturday mornings in the northern Thai province of Chiang Rai. This region is known as the Golden Triangle because of its shared borders with Myanmar and Laos, as well as its notoriety for being a prime location for smuggling drugs between those borders. The political boundary cuts through the village of Mae Sai but does not divide its people, who live harmoniously and depend on each other to work

Location of Tham Luang Cave in Chiang Rai, Thailand

towards a common goal. Their lives are intertwined with the physical environment and the myths that have been embedded into it; the caves, mountains, forests and rains are imbued with mystical powers and warnings for the local residents.

The Wild Boars[9] youth football club was founded to give boys in the community a place to go after school. The members live simple lives, some are stateless,[10] and many of the players attend school together. The team's head coach, Nopparat (nicknamed[11] Nop), sees his players more days than not – training them in soccer, helping them with schoolwork and even taking medicine to their homes when they are sick. They are more than teammates; they are family.

The 23rd of June 2018 began like many other Saturdays. The team trained together for a few hours in the morning – playing a pre-match warm-up – and then some of them departed for home while others planned what they were going to do next. They were all looking forward to spending the evening together, celebrating teammate Peerapat Sompiangjai (Night)'s sixteenth birthday and the boys who remained wanted to find something to fill the hours before the party. Ekkapol Chantawong (Ek), their twenty-five-year-old assistant coach, suggested that they could ride their bicycles to the nearby mountain to explore Tham Luang Nam Nang Non (Great Cave of the Sleeping Lady), a cave system where some of them had been before. In a few weeks the monsoon would begin, and then the cave would be closed off to visitors for the remainder of the year, but today the sun was shining and the sky was clear.

Still wearing their football strips and with their backpacks slung on their backs, twelve Wild Boars, led by their assistant coach, set off by bicycle for Doi Nang Non (Mountain of the Sleeping Lady).[12] Included in the group were: Ek, Night, Pornchai Kamluang (Tee, 16), Pipat Pho (Nick, 15), Prajak Sutham (Note, 14), Adul Sam-on (14), Ekarat Wongsukchan (Bew, 14), Nattawut Takamrong (Tern,

14), Mongkol Booneiam (Mark, 13), Panumas Sangdee (Mig, 13), Duganpet Promtep (Dom, 13), Somepong Jaiwong (Pong, 13), and Chanin Vibulrungruang (Titan, 11).

The boys were looking for a mini-adventure, a fun way to pass the afternoon. For the next eighteen days, the world would be watching to see how it all would end.

Outside of Tham Luang's entrance stands a sign – boldly printed in both English and Thai – which provides a clear warning that the cave succumbs to annual flooding and will be closed from July to November. In 2018, the rain began earlier than predicted. Just prior to the boys' arrival in late June, three days of heavy rain had fallen, filling the surface streams with water that sank into the mountain. This should have set off alarm bells, and somebody should have considered the rain's implications for the cave inside, but the posted months were never questioned, and the park remained open.[13]

Petch is the name of the park ranger who was working on the Saturday when the boys entered the cave. He began making his rounds at 5 p.m., preparing to close up and go home, but the sight of a motorcycle outside the park delayed his departure. He re-entered to track down the straggling visitor who had stayed past curfew, expecting to find the owner of the motorbike inside. What he found instead was a row of bicycles, leaning against a handrail overlooking the cave's entrance. These alarm bells could not be ignored, and Petch immediately entered the cave.

The search had begun.

In the village of Mae Sai, Night's birthday party was paused, waiting for the guest of honour to arrive with his friends. Although the boys made a habit of staying out together for long stretches of time, their parents began to worry when they hadn't arrived for the party. Phones began ringing between homes, trying to track down the whereabouts of the missing boys. A Wild Boar who had gone home after practice, instead of joining the others at the cave, finally revealed the team's plan to visit Tham Luang. Night's SpongeBob SquarePants birthday cake was left sitting on a table, its candles unlit, as parents rushed to the cave.

They were greeted at Tham Luang by the sight of the boys' bicycles. Next, the parents were met by three park rangers[14] who were exiting the cave, carrying backpacks and pairs of shoes that had been found inside. The parents identified these items as belonging to their sons, and everyone's fears were confirmed. The boys had gone inside.

Were they still in there?

The time was 8 p.m. Rain was falling heavily and had been doing so for a number of hours. The situation was looking grim.

Sunday, 24 June 2018

Early on Sunday morning, in the first of a number of key factors which led to the rescue's ultimate success, the head coach of the football club called Vernon Unsworth to the cave. Vern, a British ex-pat and experienced caver who lives in Thailand with his partner Tik, had spent six years mapping the furthest reaches of Tham Luang. He often said that he knew the insides of that cave nearly as well as he knew the insides of his home.

The cave's entrance, where the boys' bicycles had been found, is on the eastern side of the mountain. The initial passage trends westward for 1,600 metres before turning south at a T-junction known as Sam Yaek, or Monk's Junction,[15] and continuing deeper into the cave. Approximately 700 metres along this southerly path lies a rising off-shoot, which is effectively a ramp that rises above monsoon water levels.

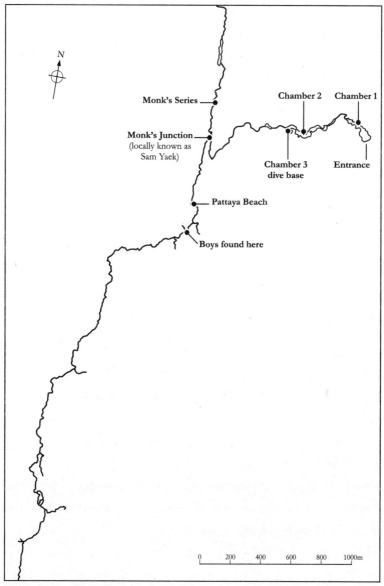

Tham Luang Cave System

Vern immediately knew that this ramp, being the only area of the cave that sits higher than the main tunnel, would be the boys' best chance for survival; his search would be focused there, with the hope that the boys had managed to reach this place and find safety from the rising waters. During his first trip inside on Sunday, Vern was able to walk to Monk's Junction but did not get beyond because the passage was cut off there at a sump. The floodwaters were advancing. He brought in sandbags, in an attempt to stem the flow that was issuing from Monk's Series, but the effort was futile.

Many volunteers soon arrived to join in the search, and none of them got any further than Vern had. One diver, part of a volunteer rescue team, was the first to dive into the sump beyond Monk's Junction on Sunday evening, and he quickly encountered difficulty underwater. He was trying to locate and pass through a low passage that was the tunnel's continuation but, without the requisite skill set for navigating in caves, he was unable to orient himself. Vern – a dry caver but not a diver – was familiar with the passage and repeatedly described its location, but the diver's attempts were unsuccessful. The search was eventually stopped when the volunteers realized that they were at their limit, and the Thai authorities called in help from a locally garrisoned unit of Royal Thai Navy (RTN) SEALs. By then, local news outlets had heard of what was happening at the mountain, and press had begun to arrive.

The effort was steadily growing at Tham Luang, but there was nothing more to be done for the day. After taking active part in the day's search efforts, the parents of the missing boys prepared to spend the night at the cave's entrance, taking shelter within the same structure that was holding their children.

Monday, 25 June 2018

On Monday morning, Vern returned to the cave and was one of the first in to continue the search. Aware of the dangers he faced by walking into a flooded cave while rain continued to storm down outside, he left a note with his partner Tik (Woranan Ratrawiphuk-kun). 'In case I don't come out,' he told her, while pressing the folded sheet of paper into her hand, 'make sure somebody sees this.'

Growing crowds of concerned neighbours and local press had gathered around the entrance of the cave, and soon the main detachment of RTN SEALs arrived by plane from their naval base in the south of Thailand. The impressive and well-trained military men were expected to succeed, but they ran into the same difficulties as the others who had tried before them. However, their elite training had prepared them to persevere through obstacles and seek solutions to unexpected problems, so they were able to make some progress in the search. For the first time since it had flooded, the area south of the T-junction was penetrated, and the SEALs travelled beyond Monk's Junction.

While the SEALs were conducting these searches, Vernon implored the men to place a guide rope along the route leading to the junction from Chamber 3. 'There will be no easier time to lay a line through the cave than right now, while parts are still dry and you're walking through,' he told them, but his requests and warnings were repeatedly ignored. The SEALs made it understood that they were not interested in working with Vern, or even listening to his advice.

All hopes depended on the boys having found a dry area inside the cave, beyond Monk's Junction, yet with each hour that passed, those dry areas were disappearing. As rain continued to fall, everyone was growing desperate but didn't know what else to do. This is when Amp, whose home is in Chiang Rai, called to tell me what was happening. She had been following the local news as it developed and was well aware that the situation would need outside help from experts. Despite having just met me, she'd learned enough to suspect this was something I ought to be involved in.

Following my phone calls with Amp and then John on Monday morning, I next reached out to Bill Whitehouse at the British Cave Rescue Council. John and I would need to receive an official invitation from the Thai authorities before we could become involved; to achieve that, they first had to learn who we were and that they needed us. I sent emails to local Members of Parliament, clearly outlining the events in Thailand, the skills that would be needed for the rescue and our experience using those exact skills in similar rescues. In return, I received automated responses, indicating that my request would be answered within two to five days. Brilliant. I was relieved when I finally did get through to a person in an office, only to be told that I would have to contact the MP in a different office.

Like me, Bill wasn't having much luck offering our services to Thailand. The well-oiled machine he'd established within the Cabinet Office ground to a halt when he learned that the officials he'd worked with years earlier had since left their posts. He did have success tracking down pieces of equipment from various cave rescue organizations across England, then he ensured they'd be ready and set to go when needed.

While he was doing this, I did a bit of research to see what I could learn about Tham Luang. Reading a few press releases, I came across the name of Vern Unsworth and quickly learned that Vern's caving partner is Rob Harper. I knew Rob. He and I had met on only one occasion, but it had been a pivotal meeting for me. In late 1983, Rob had been responsible for taking me into the UK's Wookey Hole Cave for the very first time. I rang him and was surprised to learn that he had just returned from Thailand, where he had been caving with Vern.

'We were planning to go inside Tham Luang this time last week but had to cancel because of the rain,' he told me. 'I just got home two days ago.' I noted the irony that he had flown to England on

Saturday the 23rd, which was the same day that Amp had flown to Thailand; this was also the same day that the boys had entered the cave.

Rob and Vern had been keeping in close contact about the events at Tham Luang as they unfolded. I asked Rob to keep me in the loop, then hung up the phone. After spending the day actively researching, planning and preparing for departure, I had nothing more to do. John and I were forced to sit and wait impatiently, hoping that somebody in Thailand would quickly understand that they needed us there.

Tuesday, 26 June 2018

At Tham Luang, Tuesday passed much as Monday had, with the SEALs and government officials on the scene, and the media presence steadily growing. Things were worsening inside the cave, as the water was rising further, and it was no longer possible for rescue personnel to safely reach Monk's Junction. Throughout the day, Vern kept trying to communicate the extreme nature of this mission, and the desperate need to call in people who had experience diving in this specific environment. The SEALs had already dissociated themselves from Vern entirely, seeming unwilling to take advice from a British civilian.

Having been raised in the world of UK caving and (through no fault of his own) having been the subject of a significant cave rescue himself,[16] Vern knew which skills would be needed inside Tham Luang. The searchers would need to be truly amphibious sump divers – explorers who were adept at carrying their dive gear through dry passages until reaching the next sump and going underwater again. In the sumps, they'd be diving blindly through an unfamiliar cave, fighting a strong current as they searched for the way on, accepting the possibility that at any moment they could be colliding with dead bodies.

Vern knew that there were few cave divers in the world who had spent their life building these skills in this type of cave, and even fewer who had managed to gather additional experience with cave rescues and body recoveries. Only three names came to mind for this mission, and with those names Vern felt like he had the missing key that was needed to unlock the problem at Tham Luang.

However, having lived for some time in Thailand, he was also aware (and respectful) of their closed culture. Thai people are very proud, and Vern understood that if Thai officials needed to ask for help abroad, they would feel a sense of shame, as though they were losing face. Despite these cultural restrictions, Vern was convinced that the precious hours being wasted could be diminishing the boys' chance for survival. With growing frustration, he tried repeatedly to get his message through to Governor Narongsak, the official who seemed to be in charge, only to find that he, too, was dismissive of the valuable information Vern was giving him.

On Tuesday evening, Vern was surprised to receive an invitation to attend a planning meeting with Thai civilian and military officials. Two members of the Thai cabinet would be present: Anupong Paochinda (Minister of the Interior) and Korusat Weerasak (Minister of Tourism and Sport). Towards the end of the meeting, one of the ministers turned to Vern and asked him directly, 'What should we do?'

After being given permission to speak freely, Vern got straight to the point. 'This rescue is not going very well,' he began bluntly. As he began speaking of the need to bring in experts, he handed over the note that he had written out for Tik the previous morning. (*'Make sure somebody sees this.'*)

The ball could have easily been dropped here. If Vern's message had been ignored, we might not have been invited over. Fortunately, the two ministers read the note, consulted with each other, and quickly agreed.[17] Vern was already holding his phone in hand and as soon as he was given the nod, he began dialling Rob Harper in the UK. When the call went through, Vern handed his phone over to the minister.

Rob, who worked night shifts as a veterinary oncologist, was awakened by the incoming call. When he saw Vern's name appear on his phone, he quickly sat up in bed and answered – despite being groggy and shirtless, and with matted hair from sleeping. He expected to see his friend's face on the phone, but was greeted instead with the face of Thailand's Minister of the Interior, who tried (not very well) to hide his look of surprise at finding Rob in bed at midday. Unfazed, the minister made the official request, via FaceTime, for help from the British cave rescuers.

'We'll see you in twenty-four hours,' was Rob's prompt reply.

Vern's largely illegible note naming John, Rob and me was re-written by the minister, who thankfully had better penmanship.

Vern passing along this note with our names to the ministers – and the fact that the information was acted upon – would comprise another pivotal element of the rescue's success. I believe it was solely responsible for expediting the deployment of Rob, John and myself to Tham Luang.

John Volanthen (forty-seven at the time) was working as a network engineer and owned a small business-to-business Internet Service Provider; in his spare time, he was a volunteer Cub Scout leader and ultramarathon runner. I, Richard Stanton (fifty-seven), had already begun collecting my pension from the fire service. Rob Harper (sixty-six) was still actively working full-time[18] at a veterinary clinic. We were all cave divers, but it was just a pastime, a hobby – although some would call it more of an obsession. None of us fitted the hero archetype by appearance or demeanour, a fact that was quickly noted in the media when our images began circulating from the rescue.

Regardless, we were the ones selected.

Like a row of dominoes falling, one by one, after the first one has been nudged, that meeting held on Tuesday evening in Thailand set off a chain of events that had been sitting in wait to begin moving swiftly towards their finale.

Rob phoned me with news of the invitation. Within an hour, the Minister of Tourism had booked the three of us onto a flight to Bangkok, due for departure from London Heathrow airport at 9.25 that evening. Bill Whitehouse deployed the prearranged caving equipment (underground communication devices) from Buxton in Derbyshire, arranging for their delivery to London in fast-response police vehicles to ensure their timely arrival.[19]

When I ended my call with Rob, I was left with fewer than four hours to prepare and pack for the trip.[20] I had no idea how long I'd be gone, nor did I know exactly what I might need while I was there. I threw a change of clothes into a rucksack, gathered and packed all of the equipment that I thought might be needed in the cave, then secured a ride to the airport from my mate Dan, a lecturer at Coventry University who typically spends Tuesday evenings Morris Dancing.

After going through my routine to close down the house before leaving on extended trips, and with everything packed and sitting by the front door, I had one last thing to do before leaving my home. With that in mind, I went upstairs to the small box room at the front of the house that I use as an office. Seeing that the street in front of the house was still empty of Dan's car, I sat at the computer and sent a message to a friend in Florida, letting her know I'd be out of touch for a while. After waiting a few minutes for a reply that didn't come, I reached over the computer to close the window. Years before, the curtain rod had dislodged itself from one of its brackets in the wall and has since sat askew, balanced precariously between the wall and the edge of a crowded bookshelf. I wrestled to keep it all from falling as I pulled the curtain closed.

Much like I've stopped noticing all of the ways my house has fallen into disrepair over the years, I also don't spend much time looking through the things I keep stored in this room. Waiting for Dan to arrive, I stood in the doorway to have a rare look around. A glass statue with the inscription 'Hero of the Year, 2011' was resting atop a rusted and dented filing cabinet. A mounted and gleaming silver axe hung on a faded yellow wall beside framed certificates. Aged newspaper clippings were pinned onto a crowded noticeboard. Piles of loose A4 paper and folded newspapers rested on every flat surface, tucked among various awards, trophies, and velvet boxes holding medals I'd been presented with over the years, some of them from Buckingham Palace.

'It's been a long road getting here,' I thought as I scanned the memories contained in this room.

Hearing a knock downstairs a moment later, I shut down the computer and closed the door behind me, then went to meet Dan. When I opened my front door, I laughed to see that he had not taken the time to change out of his Morris attire before rushing over. He stood there with shoulder-length curls, wearing a white blouse with braces, knee-length breeches and long white socks. All that was missing was bell-pads on his shins.

Ninety minutes later, outside Departures at Heathrow, as he was helping unload my equipment from his car, I couldn't help but notice the tourists entering the airport were blatantly staring at Dan. (*Is this how British people dress?*)

I pulled my last bag from the boot of his car and set it with the others on the pavement.

'See ya, mate!' Dan said glibly before driving off, showing typical British understatement. I gathered my luggage and made my way into the airport, wondering if I was properly prepared for the task ahead and knowing there was only one way to find out.

Later that evening, in Florida, my friend Karen arrived home from work and sat down at her computer. Having not heard the news, she knew nothing about what was going on in Thailand, so had no idea what I was talking about when she read the message I had sent to her a few hours earlier:

I'm heading to Thailand . . . to meet up with a football team.'

2.
First Things First

When asked why he was driven to reach
the summit of Mount Everest, explorer George Leigh
Mallory famously answered,
'Because it's there.'
When asked why they are driven to
reach the end of a cave, some cavers have played with
his answer in their own explanation,
'Because it's not there.'

If you show a cave entrance to a group of youths and a group of adults, I would place money on which group runs towards the entrance in excitement while the other turns away with disinterest. Fuelled by their natural curiosity and desire to learn, children are driven to ask questions, and they explore unknown places fearlessly. Unfortunately, these traits are often casualties of their maturation, weakening with lack of practice as a person grows older and learns to fit in to today's risk-averse society. As children become adults, they often lose the desire to explore new things and they stop asking questions. The opposite happened with me.

In my own childhood, not much had evoked my curiosity or driven me towards exploration. I had rarely felt very inspired by anything I encountered, as evidenced by my numerous school reports that criticized my tendency to spend time in class daydreaming. Not until I saw Geoff and Bear's exploration in *The Underground Eiger* did I feel a surge of excitement that I couldn't ignore, and I committed myself to learning what lies beneath – and inside – the earth. It was with this motivation that I set off from home for my first year of study at Aston University, where I quickly sought out and then joined its caving and diving clubs.

When a school friend had gone on a caving trip earlier in the year with his Venture Scouts group, I'd been eager to hear his recounting of the experience, but I'd not been tempted to join the Scouts to have the experience myself. I thought they were too organized and officious, which wasn't appealing to me at all, and I'd compared them to a paramilitary group in their uniforms. Aston University's caving club, on the other hand, was made up of a group of joyful anarchists, all connected by their common interest. The Aston Speleological Society (ASS) was haphazard and casual, which was much more to my liking. (The club's T-shirt, worn by its members with pride, sported their initials printed above an equine ass.) For maybe the first time in my life, I immediately felt comfortable with this group, as though I belonged.

Early in the first term, the club arranged an introductory trip for first-year students and novices who wanted to see what caving was all about, and I eagerly signed up. On Saturday, 20 October 1979, I was given a helmet with a caving lamp, and I entered my first cave.[1] The day was spent making a series of simple underground excursions into short caves, all of which were pleasant but not entirely committing and not at all challenging. There was a feeling of solidarity arising from the group, who seemed to be excited by the fact that they were underground in a place where most people would never go. I remained a bit apart from the others in that respect. Instead of feeling like I was having the adventure of my life, I sensed that I was only scratching the surface and I feared that I would return to Aston feeling a bit disappointed with my first caving experience.

I needn't have worried. As it turned out, the day was far from over.

The group would be sleeping at the local caving cottage owned by the Cerberus Speleological Society, but first things first: a meal and the pub. At the pub, over a round of celebratory beers, the group clamoured on about the day's excitement and discussed plans for future trips. Towards the end of the evening, one of the more experienced members offered up an additional adventure, for any who were willing. He proposed a trip to St Dunstan's Well, a nearby cave that had been avoided earlier. We were told that this cave would be more physical and committing than those we had done already, with smaller spaces we'd have to squeeze through on our bellies. Most members shook their heads and returned to their pints, satisfied that they had done enough caving for the day, while a few of us agreed that we weren't finished yet and wanted to keep going.

We entered at night, into a cave that is now described with the warning: 'Only the thinnest cavers should contemplate this trip!'[2] I hadn't been given this advice before entering, and even if I had it wouldn't have deterred me. I was exceptionally thin at that age and, even more importantly, I was exceptionally motivated.

Not long after entering, we encountered its main challenge, Domestos Bend,[3] which is a narrow U-shaped feature with a pool of water collected at the bottom of the bend. At its lowest point, only a few centimetres of airspace exist between the surface of the water and the ceiling, requiring a caver to pass through on their back, being mindful of keeping their nose out of the water. Some in the group hesitated at the sight of the restriction; others turned and left. Maybe the ale I'd drunk at the pub had emboldened me, for I approached the bend without any trepidation, confidently getting onto my back and removing my helmet before squeezing myself through the narrow chute head-first. I moved slowly and purposefully in the confined space, knowing that this was something that couldn't be rushed. Even though this was my first day of caving and my first time moving through a more difficult feature, I moved confidently, as if I had done this many times before.

As we continued on the other side of the bend, and then on our way out, I found myself anticipating each turn before we reached it, visualizing our path and testing my ability to navigate in this new landscape. Leaving the pitch black of the cave to be greeted by the surrounding darkness of night, I felt a strong sense of satisfaction and pleasure. My instincts had been confirmed: I did belong in caves. With a new-found purpose, I returned to Aston University at the end of the weekend, excited not by my upcoming classes but by the promise of future trips with the club.

On our very next caving weekend, camped on the meadow outside Porth-yr-Ogof cave system near Ystradfellte in South Wales, I would be told about the death of Paul Esser.

In the early 1970s, Bristol University had been home to a very active bunch of cave divers. On 13 February 1971, they had gone to Porth-yr-Ogof, a fairly popular destination for adventure caving and a well-known training site. Paul had been invited along as an open-water diver with his cave-diving friends to take part in an operation to clean up some old guide lines. He had no knowledge of diving in caves, no understanding of its risks. He had proven himself as a skilled open-water diver and he thought that would be enough to keep him safe inside a cave. He was wrong, and his body had later been found in an offshoot of the cave's main passageway.

By then I was beginning to learn that there are two types of cave divers. The first group – what I call 'true cave divers' – are dry cavers who begin diving only as a way to go further in the cave; when they reach a sump, they need to dive through it to reach more dry cave. The second group are scuba divers who love being under-water; for them, a cave is a new environment they'll get to experience as a diver. The differences between these two groups lie in their motivation for diving, their understanding of the cave and their awareness of the specific risks. Paul Esser was in the second group.

The conditions in the cave had been poor after his death, and every-body who had tried to recover his body had been unable to complete the mission. One diver had nearly died himself, which led Paul's parents to call off any further recovery attempts. They didn't want to feel respon-sible for another diver's death.

Nine years later, as we were camped immediately outside the entrance closest to where his corpse was still lying, I listened as Steve Joyce, our trip leader, told us the details of Paul's death. I was eighteen years old and had not yet encountered a dead body any-where, much less in a cave. I had never lost anyone, and I guess I had never given death much thought. I had never had to, really, until that night when I found myself camped 50 metres from his remains. I didn't know why that bothered me, but it did.

It all felt unresolved, unfinished.

$$\oplus \quad \oplus \quad \oplus$$

In simple terms, caves are formed by rainwater acting on soluble rock. As each raindrop falls towards the earth, it collects carbon dioxide from the atmosphere, then more carbon from the vegeta-tion in the soil. This mild carbonic acid penetrates the joints, fractures and beddings of the limestone, dissolving the rock in the process. Over the course of aeons, this process gradually creates a cave. The dream of every caver is to follow the water from where it sinks in the ground to where it comes out again, at its resurgence. That is the pinnacle of exploration – the pure pursuit – and to complete it, you often have to be able to dive, because there will inevitably be a sump at the lower reaches of those active caves.[5] This is where the true cave diver is born: when a dry caver needs to dive to continue beyond the sump.

I first experienced this union of caving and diving during a trip to Swildon's Hole in the Mendips. After descending into the cave and travelling on foot through waterfalls and streams, straddling crevices and climbing walls to go onward and downward, our group reached the first sump, where the cave appeared to end at a pool of water. This sump is short, just a quick duck underneath a rock 'wall' that descends into the pool. I laid myself in the shallow water, grasped the rope that was my guide, inhaled deeply and then went under.

With my hands on the rope, I pulled myself along for about 2 metres, passing underneath the submerged rock and emerging on its other side. *My first sump dive.* This is a dive that anyone can do – thousands of people have done it, even first-time cavers – but it was still quite momentous for me, a rite of passage. Now I truly felt like I was inside – cut off from the outside world by both earth and water.

On that day, we continued for a few hundred metres more before reaching the second sump, which was longer, and we were unable to continue. We turned around as a group and headed out, but I knew I'd be returning soon to go in further. Before then, I'd need more preparation. It was time to learn to dive.

I'd first suspected that I was a water person when I was still young, drawn as I was to anything involving aquatic adventures. I was always a competent swimmer, absolutely comfortable in the water, and I kind of instinctively knew that I would also feel natural staying beneath the surface for extended periods of time. I believe it was this part of me – this water person – that had been given direction when I watched Geoff Yeadon and Oliver Statham don their equipment before slipping beneath the water's surface to follow the underground river in the Yorkshire Dales.

Now with a clear purpose for diving, I was eager to get started. On my first pool session with the university's diving club – overseen by the British Sub-Aqua Club (BSAC) – my suspicions were again confirmed. I loved it. I think everybody who dives remembers that first unnatural inhalation when their face is underwater. Some people can't get over it and panic, while others need time to acclimatize, but I immediately found it really relaxing and enchanting. I always have.

BSAC was strict in its requirements that all members be able to demonstrate technical skills that exceeded the requirements for recreational scuba-diving certification – treading water while wearing a laden weight belt; swimming for increasing lengths on a single breath of air; free diving to the bottom of the pool to collect my diving gear which was lying there, then donning the gear at depth before ascending to the surface. Many dreaded running these drills, finding them tedious and unnecessary, but I immediately recognized the value of learning these skills, which may be needed in an emergency. The repetition of the skills helped us to gain confidence while building task memory.

I instantly loved diving and went to every weekly pool training session, where I performed competently, but I remained aloof from the other members, staying on the sidelines. Once again, I was very shy, anonymous, like I had been in school. The instructors were more interested in focusing their energy on the females than bothering to pay much attention to me (which was fair enough). I felt no bond with any of them, nor they with me. When the lessons moved beyond the pool sessions and they began making trips to the sea, I lost interest and left the club. I'd already learned what I needed.

Aston University, in Birmingham, is located in the West Midlands region of England. Being close to the geographic centre of the country, it is nearly as far from the sea – in all directions – as one can be on this island, but that didn't bother me. I wasn't interested in the sea. Aston's central location made it convenient for reaching any of the caving areas scattered across the country: from the Mendips and South Wales in the southwest, to the Derbyshire Peak District and the Yorkshire Dales in the north. With easy access to student-union minibuses, which allowed the club to plan trips to each of the regions, I quickly learned the geography and features of caves specific to each area. I also became familiar with each region's caving huts, similar to the cottage offered by the Cerberus Society. These sparsely furnished houses, comprised mostly of bunk beds and communal rooms, are owned by each area's local clubs and are opened to visiting cavers, providing us with a place to wash, rinse gear, eat, drink and sleep after a day of caving. Not necessarily in that order.

Leading many of the club's weekend trips that year was Steve Joyce, a third-year student who quickly and naturally took on the role of our leader. We all watched how he turned a thought or an idea into a plan and then made that plan become a reality, using whatever resources were available. Having spent my childhood either alone or on the outer fringes at school, and then continuing this tradition at university, where I quickly fell in with the group of cavers, I appreciated Steve's ability to communicate equally well with both immature students and professional adults.[4]

Amusingly, Steve drove a trusted and well-travelled bright-yellow Reliant Robin, which we'd use for an ad hoc trip on the weekends when there wasn't an official club trip planned. The compact three-wheeled van was ridiculous-looking and totally impractical, but it always managed to transport us and our equipment to and from the caves. Riding with Steve in the Robin was always more fun and gave us more autonomy, so even when the minibus was available, we'd often opt to make our own way there.

On the weekends when there was nothing else planned, we held local training sessions to practise Single Rope Technique (SRT), the methods frequently used for travelling vertically. A group of us could often be found hanging below a busy road bridge in Birmingham, ascending and descending on ropes that had been rigged to the parapets. We crammed in quite a bit of learning that first year, and nobody ever tried to hold us back. I was fortunate to have found an active group of cavers to learn with – led by Steve, who was always willing to go caving, take us with him, and teach us a few things. As Steve will say, it really was a matter of 'the right people at the right time . . . There was a nucleus of students who really wanted to go caving, so we got on with it.'

For the first time, I felt a sense of belonging and purpose. I felt a connection with the members of the club that had eluded me with others up until then, and I was spending my time and energy engaged in an activity that was quickly becoming an all-consuming passion.

I was having the time of my life.

Between the caving and diving clubs, I was steadily building a strong foundation of skills. I wasn't really planning how or when I was going to use them – I couldn't have predicted the path my life would take – but I have always believed that learning those skills early, practising them in a safe environment, helped to prepare me for the challenging skills I would need to use later when I was diving through unexplored sumps. I was already beginning to develop my ethos of: prepare, plan, practise, perform. Over the years, I would adopt the military's amusing and alliterative adage of the seven Ps: Prior Proper Planning Prevents Piss-Poor Performance.

Probably.

Perhaps it's ironic, then, that the instructional sessions held that year would be the last time that I really participated in any organized classes or training. Since that year of learning the basics at Aston, I have been almost entirely self-taught.[6] To this day, I've never bothered gaining any formal diving certification.

A few years later, I'd become active with the UK's Cave Diving Group, which places strong emphasis on its mentorship programme to provide support and guidance to novice cave divers. The CDG shares my belief that the only way to truly learn something is through experience. They understand the value of using trial and error to find what works, while recognizing that sometimes you'll need to create what works yourself. Unlike most profit-driven certification agencies, the CDG actively promotes the critical skills of self-reliance, problem-solving, risk assessment and innovation. These skills, I believe, are the ones that keep cave divers alive, and they are difficult – if not impossible – to teach on a training course.

People are surprised now when I tell them that I largely taught myself what I know, but the reality is that I really didn't have much choice. I knew that I wanted to be an exploratory cave diver, but in 1979 there were limited relevant resources, and I had no contact with any active cave divers. The closest thing I'd had to any instruction had been watching *The Underground Eiger*, learning what I could from Geoff and Oliver. After that, I'd just been going caving and figuring things out as I progressed.

That changed in 1980, with the arrival of Martyn Farr's seminal book *The Darkness Beckons: The History and Development of Cave Diving*. I'd eagerly awaited its publication, knowing that it would be hugely important for me. On 28 June 1980, I went to a climbing shop specifically to purchase the book and I started reading before I'd even left the shop. I spent hours and hours on this book. Countless hours. For a year. I pretty much spent all my time reading it and studying it. This was the first documented history of cave diving, and it was largely based in England. It was loaded with photos and stories, so I could finally look at and picture what cave divers were doing. I read it from cover to cover, scrutinizing every photograph, doing a lot of visualization. I had identified my goal, and now I could begin preparing to reach that goal.

I returned for my second year of university, but my energy and focus had already shifted entirely to caves, at the expense of just about everything else. I had no social life apart from the caving club, my academics suffered, and I rarely went home. I wondered if this is what my teacher had been referring to when he'd identified my economy of effort. In my opinion, a thing is worth either all of my effort, or none at all.

All of this had a natural – and expected – consequence. After spending most of my second year studying Martyn's book instead of my professors' textbooks, I decided not to return for a third year at university.

By then I had moved into a flat with my caving friend Chris Cooke. The place was cheap and it suited us just fine, so I stayed there even after dropping out. I also continued caving with Steve and members of the Aston University club. Really, my life didn't change all that much – it wasn't like I had been spending much time studying, anyway. Now, I just had more time to go caving.

Steve and I had begun spending our summer holidays caving abroad, and during the summer of 1981 we visited the caves of County Clare. On our return drive to Birmingham, we stopped off at a dive shop to purchase glue for some much-needed repairs to our wetsuits, which had just suffered a week of abuse crawling through the Irish caves. I've always been very frugal – not much of a shopper[7] – but on that day I made an impulse buy of a second-hand 3-litre diving cylinder, similar to those I'd seen in *The Darkness Beckons*. I followed this a week later with the purchase of a second-hand regulator (also called a demand valve) from a different shop.

With no bus service to the shop, I'd had to walk ten miles along the canal to purchase the Poseidon Cyklon. This specific regulator is the preferred choice for most UK cavers because of its simplicity and ruggedness. I wish I could say that I had purchased that first one intentionally and with prior knowledge, but the truth is that I didn't know what I was looking for back then; I'd just bought the one that was on sale. (That very same regulator has proven its dependability time and again. It remains my preferred model, and I now own fourteen of them.)

My caving gear then consisted of a neoprene wetsuit, wellies,[8] a helmet and light, with a belt carrying the light's battery. Now I also had the bare minimum needed for breathing underwater: a cylinder to carry compressed gas and a regulator to breathe it through. Having spent two years dry caving and free diving through short sumps, it wasn't long before I progressed to proper cave diving.

> 'Hell's Teeth! It's like being in a
> depth-charged submarine.'
>
> Clive Westlake

Wednesday, 27 June 2018, Thailand

Within Britain's search and rescue community, it is well understood that the only people who can rescue cavers are other cavers. Following this logic, when there is an incident in a difficult underwater cave that is beyond the reach of most cave divers, I'm typically called directly to help. My first step is to get John Volanthen and/or Jason Mallinson on board. My next call is to Bill Whitehouse of the British Cave Rescue Council, who has accumulated forty years of experience sitting on national search and rescue committees.

John, Jason and I are cave divers by hobby, utterly unprofessional, and none of us can be bothered dealing with bureaucracy. Therefore, working under the auspices of the BCRC and being officially deployed by the Cabinet Office as the 'cave rescue experts' gives our involvement a sense of legitimacy, of national authority. This identity makes people take us seriously. Upon arriving, we are usually given the freedom and autonomy to proceed the way we choose, without having to get clearance or permission from any lingering bureaucrats. I'd grown accustomed to having this understanding in place before I arrived at a rescue. I'd also come to expect a sense of order and organization being in place.

Promptly after our plane landed in Chiang Rai, I was given my first clue that things on the ground in Thailand were going to be different. All the other passengers were ordered to stay seated and wait while we disembarked first. After stepping off the plane, the three of us were invited to board one of those electric airport shuttles, the kind normally reserved for people with mobility issues. Going against all of our natural instincts, we agreed and climbed aboard. The cart was meant to transport us an embarrassingly short distance through the airport as a mark of respect, but it quickly became stuck negotiating a tight corner while trying to get into a lift. We were left sitting hopelessly, while everyone else who had been on our plane walked past us, looking at us quizzically as they went by, undoubtedly wondering what the hell we were doing.

It was a fair question.

Our next clue arrived as we walked down the airport stairs and were confronted by a reception committee. Airport staff were holding a grand banner, complete with full-colour photographs of ourselves[9] and the modest greeting: 'Welcome to the world's best cave divers!'

'No pressure then,' I muttered to John as we stared at the display in disbelief.

'Right,' he laughed as we were led into a room for our first briefing from the Chiang Rai provincial governor, Narongsak Otanakorn.

Since our first phone call on Monday, two days earlier, John and I had been intently discussing possible courses of action. We had read any information we could find about the cave (much of which had been provided by Martin Ellis and Rob) and we had discussed what personal equipment we'd be taking.[10] Most of our planning had been based on conjecture and speculation. There were some details – about the cave, the boys and the conditions of both – that we would need to know before we could confidently put together a detailed rescue plan.

John and I were pleased to be meeting with the one in charge of it all, the one who could finally give us this crucial information to fill in the missing pieces and allow us to begin planning. We sat down for the briefing with the governor, eager to hear the details of what we were about to encounter. I had thought to bring notebooks and pens with us – giving the illusion that we were being professional – and I had them sitting out on the table in front of us.

I didn't know who Narongsak was, and when I first saw him I never would have guessed that he was the governor. Although he holds multiple degrees (including one in Geology) and a government position, his voice and presentation resembled those of a cartoon character.[11] Dressed as he was in a khaki uniform with badges, a yellow neckerchief tied neatly and a blue cap, he appeared like an overgrown Cub Scout more than a political leader. I was rather surprised when he took his position at the front of the room, flanked by senior officers from the military and police. *Blimey, he's the one in charge.*

After welcoming us warmly and thanking us for coming, he announced to the officers and members of the press that his briefing was about to begin.

'We have a situation,' he began dramatically. John and I sat a bit straighter and picked up our pens, with our ears perked as we waited to hear his words.

'There's a football team and their coach, and they're stuck in the cave.' I waited for him to continue, but he had stopped talking and stepped back, apparently satisfied that his briefing was over. I put down the pen and closed my notebook.

For fuck's sake.

There was a moment of dumbfounded silence at the table as we took it in. Then, to keep things moving, I cleared my throat and brought up the matter of weather. 'This whole situation is going to depend on the rainfall. We'll need constant weather updates.' In unison, the officials picked up their phones and began checking their mobile weather apps. *Not on your bloody phones!* I realized they'd require clearer instructions, so I told them we'd need national meteorologists feeding timely, reliable information to the rescue site.

My next concern: 'What about the children? We'll need to know about their health, any medical conditions they might have.' I was thinking specifically that – being active and lean Thai boys – their lack of body mass, combined with the threat of starvation, would be a major cause for concern. I also inquired if there were any illnesses or conditions we should know about. (The truth is, I haven't spent much time around children in my life,[12] and the young age of the people I'd be rescuing was the only part of this mission that was entirely unfamiliar to me. I was grateful that John was both a father and a Cub Scout leader. He often takes his group of Scouts on caving trips, so he was in his comfort zone here. I could only hope that John's comfort and experience with young people would make up for my general aversion to them.)

The officials looked confused by my concern. 'Well . . . they're young boys. Why would they have problems? They're all healthy.' He didn't seem to be going off of any known information, just an assumption that young boys raised in that environment must be healthy. I hoped he was correct.

After the meeting dispersed, we left the airport and were shepherded onto a minibus that was waiting to take us to the cave. Our gear travelled behind us in the flatbed of a pick-up truck, and we were led by a police escort. During the thirty-minute drive, heavy rain began to pour down, providing us with a more ominous – and perhaps more appropriate – welcome to Mae Sai. What we saw when we arrived at Tham Luang would continue the trend of preparing us for the unusual manner in which this operation would be run.

The scene was utter chaos.

Hundreds of people were crowded around the buildings on the park property, walking around in what seemed to be circles.

Although I'm sure they were doing something, I couldn't discern what it might be. Everyone was soaked to the skin and covered in mud, as rain continued to fall. For the life of me I couldn't tell who was in charge. One news video catches me on camera saying to John, 'Where are the people who were supposed to be leading us and showing us? We've sort of been thrown to our own devices.'[13]

Thankfully, at that point, Vern Unsworth emerged out of the crowds. 'Long time,' he said to Rob with a smile as they shook hands, and I remembered that Rob had been here with Vern just days earlier. Neither John nor I had met Vern before, but we had common friends in the world of UK caving, so I knew I could trust him. I was grateful to finally be in the presence of someone who was familiar with the cave, cave rescue and Thai culture.

All this time, our equipment had been sitting – exposed and unsecured – in the back of the pickup truck. Knowing that we wouldn't be much good there without our diving gear, I grabbed a man in uniform and directed him to watch over it. He did not speak English, and I hoped he understood the point I was trying to convey. Suddenly, a man appeared at my side. 'I speak good English,' he offered. 'I can help you as a translator. My name is Max.'

I was trying to get an overall sense of the command structure, so I asked him who was coordinating what he was doing. He told me that he wasn't working for anybody. 'I'm here as a volunteer. If I see something that needs to be done, I do it.' He paused and then stated the obvious. 'I can see that you need a translator.'

I respected his forward-thinking approach and gratefully accepted his help. As Vern led us through the crowds, the people who had previously been milling around aimlessly were soon following and filming us. They somehow knew that we had been brought in for a purpose, and as our crowd of followers grew, expectations seemed to shift onto our shoulders. After a short trek beyond the police cordon and into the restricted area, Vern presented us with the room that had been set aside for us inside the 'Rescuers' Area' of the national park headquarters.

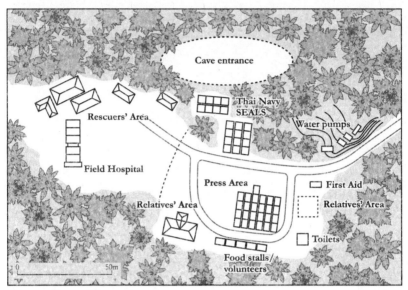

Rescue Camp, Tham Luang

Before we had a chance to sit down on the plastic garden furniture inside the room, the pick-up truck arrived, and we began offloading our gear while Vern told us briefly about the attempts he had been making to get into the cave. Initial rescue operations had started on Sunday in the region of Monk's Junction (1,600 metres into the cave), but since Monday night the encroaching water had been pushing everybody back. 'We're quickly losing ground,' he told us. 'By Tuesday, the section of cave beyond the third chamber had been evacuated.'

John and I wanted to enter immediately, to see what we could learn before we lost more time and dry cave to the continuing rain. We set to work preparing our gear. I didn't give much thought to Larry Risser when he first poked his head through the door to introduce himself, but when he stepped inside, I stopped and took notice.

An exceptionally large Thai man wearing a high-visibility yellow safety jacket, Larry couldn't help but stand out, and I soon learned that his physical size was equally matched by his larger-than-life persona. My impression of him would shift in the days to come, with each thing I learned about him succeeding in adding another layer of intrigue.[14] As the rescue progressed, Vern began referring to him affectionately as Larry the Lounge Lizard, which I thought was an appropriate moniker for a man who seemed to defy labels and was hard to miss in his large yellow uniform.

After introductions and a bit of small talk, Larry stepped forward with a bold statement. 'If there's anything you need,' he said confidently, 'I can get it. All you have to do is ask. If you can't find me, any policeman on site will be able to get in contact with me.' I was inclined to dismiss this, after the chaos I'd already witnessed, but very soon I was obliged to put his claim to the test. 'There is one thing we need right now,' I told him. 'We need a compressor to fill our cylinders.'

Within minutes, he presented us with an air compressor – old and knackered, but still working. We filled two cylinders before setting off for the cave as a group: myself, John, Rob, Vern, a German cave diver,[15] Max the translator and a few Thais whom Vern had recruited to help carry our gear.

Tham Luang is a show cave, and as such it is open to the public during the months that fall outside the rainy season. The entrance to the park is accommodating to visitors, with a large, flat, open expanse on the hillside that is typically used for parking but was already overrun with press and rescue volunteers. Cut into the mud[16] and lush tropical vegetation of the mountainside, a staircase rises towards the cave, ending at a walkway with a handrail signalling where the visitor descends to enter the cave.

As we were leaving the flat and heading towards the staircase, I saw for myself the warning sign, stating that the cave is flooded from July to November and would be closed during those months. 'But then, the monsoon doesn't run to a precise calendar,' I thought to myself.

We passed the boys' bicycles, still leaning against the handrail along the walkway overlooking the cave's entrance. I was surprised by the relative good quality and condition of the bicycles, which I took as a promising sign that the boys might also have robust torches with them. The opening of the cave's entrance on the side of the mountain was like a carnivorous mouth, a wide-open space that narrowed at the back into the ongoing cave passage, like a throat acting as a portal into the mountain.

The inner walls of the entrance cavern were lined with electric lights, fed by cables from generators. I glanced uneasily at the snakes' nest of wires, knowing that the flood was approaching and surprised that nobody seemed concerned by the risk. The area was packed with hundreds of military personnel – all of them sitting or lying on the level ground and sloping side walls, looking utterly exhausted. Any space where a person could comfortably rest was occupied. Vernon had told us that a diesel-powered water pump had been set up close to Monk's Junction on Sunday, in immediate response to the news of the trapped boys, and we saw the pump workers and electricians laying out hoses and more wires.

Who would run an internal combustion engine inside a closed space? That is utter madness.

There was a large Thai SEAL standing at the cave's throat, where the open cavern began to taper into the tunnel of the cave. We nodded at him as we began walking past, but he moved to block our entrance, refusing to let us into the cave. I stared at him in disbelief as Vern and John – assisted by Max – tried reasoning with the man, to make him understand who we were and why we were there.

John: 'We've been brought here by your government . . . We know what we're doing . . . Let us do our job.' By then it was becoming clear that we were the best chance those boys had for survival – if they were even still alive.

Vern: 'These men are divers from Britain who were brought here to rescue the kids . . .'

When the SEAL failed to respond to reasoning, John moved in closer to him and addressed him more assertively: 'Do you understand that there are thirteen children inside?'

I stood back and watched, with John later pointing out to me that I had remained noticeably silent and unhelpful during this exchange. 'There's no point arguing with the gatekeeper,' was my thought. This SEAL had been given an order not to let anyone through, and his job was to follow orders. He wouldn't budge.

I checked my watch impatiently. It was past 10 p.m. on Wednesday. We had already been in Chiang Rai for five hours, and the boys had been trapped for about 120 hours. We were exasperated, knowing that precious time was being wasted. Vern left to speak with somebody in authority; the discussion ended with the words, 'Let them go kill themselves if they want to.' When we returned to the cave some thirty minutes later, the SEAL had clearly been given the change in orders and he begrudgingly let us walk past him into the cave.

As I entered Tham Luang, I was reminded of a time I'd been in a flooding cave with a friend who had compared the experience to being inside a depth-charged submarine. Although there was no sign of a river in this part of the cave, there was water showering down on us. 'This cave didn't fill with the water from one rainstorm,' I thought to myself. The mountain had been collecting water like a sponge and, now saturated, the continuing rain was causing the water to flow out of the mountain itself, into the cave passage, which was acting as a conduit to funnel the water through.

Approximately 700 metres into the cave, the second chamber ends at a pile of boulders, through which a gap descends to a U-bend. At the lowest point of this bend, the ceiling of the cave dips down sharply and narrows into a small opening, forming an archway about a metre high.

Rob and I were the first to approach this archway. As we stood there, a lake was forming around our feet, and I heard a rush of moving water from the space beyond. 'This isn't right,' I thought, just as Rob went ahead and ducked under the arch. The water was already at my ankles and rising. *There shouldn't be any water here.* I've been trapped like this before and I knew we shouldn't be going forward. Vern came down beside me and agreed with what I was thinking.

'This absolutely isn't right,' he said, as we stood in water that was now shin-deep. Rob had been so focused on going forward with the search to find the children that he had forged ahead blindly, oblivious to the danger.

'Rob's just gone through that arch,' I told him. 'We need to get him back.' As we watched, the water level rose steadily towards the top of the arch that Rob had just ducked under. Soon we were standing in a knee-deep pool of water. I took further note of the wires that were channelled through the archway on their way to Chamber 3. There were fluorescent lights and junction boxes everywhere, adding to my uneasiness. I presumed there were trip switches but didn't know for sure; I had no idea about the nature of the electrics and whether the water was going to go live.

'Rob, come back! Come back!' we shouted, but he could no

longer hear us against the noise of the water. As we waited, the water filled almost to the top of the archway. Rob's clear exit was rapidly disappearing. My diving gear was in the tackle bag that Rob was carrying, and, not knowing the layout of the cave, I didn't know if a free dive would be possible. I stood there helplessly as the water rose towards our thighs. Vern was with me, but he isn't a water person and doesn't dive. John was further behind me with his own diving equipment, still at the boulders with the rest of the group, unaware of what was happening ahead.

After about five minutes, Rob reappeared, looking a bit flustered. He'd had to hold his breath and free dive his way back through the sunken arch and in the process of hurrying back to Chamber 2, he had let go of the tackle bag he'd been carrying. *That bag has all of my kit in it!* I imagined it being swept between boulders and lost.

I had a few distraught moments here, standing in my ordinary clothes and waiting for John to catch up. I shouted to him that all of my diving gear had been lost in the sump, but he didn't immediately understand the urgency. He seemed to take forever getting into his wetsuit and cylinder harness, before he was able to dive down and rescue mine. The German who had come in with us was visibly shaken by the commotion and the rising water; without a word, he turned on his heel and scurried towards the exit, leaving us behind.

As we made our way out, Vern explained what had just happened. Chamber 3 had been acting as a dam wall, effectively containing the rising water arriving from further upstream and creating a large holding reservoir. At the moment we had reached the U-bend that night, the reservoir had filled high enough that the 'dam' had been breached, creating a flood pulse that had poured towards us.

Imagine a long hose running through your garden, undulating up and down over rocks and shrubbery or whatever. One end is held aloft and water is poured in through a funnel, while the other end is fitted to the base of a bowl that's resting on the ground. As water enters, it will pool in the low-lying sections of the hose. The dips closest to the funnel will fill first, before pouring down into the next low section. Finally, when all sections of the hose have filled completely, the water will pour out of the hose and into the bowl.

This is how Tham Luang filled with water. The source of the cave's streamway (where the surface streams that channel the rain-water falling onto the mountain disappear underground) was the funnel; the main tunnel of the cave (with the undulating parts becoming either sumps, canal passages or dry chambers) was the hose; and Chamber 3 was the bowl, finally accumulating water after the cave behind it had filled.

In the early days of the flood, the water from the source had been running through the cave, filling the low-lying sections and creating sumps. By Tuesday night, after these low-lying sections of cave had filled, the water had finally begun draining into Chamber 3. When we were back there on Wednesday night, Chamber 3 had finally filled and begun overflowing, and this is when Rob had got caught beyond the archway. The water spilling out from Chamber 3 had then continued its journey towards Tham Luang's entrance, like water running down the garden path after spilling over from the bowl.

'The cave beyond Chamber 3 must have filled completely,' I thought with a sinking feeling. We exited quickly, while the water continued to rise at an alarming rate. The flood would now be pouring between the boulders downstream of Chamber 2, and from there would flow to the entrance. When we were leaving the cave, well past midnight, Vern relayed an urgent message to the military officials who were waiting in the entrance chamber.

'You've got about four hours, I reckon. All your equipment here needs to be taken out. By tomorrow morning, there'll be a neck-deep river flowing through here.' Absolutely no one had been through this cave before while it was flooded and there was no record of how it would flood, but we trusted Vern's word and were confident that his prediction would prove to be correct. The SEALs, refusing to engage with the situation, responded with indifference. I looked around the chamber, which was still packed with men and equipment. In a few hours, all of this would be an underground lake, and they didn't seem concerned. Four hours later, when the flood arrived right on time, they were all caught by surprise. I really wish I'd been a fly on the wall to see them making a mad scramble to gather up their equipment and run out as the chamber became inundated with water.

I had only known Vern for a few hours, but I could already tell that he was at the end of his patience with the SEALs who had been dismissing his advice all week. I later learned that there had been a bit of an incident between Vern and the SEALs days before, which might have explained why the Thai military had seemed to take an immediate dislike to me and John when we arrived.[17]

For one last sickener to welcome us to Tham Luang, a Thai man carrying our gear had wandered off somewhere between the cave and our gear room, taking with him one of my cylinders. I was furious to learn that my cylinder was missing, but too exhausted to deal with it at that moment. I was going to have to learn to cope in this disorganized environment, and it was pissing me off, because I could already see it was affecting our ability to operate.[18]

With enough obstacles being given to us by nature, we didn't need further unnecessary ones caused by people.

The three of us left Tham Luang in the pre-dawn hours of Thursday morning, seated in the back of a pickup truck to be taken to the local resort where we would be staying. We were already exhausted with jetlag and before long we were soaking wet from the rain, covered in mud from the cave, and literally shivering in the chill of the early hours. *It won't be very good if we catch a cold our first night here and aren't able to dive.* None of us had eaten, and as the driver circled the streets trying to find where he was supposed to be taking us, we were all feeling completely discouraged. *What the hell are we doing here?* Everything was looking pretty grim, including us.

Then we arrived at the resort.

I wasn't expecting to find luxury, but I have to admit I was disappointed when we were presented with a single ramshackle room that the three of us were meant to share. It was small, damp and sparsely furnished with only two beds. Rob immediately spotted the shortfall and quickly placed his baggage on the single bed, leaving John and me to work out what we were going to do with the double.[19] To continue the mood, heavy rain was beating down loudly on the corrugated metal roof of our chalet.

Despite my exhaustion, I lay awake for some time, trying to gather my thoughts. Both Vern and Martin Ellis (a British caver who's documented Thai caves) had assessed the deeper parts of the cave as being flat, level passages with only small areas that might have contained air pockets. This implied that, with the cave beyond Chamber 3 now flooded, there was little hope for the boys' survival. Furthermore, the speed with which the water had risen from Chamber 3 signalled that a strong flood pulse was surging out from deeper in the cave. A flood pulse is bad news.

I had read of an incident involving a flood pulse in a cave in southern Thailand (Nam Talu cave, in 2007), when a group of European tourists had been inside at the time of a flood caused by the seasonal monsoon. As the pulse surged through, six of them had immediately been washed away and drowned; another had succumbed to the same fate as he attempted to summon help; the lone survivor had managed to cling to a ledge for eighteen hours while waiting to be rescued. I thought of this story as I imagined the flood that was washing through Tham Luang. I wondered if any of the boys would find a sanctuary . . . and how long they'd be able to hang on as they waited for us to arrive.

I was trying to stay focused on planning the next day's dive, but I was powerless to stop the waves of pessimistic thoughts that were forming. I knew that I needed to stay optimistic for the sake of maintaining motivation – not to mention keeping up appearances for the media, government and families – but I also have learned, through experience, that false hope can result in devastating let-downs.

Nightly Correspondence:
Wednesday, 27 June 2018

From: Richard Stanton
To: Bill Whitehouse

Arrived safely, immediately went into cave with dive gear.
Cave waters rising rapidly, not possible to get anywhere near the limits of where they reached on Mon. We retreated.
Heavy rain predicted and now falling for all of tonight, and much of next week.

From: Bill Whitehouse
Replying to: Richard Stanton

That doesn't sound good!

From: Martin Ellis [explorer of Tham Luang]

To: Emma Porter [secretary of the BCRC, and passed along to me]

I have only been in the cave as far as 'Monk's Series'.

Personally I don't like the cave. It is one of those places that I think gives off a bad vibe, but the entrance series isn't bad.

The system is very under explored due to a lack of cavers and the limited safe exploration season. The hydrology is also a mystery. The known main resurgence is near the entrance to Tham Sai Thong. The cave flooded via Monk's Series and the streams that sink in the north.

3.
Finding What Works

'Rick Stanton . . . Who's he?'

Whenever I was doing anything that involved risk, I always remembered my father's phrase: 'Mind what you're doing.' When he was serving as a firefighter in London during the Second World War, the phrase hadn't just been a cliché. They were words to live by. 'Give everything your full attention,' he had taught Jane and me. 'Know the risks in advance and have a plan for them.' I combined his words with my own practice of focused preparation and taking incremental steps when learning new skills. *Never take on more than you know you can handle at any one time.* I applied these strategies while preparing for my first cave dive.

After purchasing my first pieces of dive equipment in the summer of '81, I spent the rest of the year playing with them and learning how they worked. First, I dived in open water – a river, then a flooded quarry and then in the entrance cavern to Keld Head – before I felt ready to progress underground. For my first cave dive, I chose two short sumps in Old Ing Cave, Yorkshire. I'd already free dived both sumps, so I was familiar with their layout and knew what would be involved. In January 1982, Steve Joyce and I went there to dive, with three of our university friends coming along to help us carry our equipment.

When free diving these sumps earlier, I'd grabbed on to the rope and pulled myself through as quickly as possible on a single breath-hold, like an ape on a rope. Now with scuba equipment, I took my time moving through and became absorbed in the underground landscape. I enjoyed the feeling of being in a three-dimensional environment for the first time. 'Gravity confines us to walking on the floor, climbing up stairs,' I thought as I hovered weightlessly, 'but underwater I can move freely up and down at will. I can float up to the ceiling.' I felt like I had my own jet pack. Even more than that, I enjoyed the feeling of being in the water. Immersed, underwater and underground. Instead of feeling uneasy in this new environment, I felt like I had been there before, like I was arriving back home after a long time away.

I continued to build up experience alongside Steve, progressing slowly through caves and sumps we were already familiar with. I dived Old Ing again before moving on to Dido's Cave[1] in Derbyshire. I went back to Swildon's and this time I went all the way down to its ninth sump. I returned to Keld Head – the site of Geoff and Bear's record dive, where I'd practised with my gear at the entrance – and this time I went inside. Diving alone, I finned along the murky tunnel from the exit pool for 300 metres before turning around and heading out. This was my longest dive to date.

Steve and I were learning, together, how to advance. We would isolate a specific skill we wanted to build, or a particular site we wanted to explore, then we'd develop a plan to move systematically through the steps required to finish the task. Because it was early in both of our learning curves, we made mistakes, which we used to progress our knowledge. *What went wrong? How did I respond? Did it work? What else could I have done?* Mistakes are always where the most learning occurs, and in those early years I learned a lot of valuable lessons.

The majority of our trips together were in British caves, but from the beginning of our friendship we had taken advantage of our summer holiday for trips abroad. In the summers of 1980–82 we had gone to County Clare in Ireland, and it was there, in 1982, that I made my first exploratory dive, using the cylinder and regulator I had purchased the previous summer. After doing some careful research, I'd selected Poulnagun Cave, whose stream was believed to come from the nearby Coolagh River. I thought that if I could pass through the sump that marked Poulnagun's present limit, I'd find a lot more beyond, waiting to be discovered and explored.

Although I never made that connection from Poulnagun, I managed to extend the existing line for 20 metres, thus marking my first exploration. Upon returning home, I submitted my dive report to the CDG's impressive leader, Oliver Cromwell Lloyd, and I was delighted when my report was accepted for admission into their newsletter. Having my exploration noted in print by the CDG was almost as satisfying as the exploration itself had been. Almost.

As Steve and I travelled around the UK in search of caves that would provide suitable locations to progress our diving skills, I became even more intimately familiar with the caves that I had first encountered during my early trips with the university's club. Part of any cave's allure is its complex path, which has been shaped into the earth naturally over centuries. The ripples in the sediment on the floor, the positioning and poise of a gravel slope, scallops in the cave walls . . . these all tell a story. A natural cave can be read to reveal its secrets, and I found that I had a knack for uncovering the clues.

This is lacking in man-made mines, and so I have never been particularly interested in them. There was no mystery there for me to unravel, nothing new to discover, and I found them to be a bit boring. I was caught by surprise, then, when a significant portion of my learning in those formative years ended up occurring in the Dudley limestone mines.

I first dived there in spring of 1983 and found the mines were unlike anything that most British cave divers experience. My previous dives had taught me how to move through smaller tunnels while looking for the way on in the rock, but this was different. In British caves, most of which are small, a diver is typically in intimate contact with a wall or floor, or both. Yet here, in the open chasm of the Dudley mines, I was able to travel distant from these reference points and had the rare opportunity to fine-tune the skill of buoyancy control. I'd recently picked up a cheap second-hand drysuit, and this was my first time using it. Although the suit wasn't very dry, it held air well enough to control buoyancy.

The first descent was like taking an elevator into the earth. Upon reaching the bottom at −25 metres, I inhaled through my regulator and got nothing. No air. I had just begun the dive, so I knew there was plenty of air left in my cylinders. The demand valve must have frozen. Having just completed an exhalation, I had no air in my lungs and I panicked. Without thinking through my options, I shot for the surface.

The reflective glimmer seemed to approach with maddening slowness as I pumped my legs furiously, racing against the burning pressure that was building in my lungs, biting into the mouthpiece of my regulator to keep my lips closed around it. Finally breaking surface, I tore the demand valve from my mouth and gulped in air. As soon as my brain was no longer starved of oxygen, I began mentally ticking off the 'Rules of Diving' that I had just broken, the most critical one being: don't panic.

Any problem encountered on a dive must be considered calmly and with a clear head. As soon as panic sets in, a diver is doomed. Thoughts race, pulse and breathing rates increase, and the ability to think rationally decreases. Problems quickly become compounded as mistakes are made. Had I stopped for two seconds to think calmly when my primary valve froze, I would have considered the spare regulator attached to my second cylinder, replaced the first valve with the second, and continued breathing normally as I made a safe ascent to the surface.

I was mortified by the mistake I'd made but was able to take away from the dive a valuable lesson. Two lessons, in fact: (1) every problem has a solution, and (2) don't panic. I'm happy to say that this would be the one and only time I've panicked underwater. It was a mistake I only needed to make once.

Undeterred, I continued diving at Dudley for another two years. The large open mines provided the perfect setting for learning and practising techniques that couldn't be done in British caves, and my time spent in these mines played a substantial role in my self-instruction. Significantly, the nature of the passages was very reminiscent of continental cave diving and would prove to be hugely beneficial for future projects.

Steve and I went to France for our summer trip of 1983, along with Stuart Gillet (an old friend from Aston) and Alastair Hill. I had planned a long dive in the nearby Guiers Vif and I was pleased that Alastair wanted to come along. I'd spent weeks preparing for this dive back at home, using my typically low-budget methods. I'd cut out sheets of neoprene and glued them together to create a new wet-suit, then spent hours and days tightly stitching each of the seams. I'd found hundreds of metres of 5mm polypyrene rope, used drawcord that had been abandoned at a worksite. The cord was in a great big tangled mess, and I'd spent weeks untangling it all. Standing outside the cave with Alastair, the salvaged drawcord was now neatly spooled and ready to be repurposed as our guide line.

Before passing the first 240-metre-long sump, Alastair decided that he'd had enough and he signalled to me that he was turning back. The long river cave was filled with melted snow from the

Alpine meadows, and we should have been wearing drysuits with thermal undersuits, instead of the thin wetsuits we each had. We were both underdressed and really cold. I understood why he didn't want to continue and I acknowledged his exit, then signalled that I would keep going alone. I had made a plan and I wanted to see it through.

I continued through several sumps, each with significant dry passages between them. I shivered as I lugged my diving gear over the dry land, before having to slide back into the frigid water. I had the additional and time-consuming task of laying line through the sumps as I passed through them. The dive was slow, and I felt like that cave was never going to end. It wasn't fun.

I emerged in the middle of the night, twelve hours after I'd entered, to find that everyone had gone. I changed into the dry clothes that I'd left and then bivvied down in my sleeping bag. For a little while, I lay awake in the entrance chamber and thought back upon the dive I had just completed. I knew I'd stuck my neck out on that one, more than I should have. I'd been full of innovation and creativity for what I could do and how to get it done; I'd just had no imagination for the difficulty of it.

After that trip in the summer of '83, I found myself diving alone with increasing frequency as the others dropped off for one reason or another. Although I was comfortable on my own – and in many ways I preferred it – I did miss the camaraderie I'd had. There is something to be said for establishing a working partnership with one or two people; sometimes it helps to keep things going. What's that saying? 'If you want to go fast, go alone. If you want to go far, go together.'

I wanted to go far.

⊕   ⊕   ⊕

Stuart Gillet had introduced me to his caving friend Chris Danile-wicz, who was quite gregarious and already well known in the caving world, and we began caving together quite a bit. After graduating from Oxford University with a degree in Geology, Dani had gone on to serve as an Army officer, where he became active with the Army Caving Association, and he was soon offering to take me on trips with the Army cavers. I was eager to join them, but one thing stopped me. By then, my hair had grown quite matted and long, hanging a few inches down my back, and I knew I'd have to cut my hair so I wouldn't stand out so much in the Army crowd.

When I mentioned this, Pip – a girl from the caving club – offered to cut my hair. I let her, and it didn't go very well. She started on one side and cut around the back of my head to the other side, then stepped back. After hacking off my long hair, she had no idea of how to shape it into something vaguely acceptable. 'I don't know what to do next,' she admitted, and I burst out laughing. Fuck. I was left with a ridiculous, lopsided, chin-length pudding-bowl cut until another caver, Kath Davis, fortuitously came by and saved the day

Before Pip and Kath were let loose on my hair.

by cutting my hair properly. Now looking respectable with my short hair, I felt ready to join the Army cavers.

I spent the next few years doing a lot of great caving with Dani, his civilian friends who were cavers up north in Yorkshire and his mates in the Army Caving Association. Most of my diving up to that point had been done on my own, and this is where I first entered the level of other established cave divers. Through Dani and his contacts, I went on more involved trips – including to classic Alpine caves such as the Berger. These trips abroad looked like a *Who's Who* list of Yorkshire cavers, with significant members of the Cave Rescue Organization. I consider those to be my establishing years, where I was starting to become a part of the wider British cave community. These were really experienced cavers, and I was easily able to hold my own with them.

During a trip to the Picos de Europa in Spain in 1985, I reached the enormous milestone of diving through a sump that had never been passed before. This is what it was all about: true exploration. Being the first person to ever reach the unexplored cave beyond a sump is nearly indescribable, and I achieved this feat twice during that trip – first in El Gueyo Renaso and then in El Hoyo la Madre. Raising my head above the water's surface on the far side of the sump, I knew that I was breathing air in a space that nobody had breathed in before. For a moment I was filled with disbelief and wonder at how far I'd come in such a short amount of time.

That trip to Spain was also significant for introducing me to Dani's friends Barry Sudell and Pete Riley. They welcomed me into their circle, and once we were back in England, I quickly began caving with their club, the Northern Pennine Club in Yorkshire. I was pleased to see that the group was highly motivated, active and intent on new exploration, and heavily biased towards cave diving. It was a good fit, and I had found my base for UK caving. (I still consider

NPC my primary caving club, and their caving hut, named Greenclose, quickly became like a second home to me.)

A few months later, in the autumn of 1985, Barry asked for my help on a project. He was attempting to pass the sump at the bottom of Notts Pot, one of the significant potholes in Yorkshire. He had been working on this project for some time with Rupert Skorupka, but now Rupert was going abroad for three months, and Barry needed someone to fill his place. Although I'd only just met Barry that summer, he'd seen that I was a competent caver and he knew I would be an asset. (Another influencing factor was that I was unemployed, so I had the time to commit to the project.)

When Barry came to me with his plans, I was intrigued. When I began researching Notts, I was convinced. There's a caver's saying – 'caves are where you find them' – but there are clues suggesting where unexplored passages may lie, if you know what to look for. The distance water has to travel between the end of a cave and the resurgence are big clues. If they're a kilometre apart and with a big height distance between them, then you know it's going to be a good streamway. If they're at the same height, it's all going to be underwater, sumped.

The sump in Notts Pot lay a considerable distance from where the water resurges at Leck Beck Head. Even more significantly, the sump was perched at an elevation 45 metres higher than the resurgence. There was more to be found there. Barry had found a worthy project, a cave with potential.

Reaching the cave required a moderate walk on the remote Leck Fell and – due to grouse breeding season – we only had access in winter, so it was always dark, cold and icy. Once inside, the trip to the sump included nine sporting vertical pitches, just to get to the start of the dive. There were a number of things adding to the overall difficulty of this project, and we assembled a support team – many of whom were NPC members – to carry our diving equipment (including our steel cylinders) down to the sump for us.

Inside the sump, we had difficulty finding the way on but we persisted, making slow and steady progress over repeated trips. Eighty metres from our dive base, we reached a low, silty slot that was the way on. As soon as one of us had passed through, the disturbed silt clouded the water like the snow in a shaken snow globe, leaving a silt-out[2] for the second diver to move through. I was alone on my seventh dive in Notts when I found myself at the bottom of a gravel slope, looking up a steep hill of tiny pebbles. There was a narrow arch I'd have to squeeze through to get into the ongoing passage, which continued on an incline. I've seen these before and knew their significance. The way on lay beyond that gravel squeeze.

I made my way up the steep slope carefully, mindful of not setting off an avalanche. At the squeeze, I had to dig away at the loose gravel floor to make enough room to get through the low arch. It was like moving through a narrow tunnel of an underwater ball pit. If I continued at that upward angle, I would almost certainly surface, but I didn't want to take that away from Barry. This was his project after all, and he deserved to be the one to finish the dive. With a heavy heart, I dived back down the precarious slope and made my way out, confident that we'd be surfacing on our next dive.

Barry and I returned the following day, for what I hoped would be the breakthrough dive. Barry went first up the gravel slope and I was close behind. Ascending the inclined passage after the gravel squeeze, I saw the tantalizing glimmer that signals water meeting air. This was it. The end of the sump. We broke surface into an open, gloomy canal, then swam through the half-flooded passage before reaching dry land in a domed chamber of clean, black limestone. Beyond the sump was a large inviting passage, waiting to be explored, and explore it we did.

Together, Barry and I shared the privilege of being the first to walk through these previously unseen tunnels and chambers, for what was one of the finest walks through a cave I've experienced. Walking through a new cave is an entirely different experience from moving through one that has been well travelled through. Often a pristine cave is quite a delicate environment, and the floor is quite slippery because it's never been walked on, and any feature you encounter could easily break or move. In anticipation of success, I'd brought my wellies with me on this dive – rolled up and attached to my cylinders. With them on my feet, I was able to scurry up side passages to investigate leads, while Barry cautiously crept along in his neoprene socks, moving gingerly along the virgin cave floor. I managed to see a lot more of the cave than he did. (I'd told him to bring his wellies with him too, but he hadn't believed that we'd pass the sump so soon.)

We travelled nearly a kilometre and a half down the new streamway. One particularly spectacular area was adorned with pure white stalactites descending from the ceiling and gleaming flowstone curtains blanketing the walls. Finally, we reached a waterfall. After climbing down the cascade, the cave lowered and we crawled along a floor lined with cobblestone before the roof dipped beneath the surface of the water. A second sump. We turned and exited, excited to tell others about our day underground and what we had discovered. It remains a source of lasting pride that Barry and I were the first human beings to wander down that magnificent section of cave.[3]

That evening at Greenclose, the Northern Pennine Club's committee meeting was being held, and one task was to vote on prospective members. As each name was mentioned, the members of the committee reviewed their history with the club and then voted on their induction. Towards the end of the meeting, the last name on the list was read, and Bill Pybus spoke up. 'Rick Stanton . . . Who's he?'

Moments later, Barry and I arrived with our news of having found Notts 2, causing Bill to exclaim, 'Christ, it's going all the way to Kleine Scheidegg!' By naming the mountain railway station beneath the north face of the Eiger in Switzerland, Bill inadvertently christened the last chamber before the second sump with its name.

A group of Pennine members worked together surveying and mapping the new parts of Notts Pot, making dozens of trips in over the next three months. The teamwork was infectious and fun, and I really enjoyed being a central part of it. When our work in Notts Pot was completed, my membership as a Qualified Diver in the Northern section of the Cave Diving Group was secured, and my place in British caving history was cemented. The overall sense of achievement was greater for me than the sum of the project's individual components.

It's rare for a discovery to garner as much excitement and acclaim as this had done, and my status as a relative newcomer on the scene made my involvement even more meaningful. Back at the caving hut after one of our trips underground, John Cordingley – one of Britain's most active and experienced cave divers, who had joined our surveying team – took me aside and sagely imparted, 'Savour this, Rick. You're only at the start of your diving career, but you're unlikely to experience a project quite like this again.'

I appreciated his words, but it felt like a bit of a blow. I stood alone in the hut as the others mingled and chatted, thinking about the implications of John's words. Had the highlight of my career already come and gone?

Now what am I going to do?

'The rain is pissing down. If the boys weren't dead
already, they probably are now.'

Thursday, 28 June 2018, Thailand

Our first full day in Thailand began with a phone call. My friend in
Florida had replied to the message I'd sent to her before leaving
home. She had questions, of course, so I rang her to fill her in on
what was happening. I recounted our aborted attempt to get into the
cave the evening before, then described the flood inside the cave
that had turned us back.

Next, I told her that the Americans were coming to save the day.
We had been told the US military would be arriving at Tham Luang
today, with a plan 'to make the caves bigger' using explosives. Karen
laughed when she heard this, sensing my concern that they were
going to try to take over control of the rescue mission. 'Well, hurry
up and find the boys before the Americans get in there and mess
everything up.'

In the first days of the search – before we'd arrived – two Thai
SEALs had managed to reach 135 metres beyond Monk's Junction, so
John and I knew that any hope for finding the boys would lie beyond
that point. We were now familiar with the cave up to Chamber 3, but
reaching the T-junction would require another dive, through 800
metres of unknown cave with poor visibility. That was our goal for
the day, and we wanted to sit and talk with Vern before we attempted
to dive.

Vern's partner Tik had collected a breakfast for us all, and they
arrived at the resort early in the day. John, Rob and I gathered around
the table on the wooden deck in front of our cabin, while Vern and
Tik laid out the meal they'd brought. I'm not choosy when it comes

to food so I eagerly dug in. I glanced at John, who is a notoriously picky eater, and saw him halfheartedly pushing the vegetables around his plate. I didn't know how he was going to manage living there, being served food cooked by locals, for however long we'd be there. *Crikey, he's thin enough already; that's why he gets colder than me on any dive.*

While I worked at cleaning my plate, and John ate some rice, Vern began to tell us about Tham Luang, sharing the knowledge he'd gained through his years of exploration. We looked over his notes and maps, and I shared information from Martin Ellis that had been passed along to me. Vern reiterated that the tunnel beyond Monk's Junction is relatively level, without steep vertical ascents or descents, which meant that none of the dives would be very deep (which was good), but also meant there'd be few places that could have provided much safety from the previous night's flood (which was bad).

Vern told us about one elevated chamber he thought might be worth searching: a spot he had been told was named Pattaya Beach, which lay about 700 metres beyond Monk's Junction. Martin had also described this area: 'After about 600 m [the cave] opens up into a walking sized passage which ends at a chamber with a high aven.' I picked up the map to look for Pattaya Beach's location. I couldn't be bothered to fetch my reading glasses, so I used my tried-and-tested pinhole technique for improving my vision, ignoring John's withering look when he saw me raise my fingers to my eye and squint through them at the paper.

As my eyesight had begun to deteriorate with age, I'd learned that looking through a pinhole formed by my thumb and two fingers of one hand helped focus my gaze enough to allow me to read fine print. (Try it – it does work.) I know that it looks a bit daft, but the method proves handy when I'm caught without glasses, and it had become second nature to me. Most of my friends laugh at me when

I do this, and on the flight over John had pleaded with me not to be caught in front of cameras doing it while we were in Thailand.

'That thing you do to read,' he'd said on the aeroplane, 'would you mind not doing it in front of the cameras? It makes you look a bit . . . eccentric.' I knew he was being kind.

'I'll try not to do it in public,' I'd assured him, as if I needed an additional thing to be concerned with.

Our journey over had been interesting. Although we'd been put on an overnight flight, the three of us didn't get much sleep, and for a while neither did any of the passengers who'd had the misfortune of being placed close to us. Undeterred by the fact that we were stretched across a row of seats in the business-class section, John, Rob and I immediately launched into discussions of the incident.

At the time of the flight, news about the football team in Thailand had just spread to England but was not yet a top story, so many of our fellow passengers likely didn't know what on earth we were talking about when they heard us discussing diving equipment, possible conditions in the cave and what our first steps should be. John voiced the possibility that we'd probably find the children's dead bodies in one of the sumps, and we agreed that we'd leave them in there.

'If they're all dead, they're staying in there. We're not going to spend days swimming around with dead bodies. That's not our responsibility, and we're not going to traumatize ourselves with bringing thirteen bodies out of a cave.'

'Can you imagine if they've been in twenty-three-degree water for days? They'll be in a disgusting state, ready to break apart. Their heads will be dropping off and all sorts.'

It was at this point that a flight attendant finally stepped in and asked us if we might prefer moving to a different row, where we would be in adjoining seats.

'No,' John and I replied in unison. As it was, we were comfortably spaced out with consoles separating us; we didn't want to be spending the night in each other's personal space.

After the flight attendant left, we continued our discussions. This would be multi-sump diving – an amphibious combination of diving and dry caving – which is the exact sort of caving that has become our specialty over the years. As we discussed the dives we'd be doing and John considered my preferred diving kit, a sudden realization brought up a new concern.

'You haven't packed that inner-tube wing, have you?' he asked, already suspecting the answer. 'You're going to look a complete cockwomble wearing that.'

He was referring to my preferred buoyancy device. Instead of a fancy and expensive one, which can now be purchased from any dive shop, I chose to use a homemade contraption that I'd devised years ago from the inner tube of a motorbike tyre. Mine was simple, durable and effective and has travelled with me on countless dives, including several rescues that have ended successfully.

'Of course I brought it,' I told him. 'It's my lucky wing. It's already helped me save six people.'

He cringed and closed his eyes, taking a breath to calm himself, as if he couldn't believe he would be associated with me and that thing publicly. I ignored him. John and I have different styles of diving, but we know not to mess with each other's preferences because what we do works for each of us. That doesn't mean he isn't embarrassed to be seen with me sometimes, though.

⊕   ⊕   ⊕

After breakfast with Tik and Vern, we were driven to Tham Luang by the two officers from the Tourist Police Bureau who had been selected as our personal chaperones. The same ones who had driven us from Chiang Rai airport, they apparently were going to be along-side us for the duration of our stay, whether we liked it or not. We were initially uneasy with the thought of having our every move-ment and discussion monitored, but Tom and Bas quickly allayed our fears. They proved to be indescribably helpful parts of our mis-sion, providing a vital link to the Thai government,[4] while also being good people whom we quickly learned to trust as friends. John and I can be a bit standoffish, and there were times when we were under tremendous amounts of external pressure during the rescue, but Tom and Bas were always easy-going and a constant source of support. I don't know if they'd been specifically selected for their compatibility with us, or if it had just been the luck of the draw; however it hap-pened, I couldn't imagine a better selection. Their presence absolutely contributed to the success of the mission.

Not all aspects of the rescue would run as smoothly, though, and we were soon reminded of the chaotic state of things at the park when we arrived at our gear room to find that the compressor had disap-peared. Rob and Vern's description of the cave, combined with the amount of rain that had fallen, had led us to expect longer-range dives than we had previously envisaged, and we had quickly realized that the operation would need more cylinders and gas supplies than were available. When I had sent Larry off to find a compressor the night before, he had taken the one from the Thai Navy SEALs' area,[5] set-ting off what would become something of a clandestine game of hide-and-seek as the SEALs and I each tried to claim ownership of the compressor.

After tracking down the compressor outside Governor Narong-sak's office, we immediately set to work noisily filling our cylinders. An official soon came running out of the building, complaining that the noise of the compressor was drowning out the press conference being held inside. Without a word, John and I carried the compressor and set it up outside our room again, which is where we'd wanted it all along. A compressor is often the scourge of any diving expedition, and this one was proving no exception.

Tanks filled, we changed into our diving kit and went to the cave. As we walked the short distance between our gear room and the entrance, we passed through a crowd of press who began snapping our photographs and yelling questions to us. One reporter shoved a microphone into John's face, which he quickly brushed aside with the curt response, 'We've got a job to do.'

I glanced over at John quickly, to see how he was taking all of this. His brows furrowed, he seemed even more aggravated by the chaos and crowds than I was, and it wasn't long before we were being referred to in the press as 'the stony-faced Brits' – which is not the worst thing I've ever been called.

I wore an old one-piece wetsuit (well-worn with various unpatched holes), neoprene socks, caving kneepads, a helmet with lights, and standard green Dunlop wellies. I carried my fins, which would slip over the boots while diving. A home-made harness strapped round my waist carried some lead blocks and allowed a cylinder to be slung on each hip, in the side-mounted configuration commonly used in caves. Attached to each cylinder was a Poseidon Cyklon regulator, identical to the one I'd first purchased with Steve Joyce thirty-seven years earlier. John was dressed similarly, except for one crucial difference: I was wearing an inflated rubber tube on my back.

My lucky wing.

'Rick,' John sighed after we'd walked past the reporters and their cameras. 'You look like you don't even know how to swim.'

Inside the cave, we found the entrance chamber had changed drastically from the night before. It was now a large lake, with a river cascading noisily in from the cave's throat – just as Vern had predicted. There didn't appear to be anybody operating in the flooded cave beyond the entrance chamber, but there was nobody stopping us from entering, so we went in.

John was correct. We had a job to do.

Within 100 metres of the entrance, we encountered a sump where we'd been able to walk through just fourteen hours earlier. We slipped our fins over our wellies and went in. Immersed in the muddy water, with no visibility and a vicious current, we began the arduous task of laying line as we penetrated further inside. We surfaced at the far end of the sump, to find ourselves standing in a river that was surging against us. John and I are both experienced whitewater kayakers, and our knowledge of navigating through swiftly moving water became unexpectedly useful for us as we walked through, placing ourselves strategically to prevent the force of the current from knocking us off our feet or pinning us against the wall at the corners.

The cave back here reeked, polluted with the diesel fuel leaking from the pump beyond Chamber 3. I started to gag and retch. A further short dive led through the archway that had nearly trapped Rob the previous evening, which was now 4 metres underwater. On its other side, we began ascending through a confusion of cables and large clusters of hose towards the large third chamber. After surfacing, John and I were startled to see a flashlight and hear voices.

'The boys are here?' I wondered incredulously. 'Have some of them found a way out, in desperation?' As the owners of the voices approached, though, I saw that they were four adult men. My initial disappointment was immediately replaced with confusion, and then aggravation. What on earth were they doing there?

The men were excited to see us, and the one who came forward as their leader was the most excited of them all. Surapin Chaichompoo spoke loudly to us in Thai, and when it became obvious that John and I were foreigners who didn't understand the language, he began gesticulating wildly with his hands and arms. Somehow, he communicated that the four of them had been working on installing the water pumps there in Chamber 3. When everybody else had made an orderly evacuation twenty-four hours earlier, they had been napping in an alcove. They'd slept through it all and had awoken to find themselves trapped and abandoned.

'They must have been here when Rob popped in last night.' John said exactly what I was thinking. 'Has nobody even noticed that they've been missing?'

We took off our diving gear and walked around in our wetsuits and wellies to have a look. This side of the chamber was largely comprised of muddy, slippery slopes. Then there was a dividing rib of rock, on the far side of which lay a large sandy plateau, approximately 15 metres in diameter. The trapped men had been placing marks in the sandy rise of the plateau to track the level of the water. At the moment, this plateau was less than a metre above water, and Surapin indicated with excitement that the water had risen a half metre in the past half-hour alone.

Before taking any action, we looked at where the water was issuing from, at the far end of the chamber. Beyond Chamber 3, the water was surging. Strong pulses of upwelling water burst on the surface and swirled around, pushed out by the steady beating of the cave's heart. The force was violent. As much as John and I would have liked to continue, it seemed pointless given the conditions. Anyway, we had these men to deal with. So much for searching and laying line further into the cave today.

We needed to take the men out, but how? There were four of them, two of us, and no spare diving equipment. We didn't have time to retreat, put together a plan, find reinforcements – *who would we have used anyway?* – and return in time. Instead, we held a quick discussion.

'If we leave them here, they'll be treading water before we get back to them.'

'Besides, there is nobody else. We'd be the ones to do the rescue anyway.'

'We have everything we need with us. Let's just do it.'

Although we had not taken in spare equipment, cave divers depend on redundancy of equipment. Always have at least two of everything you need. In keeping, each of our harnesses held two cylinders and each cylinder had its own demand valve attached to it. We used hand gestures to let the men know that we would be diving them out, one at a time, with them breathing off of our spare cylinder. At first, the men seemed more concerned about their phones' safety than their own rescue. I watched as they carefully wrapped their mobile devices in plastic bags and then put them inside a canvas pouch, which they handed over to me delicately.

None of the men seemed like they'd be particularly comfortable in the water. On the other hand, they were adult men who were desperate to get out and they all seemed willing, so I didn't think we'd have a problem. I selected one of the younger men to go first. In order to help him acclimatize to being underwater, I first gave him a regulator to practise breathing through while his face was submerged. This typically proves to be helpful in calming a non-diver who would be breathing underwater for the first time, but it didn't work this time. As soon as his face was immersed, the young man began flailing his arms wildly, pulling his face out of the water and desperately gasping for air. I thought maybe he shouldn't be the first one out, and that it might comfort him to see others go first. I beckoned to Surapin, who was more agreeable to the learning process, and we soon set off underwater.

What an epic.

With Surapin breathing through the regulator attached to my

second cylinder, he was tethered to me by the hose that was providing his life-sustaining air. He would need to stay by my side. With my arm around his back and my hand gripped onto the armpit of his T-shirt, I kept a secure hold, guiding him through the difficult terrain. My other hand was tightly holding the line to keep us both from getting lost.

Remembering the jumble of hoses and wires I'd encountered on the way in, I knew that diving down to the archway on the way out would be awkward, but I wasn't expecting to encounter ledges of rock jutting out towards us. The walls and ceiling were jagged with these protruding rocks, which had gone unnoticed on the ceiling above us as we'd passed underneath and ascended. Now, heading down to go out, they kept catching us as we tried to go through. I was doing everything I could to avoid the rocks, but the dive was treacherous. Surapin's head was exposed – I had no way to protect it, and he didn't think to use his arms as a shield – and I heard an audible thud each time his head collided with the ceiling.

After finally passing through the archway, the sump's deepest point, Surapin must have sensed that we were rising, and he became desperate. Unaware that we were not beneath an airspace, Surapin tried to swim away from me in an attempt to reach the surface more hastily. I could sense that he had lost control. The rescue turned into an underwater wrestling match.

I struggled to keep a grip on him with one hand while keeping my other hand securely fastened around the line. If he escaped from me, I knew he would have been unlikely to locate the airspace that lay ahead of him, and I would have been hard-pressed to find him. Had I lost the line, we would both be lost. Just as I knew we were close to breaking the surface, the struggles became too much and I released my grip on him, knowing I'd deal with the consequences in a moment after I'd gained my bearings.

The area where he surfaced was low, with maybe 10cm of air-space between the water and the ceiling. I hoped he'd figure to turn onto his back and keep his nose up, but I heard his head strike the roof as he tried to burst out of the water, followed by the sounds of him spluttering for breath and spitting out water. I ascended and surfaced along the line, gained my bearing and made my way back to him, then twisted his head so his nose was sticking into the airspace.

After a few breaths helped to calm him, I led him to an area that was large enough for him to breathe more comfortably. I guided his feet to a sloping ledge where he could stand while he regained his composure. Then, when he was safely on dry land, I clipped the spare reg to its D-ring on my neck strap and dived back to Chamber 3. John was waiting to see how it had gone.

'That was quite exciting,' I told him drily. 'Not in a good way.'[6]

While Surapin and I had been off on our adventure, John had re-evaluated the situation and assessed that the first worker would have been a lot calmer if he'd been wearing a mask. I'd lend my mask to the next worker, and John would come back with it after the dive, then John would lend his to the next man I dived with. John's mask has prescription lenses and he was hesitant to hand it over – 'If this gets lost, we're fucked' – but he knew there was no other choice. This situation wasn't ideal, and we were having to improvise as we went.

The remaining three dives from Chamber 3 went more smoothly than the first had. By the time John and I made our last exit, the current was considerably stronger and swirling around us in pulses. I wondered if the men had noticed how much the water had risen in the twenty minutes since we'd first arrived.

We found the men were much calmer when they were together again in the second chamber; I was even struck by their resourcefulness when they unplugged one of the electric lights to augment their own weak torches. The final dive of the rescue was once again Surapin and me together, leaving for the cave entrance. Despite what had happened earlier, I presumed he still trusted me – he didn't really have any other choice – but then as poor luck would have it, my light switched off just after we began descending beneath the surface of the water. I briefly debated continuing in darkness, but thought it more prudent to turn around and get the light sorted before completing the dive.

When we surfaced, back where we'd started, Surapin thought that we had reached safety. He tore away from me yet again, running off up the passage in search of the others. I let him go while I fettled with my light, confident he would sort himself out. I knew he didn't have anywhere to go. Soon he realized this too and came back to me with a quizzical look, not understanding why his friends weren't there. When my light was fixed, I signalled that we still had to dive out. To his credit, he accepted this relatively calmly.

When we had all successfully reached the entrance chamber, we approached the nearest Thai SEAL as a group. 'We found these four men in Chamber 3 and brought them out.' When I heard John say those words out loud, I was struck by how utterly ridiculous the past hour had been. The Thai SEAL looked unimpressed and, understandably, a bit bewildered. Fortunately, we had Surapin – who was never short of words – to explain the situation to them. Before leaving, the four men thanked us repeatedly for saving them, wanting to be sure that we understood their gratitude in spite of the language barrier. I handed over their phones optimistically, and the four men disappeared into the crowd.[7] That day's unexpected rescue mission, full of drama as it had been, provided valuable lessons that would go on to inform many of the decisions we'd make the following week while planning the boys' rescue.

What did we learn? What would we do differently? Our gears were already turning. The boys couldn't be expected to stay calm during a series of dives that would be much longer and more challenging than the dives these men had just struggled with. We'd have to find a way to account for the panic. Although neither of us held much hope for finding the boys alive, we were nevertheless appreciating that today's rescue had provided us clear lessons for what would need to be done.

Securely fitting masks . . . Something to protect their heads during the dive out . . .

We returned to our gear room in silence, still trying to process everything that had happened and wondering what could possibly go wrong next. As we stepped out of our muddy boots and harnesses, John finally let rip with what we were both thinking.

'Fuck! Fuck! Fuuuuuccccck!' he screamed at the wall, as loudly as I've ever heard him, in a pure display of lalochezia.[8] The limits of his frustration and incredulity had been reached – and breached even – while I was still letting everything wash over me. John is more of an over-thinker than I am, and he was possibly more stressed in Thailand than I'd ever previously seen him. I had further to go yet before I'd reach my breaking point.

A few minutes later, the mood was lightened a bit when Vern and Rob showed up to ask us what had happened on our dive. As we were filling them in, a handful of Thais suddenly entered our room, bringing with them a man I hadn't seen in years.

Ben Reymenants is a respected Belgian cave diver I'd met at OzTek, a technical diving convention that is held in Australia. Ben runs a diving school in Phuket and works as an instructor, so I knew he would have vast experience diving in the flooded abyss-like caves of southern Thailand. I was pleased to see a familiar face, particularly a fellow cave diver, and especially one who had formed a connection with the SEALs. Standing with him was his colleague Bruce Konefe, an American who was also a dive instructor.

I've found that cavers tend to share the common traits of being intelligent decision-makers and quick, clever thinkers. These qualities had been sorely lacking in most of the people we'd encountered at Tham Luang up to that point, so now being in the presence of other cave divers – English-speaking ones at that – was a relief. John and I began conferring with them in an effort to gather information, thinking that having Ben and Bruce on our team could only strengthen our effort.

Not for the first time that day, we were about to be disappointed.

Ben began by telling us about the Thai SEALs' first dive on Monday, when they could still walk to Monk's Junction. According to Ben, the SEALs 'dived into a sump and got to a point where the passage was so tight, they had to take their cylinders off and try to dig their way forward with their hands.' He continued, 'There they got to a place where the current suddenly reversed. It started flowing away from the entrance, into the mountain.' Vern immediately interjected.

'There's nowhere that small on the route to Pattaya Beach,' he said confidently, with Rob in agreement. John and I believed Vern and Rob, who had so far only provided reliable information about the cave. As for the claim of the current reversal, we all knew that to be impossible. What likely happened is that the SEALs – being inexperienced in caves and out of their element – had become disorientated. I thought the SEALs must have been off-route and to the side of the main passage, where it would be quite plausible to find a low section. Ben's report had only made me more aware of the danger the SEALs were in, trying to dive in a cave that was well beyond their experience and training.

While I considered this danger, Vern was trying to make Ben understand why a current reversal is impossible. Appearing not to be dissuaded, Ben pointed to his map, saying that it was vitally important to find where the 'reversing current' exits the cave on the other side of the mountain. He thought this might provide another entrance for reaching the boys, a back door. He gathered his map and set off, presumably to start this quest. John and I watched them leave.

So much for our hopes of working together with Ben.

That evening, we gathered once again on the deck in front of our room at the resort to enjoy another meal brought by Tik and Vern. The five of us sat in the gloom to debrief about our day, all of us feeling defeated by our steady lack of progress. We'd saved four men's lives but were no closer to the boys.

After I finished eating, and in need of cheering up, I went inside to phone Amp at home. She had offered to come to Tham Luang immediately when she knew I was on my way, but I'd told her to wait until I could assess what was happening on site. I'd initially been reluctant to bring her in and submit her to the chaos; I'd also wanted to protect her from the emotional trauma of whatever we might be walking into. Disregarding my advice, she had arrived at the outer police cordon while John and I had been in with the pump workers, carrying homecooked food with her, but had been forbidden from entering into the restricted area.

When Amp answered her phone at home, we arranged for her to return the next day, Friday. This time I would be there to meet her at the outer police cordon. Knowing I'd be seeing her again, I started feeling a bit better and more hopeful than I had since arriving.

From: Richard Stanton
To: Bill Whitehouse

Confidential – complete chaos here with no control of hundreds of rescue workers or press.
Water is at the entrance chamber, current still increasing.
Today JV and I entered alone (the cave is off limits to most) passed two short siphons to reach the 3rd chamber. This is nowhere near the junction with Monks passage on the survey.
Here we unbelievably encountered a team of 4 trapped rescue workers that nobody knew was there. We had to dive them out on the spot as it wasn't clear if we could even reach this far again.
No one on the surface seemed at all perturbed.

From: Ben Svasti Thomson
To: Richard Stanton

Hello Rick,

This is Ben Svasti Thomson, I'm the British Honorary Consul for Northern Thailand.
I'm ready to provide support to your team in anyway needed.

From: Ben Svasti Thomson
To: Bill Whitehouse

It seems from talking to various people that coordination between the huge number of rescue units onsite is problematic.
I'm arranging for US team to sit down with British team and see if negotiating power with Thai authorities can be improved.
I've talked to Thai authorities to see if they can get a tighter grip on the rescue site and improve coordination structure.

PART TWO
Prepare

4.
Teammates and Rivals

In April of 1986, two cavers went inside Kingsdale Master Cave in Yorkshire. The trip was meant to be brief – they were planning to free dive some sumps – but they failed to return at their scheduled call-out time, and the alarm was raised.

When notified of their delay, the Yorkshire-based Cave Rescue Organization (CRO)[1] quickly sprang into action to assist. Volunteers arrived on scene, and a team was quickly formed and sent underground. The cave was in such flood that they couldn't progress far upstream from the Master Cave, where the missing cavers had entered; instead, they decided to drop down into Rowten Pot. A local caver named David Anderson was one of the first to enter Rowten Pot in search of the missing. David was descending through one of the vertical pitches, to approach the area where the missing cavers might be found, when a flood pulse engulfed him. He was washed off a traverse and, with a forceful waterfall pouring over him, he drowned while hanging on his rope.

Now, who rescues the rescuer?

As was quite typical for the time, police were dispatched to various local cavers' haunts, looking for additional resources. 'There are two missing in Kingsdale, if anybody is able and willing to join the search . . .' This being a Saturday evening, there were plenty of us there in the pub, and although I was not a member of the Cave Rescue Organization, I went along with the others.

By the time I arrived, everyone knew of David's fate, and there was quite a sombre atmosphere. Another team had to be assembled to go down for David, so Geoff Crossley, a locally active caver, stepped forward to take on this task. Of all the people there on the surface, he had to pick the ones he wanted for this second team. He knew this would be a tricky one, and not everyone would be suited for what would be required. He'd need people who would be able to go into a cave that was in a terrifying state of flood, yet were able to remain calm and capable of looking for the still-missing cavers, without a repeat of the misstep that David had taken. In addition, this second team must be able to cope with the presence of David's body, which was still hanging on its rope at the top of a waterfall.

We were all gathered there on the surface, standing in the rain, a group of Yorkshire cavers with their equipment piled around them. I watched as Geoff looked around at the group, trying to select the right people for the job. Standing on a field with a group of others, being sized up for consideration by a leader, reminded me of standing on the playing field while I was in school, waiting for the team captains to select the ones they wanted on their team. In school, I'd had no interest in ball sports and had never been selected, but we were not in school, and this was not a ball game.

Geoff swiftly selected me for the team, and I gathered my kit. I knew David personally, but not well. We'd been caving together once or twice – he'd been on the big Army trip to the Berger; I'd even visited his house and gone to the pub with him a few times. Still, I wasn't worried. I knew I wouldn't have an issue coping with any of it.

To approach David's body, we walked on a metre-wide ledge that ran along a wall, suspended over a big drop. A hole in the wall ahead of us had the river coming out of it, pouring over the ledge and down. This is where we found him, still hanging on his rope, in the waterfall at the top of the shaft. We needed to somehow clip a rope to David before we could cut the rope that he was hanging off, but the water was so powerful that we couldn't walk very close to the place where his body was hanging. We didn't have many options, with the cave in its flooded state, and because I was the tallest – with the longest reach – the solution was obvious. I was selected for the task.

David's body was being thrashed around by the water, and it was just beyond my reach. Watto (Ian Watson), a big strong bloke I knew only by reputation, came up with a very old-school solution. Instead of having me tensioned on a lifeline, he recognized it would be far simpler and quicker to just grab me by the back of my collar as I leaned out to clip on to David's body. Watto was supporting the weight of my body in our makeshift neck belay. I never felt unsafe, and it obviously worked, but I can't imagine this method being adopted as accepted practice.

Once we had David off the rope and resting on the floor, Watto bent over David's body and rotated his hood so that his face was covered. It struck me as odd at first that he would do that, but then I appreciated its effect. It was easier to cope with a faceless body, an anonymous parcel. When we were removing the body, we reached a narrow passage that was only wide enough for one person and we had no choice but to lift David's body above our heads. We didn't have a stretcher; we just held his body aloft as we walked him through. His body was held above us, as we carried him along like five bizarre, ritualized pallbearers. It was a very surreal moment.

After that, the team sort of dispersed. Watto and Geoff continued on to find the original pair of missing cavers,[2] another went off to advise the hauling team, and I was left with this other guy whom I'd never met before (nor have I seen him since). We were left there staring at the body, which we had to put into a body bag before it was hauled aloft. I don't know if there was a proper technique for doing this, and clearly neither did he. Between the two of us, we just sort of manhandled him into the bag. It wasn't graceful, but it got the job done.

This event was noteworthy because it was – and still is – the only time a cave rescuer has died in the UK during a rescue effort. It was also the first time I'd been on a rescue or recovery mission. I'd suspected that the encounter with a dead body would not upset me, and I had been correct. Even though I had known him personally, and he had been involved in the cave rescue community, I was able to switch off any emotions or thoughts during the recovery. His body had just been a large item that had to be removed from the cave safely; being able to consider the situation unemotionally had allowed us to do what needed to be done.

Not long after my involvement with David Anderson's death, in the spring of 1986, my mother was given the news that she was dying. She went to the doctor one day, and he said, 'You've got bowel cancer, with three months to live.' Just like that. She was fifty-seven years old, and there was nothing to be done.

I took the news of her illness in my stride and went home to visit her once while she was ill. She was bedridden by then, and so I saw her upstairs in her bedroom. Mum had become a bit of a hoarder in her later years, and she had piles of papers all over the room. At one point, she became excited and wanted to show me something. As she reached for the newspaper cutting she wanted, she fell out of bed and landed with a thump on the floor. Unhurt, she started laughing as I lifted her up – I was surprised by how light she felt in my arms – and set her back in her bed.

The noise had sent Dad running up the stairs to check on us. 'What was that? What happened?' he asked as he came into the room.

By then, Mum was tucked in and she looked up at him inno-cently. 'Nothing happened.'

That was the last time I saw her. I didn't go to the hospital when she was there, and I didn't even go with Jane to see her body after she'd died. There didn't seem to be any point. I was twenty-five years old then and so wrapped up in my own life that I wasn't very affected by her death when it happened. I just didn't see the point at the time, but maybe I should have done more. A friend asked me recently if I'd ever told Mum about how her suggestion to watch *The Underground Eiger* had directly led to my interest in caving. I was surprised by the question because it made me realize that I had never acknowledged that connection before and I certainly had never spoken about it with Mum. Neither of my parents had engaged very much with what I'd been doing. She knew I was caving and might have made the connec-tion herself, but we had never talked about it. I had never thanked her.

After she died, I felt sad, a bit pissed off about it all, but didn't slow down enough to think too much about it. I'm not even sure I was that upset at her funeral. I don't remember crying.

Sixteen years later, my father passed away and he was buried in the same grave as Mum. Being back there for Dad's burial was the first time I'd returned to the cemetery, and it affected me more than I expected. I hadn't cried when Mum was buried but I was upset at my dad's funeral. When the grave was open for his coffin to go in, I don't know if I saw her coffin, but I was thinking of Mum. We were burying Dad, but I was thinking of Mum. My girlfriend Abigail was with me, we were standing there with Jane, and as I looked at the hole in the ground, I think I said something like, 'Mum's down there.' And that suddenly sort of hit me, maybe for the first time, sixteen years after her death.

My family was always disassociated, very unemotional, and that's the way I've always been. We weren't close or connected with each other the way some other families seem to be. Ours was a very placid home. Mum provided a great nurturing environment, but our family wasn't close or warm. My parents never hugged us or said, 'I love you.' None of us did. I don't know if that's how all families were in those times, or if ours was unusual in that respect.

I've never known any other way.

$$\oplus \quad \oplus \quad \oplus$$

I was still being invited along on Chris Danilewicz's trips abroad with the Army Caving Association, and in 1987 we went to the Peruvian Andes. It was a prospecting trip, and although we didn't find any decent caves, it was worthwhile for introducing me to Ian Rolland. I'd already known Ian by reputation – mainly as part of Rob Parker's gang of divers who were pushing Wookey Hole Cave in the UK – and I was glad to finally meet him in Peru. We spent a lot of time talking there, quickly sussing each other out as worthy partners for future projects. Before long, Ian asked if I wanted to join him in exploring a cave in Wales.

There's an area in Wales, on the lush moorland above Abergavenny and overlooking the Usk Valley, where visitors enjoy breathtaking panoramic views of the rolling hillside and mountains. Cavers are also drawn to this scenic location, but it's not to admire the countryside around them. Instead, cavers are the sort to look down and feel compelled to squeeze into the person-sized hole that is found there, on the edge of a limestone face known as the Llangattock Escarpment. The casual day hiker would walk past this hole without a glance, having no idea that beneath it lie kilometres of exquisitely beautiful and remote cave passage, a massive cave system named Ogof y Daren Cilau.

Daren Cilau had been one of the early caves we had ticked off at Aston University. After squeezing through its entrance, I'd been greeted with a committing 600-metre crawl through wet rock, which required shimmying on my belly or side for most of its length. The crawl is not everybody's cup of tea and is often seen as something that 'needs to be done'. It was known as a collector's piece, just like St Dunstan's Well – completed only for the sake of it. For a long time, it was essentially a crawl to nowhere, as there was not much cave to be seen beyond it. Then, in 1984, Welsh cavers broke through with a crowbar, revealing an extensive cave beyond that was mapped for many kilometres before reaching an inlet sump, named St David's. Now that ridiculous crawl at least led somewhere.

Taking over where the Welsh team had left off, Ian and Rob Parker had found further passages beyond St David's, and they'd continued exploration to the terminal upstream sump, in one of the most remote sections of any British cave. Ian named this Seventh Hour Sump, in deference to the seven hours of hard caving that were needed to reach it. Just getting there meant you had to be a good caver and diver, with loads of stamina and energy still in reserve. Ian had identified an unclimbed lead there, which he suspected would be the way on. It was a long way to go in a day, before even reaching the challenging climb that Ian was targeting. This is when Rob had to leave the project, and Ian brought me in.

Our first trip underground together was a twenty-six-hour excursion, an ambitious day of demanding caving which showed me that I had found my match in Ian. He was as skilled in caving as he seemed to be in every aspect of life, and we moved quickly through the various sections of cave leading up to the climb. Even with our steady pace, it still took us eight hours to arrive all the way back there, and then we stood there together sizing it up. I immediately saw what he had: the cave showed clear signs of continuing above. The face of the wall rose from the cave floor, relatively smooth and featureless for the first 3 metres of ascent, before the rock became more interesting. Naturally, because he was lighter and a better climber, Ian stood on my shoulders to get a closer look at this 'more interesting' piece of rock; he was searching for any feature that could be used for aid. After a few moments he looked down at me, considering something.

'Pass me your belt,' he said.

I was wearing a band of nylon webbing around my waist, holding the rechargeable battery for my headlamp. I removed the belt, slipping off the battery with one hand, and handed the belt up to him. I could feel his weight shifting as he worked at something on the rock, then his weight on my shoulders was removed as he scaled the rock face. I stepped back and looked up to see that he had threaded my belt through a hole in the wall, secured the buckle of the harness and used the looped belt as a foothold. As I looked up, admiring his craftsmanship, his head reappeared over the lip of the rock wall.

'It goes!' Two words that are music to any cave explorer's ears.

There was new cave to explore. I'd felt this excitement a few times before, and I would feel it again many times in the years to come. It never has, and never will, become any less thrilling to me. I knew that Ian felt the same way I did, and although he was only 5 metres above me, the distance between us felt vast. I wanted to be up there, to run off with him into the unexplored cave. Knowing it was up there and I was down here was torturous, and it soon became worse with the realization that I had no way of getting up there after him. My belt loop dangled a metre above my reach.

Ian had a solution.

'There's a rope in Prawn Cracker Passage,' he yelled down, naming a passage he had pointed out to me twenty minutes earlier. Ian had proved to be reliable, and I had no reason not to trust him, but as I ran for the rope I had the sinking realization that he could easily set off without me, leaving me stranded at the bottom of the climb while he explored his new passage alone. I ran through the cave as quickly as I dared, bearing in mind that we were in a spot so remote that an injury to one of us would be disastrous for both of us. Returning twenty minutes later with rope in hand, I saw he was still there, his head poking out from over the rock.

'What have you found so far?' I called up to him.

'I haven't moved,' he answered. 'I'm waiting for you.'

Standing below, I tossed the rope up to him, and he found a suitable anchor to tie it off. I ascended the climb (which we would name Jacob's Ladder), collecting my belt on the way up, and within seconds I was standing by his side again. The rest of the cave lay ahead of us, and we set off for it together, two boys alone on a magnificent playground. We passed through large chambers that were filled with stalagmites, stalactites and flowstone curtains, some of which were stained turquoise by some mineral impurity. After a few hundred metres, we had to stop our exploration when we reached a drop. We saw that it would be easy enough to negotiate, but we had no remaining rope with us, so we had to turn back.

I didn't mind. I was thrilled with what we had accomplished on that trip, having discovered unexplored passage that had taken us as far underground in Britain as anyone had been. We called this new cave passage Agua Colorada, named for the camp in Peru where we had first met.

Ian and I were about as different as two cavers can be. We shared passion, enthusiasm and skill in long-range caving; and that's about where the similarities stopped. I was tall and lean, quiet, often described as being closed-off and intense; Ian was short and muscular, gregarious, vivacious and full of energy. He was even a good footballer, which is rare for most cavers, who are generally known for their abysmal hand–eye coordination. (This might be the reason why most cavers tended to avoid the team sports at school – for fear of peer ridicule.)

Ian has been described more than once as being 'a force of nature'. Although he was three years my junior, he was quite far ahead of me in terms of meeting life's more conventional objectives. He had established a career in the military as a sergeant in the Royal Air Force, where his job was servicing fighter jets; he was already married to his childhood sweetheart Erica, with whom he had three young children; and – most impressive to me – he was already taking the lead on a significant exploration project. I didn't understand how he had the time to fit it all in; I still don't. At the time, I had a girlfriend and I had caving, and not much time or energy for anything else.

I was excited to have a new partner for my adventures, and it was thrilling to have found somebody with the same mindset for caving as I had – the one I had first learned from Steve. A true caver, Ian was enthusiastic, motivated and self-sufficient. Most critically, he wouldn't stop with a project until it was finished. Although our lives on the surface couldn't be much more different, we moved in sync in the caves.

Except in one way.

On this, our first trip underground together, it had quickly become apparent that my physical stamina was no match for his. On our return trip through Daren Cilau, I felt like the pair of us were acting out a live-action version of the 'Tortoise and the Hare' fable. He'd dash off at a sprint with boundless stores of energy while I plodded along behind, moving slowly, evenly, carefully. I'd never considered myself to be slow in a cave, but I just couldn't keep up with Ian. I didn't even try to, and we quickly established our routine. He'd finish a crawl or a climb, then patiently stop and wait for me to catch up to him, and then he'd shoot off again. Repeat as necessary.

The only time I was ahead of him during our return trip was at an awkward bit that was going to take some time to pass. He didn't want to be stuck behind me, so he indicated he'd rest while I went in first. I passed through and then waited on the other side for what felt like a reasonable amount of time, and he never turned up. Finally, I went back looking for him, shouting his name ahead of me, and before long I heard his voice.

'I'm here,' he laughed. 'I fell asleep.' A moment later, he went whizzing past me on his way out, and I set off to follow.

After leaving the cave, the morning sun was a bit of a shock. We had been underground, almost constantly in motion, for a full day. I thought it was pretty impressive, for our first trip together, and looked forward to more. But first, I looked forward to sleeping. I drove home to Coventry, struggling to stay awake on the drive, and collapsed into bed. Ian, on the other hand, dashed home, took his dog for a walk and then went out shopping with his wife.

A force of nature, indeed.

Another similarity in style that quickly emerged was our appreciation for simplicity and the spartan Alpine style of caving, of which Ian was a master. Embodying our ethos to keep things simple, we only carried in what we absolutely needed; when possible, we'd share one between the two of us. This allowed us to move more quickly and efficiently, travelling as lightly as possible. We appreciated this as another challenge, another part of a caver's mindset – to see how far we could go with how little equipment. (This mindset led to me doing the length of the trip wearing the same neoprene wetsuit – which saved me from having to carry dry caving clothes, but resulted in some unsightly and painful rashes of raw skin behind my knees, caused by the sand that inevitably seeped into the suit during the entrance crawl.)

We continued our exploration, with our ensuing trips being extensions of the first: always challenging, with longer durations underground, and much new passage explored. We moved quickly and efficiently when we caved together, usually with Ian setting the pace. In the beginning we had this part of the cave to ourselves, but that soon changed with the arrival of a group of cavers who called themselves the Rock Steady Crew. The Crew, made up of dry cavers who did not dive, had been working in the cave for months before Ian and I had explored Agua Colorada. Their efforts were focused on bypassing St David's, in an attempt to find a dry path around the sump to reach our cave beyond.

Anathema to Alpine caving, the Rock Steady Crew had set up a luxurious and opulent campsite before the sump, replete with many of the comforts from home. A well-equipped camp kitchen allowed them to dine on fully cooked meals, which they washed down with liquor. Thick sleeping bags on air mattresses, with cosy camp clothes and slippers, afforded a comfortable night's rest. They were enjoying themselves too much, and they weren't appreciating the beauty of simplicity. Ian and I judged them harshly, and this incited our sense of competition with them.

Before long, they were successful in their mission, breaking through at a tiny squeeze that they named the Micron. They now had access to the divers' section of the cave and Agua Colorada, which they began eyeing up for their own exploratory push. Feeling a bit possessive of the cave that was yet to be explored beyond Agua Colorada, and with them close on our heels, we knew we'd have to start making multi-day trips in the cave. I had camped inside caves before, recreationally, but never as a necessary component of an exploratory push. This all made the logistics a bit more difficult and made the experience feel more serious.

Ian and I set up our camp inside Daren Cilau in October 1987, after a ten-hour trip getting our food and gear to the far side of St David's sump via the Micron. (This trip circumvented the sump, which saved us from having to dive with our camping supplies, and I was grateful to be wearing my more-comfortable dry caving clothes.) Our spartan campsite stood in stark contrast to the opulence of the Rock Steady Crew's camp, which they had fittingly named the Hard Rock Café. The only luxury we allowed ourselves was a change of clothes to sleep in. We didn't bother with camp shoes or socks, had minimal supplies for preparing basic meals, and used thin sleeping bags. We named our campsite the Restaurant at the End of the Universe, in part as a direct contrast to the Hard Rock Café, and also as a testament to the camp's remoteness.

We spent a total of six days and five nights underground during that trip. Each day we pushed further into the cave; each night we returned to camp to sleep. Our fifth day inside was the best of them all. On that day alone, we discovered 700 metres of new cave, much of it dripping with stunning formations. We stood in silence, drinking in the decorations of these remote chambers, savouring the knowledge that we were the first to see them. We named this passage Divers' Last Stand.

As we were exiting from Last Stand to spend our fifth night at camp, the Rock Steady Crew was just setting up residence at the other side of our Restaurant. We were exhausted from the great day of caving and ready for sleep. They were full of energy and stayed up late, drinking and partying, keeping us awake. I kept yelling for them to be quiet, but they ignored me and carried on. Thankfully, this was our last night inside, so we didn't have to put up with them any longer.[3]

After that, Ian moved north to Scotland for work. Although our first project together was ending, it had been an overwhelming success. The exploration had been magnificent, the caving unforgettable, the learning experiences valuable, and the resulting friendship was rock solid. I looked forward to future projects with Ian.

'You may need to manage your expectations.'
(My advice to everyone who was still
counting on there being a rescue.)

Friday, 29 June 2018, Thailand

On Friday morning, John and I woke in our shared bed at the resort, not knowing what this day might bring. We had been in Thailand for thirty-six hours and had accomplished little in the search for the boys. We were continuing to be surprised at every turn, and our inability to settle into a routine or find any sort of order in our surroundings was leaving us frustrated. There is always chaos in the early days of a rescue – or any big event that involves large groups of people working with limited information – and in time, as the situation unfolds, a natural hierarchy typically emerges. I was still waiting for this to become defined at Tham Luang, which was larger and more chaotic than most. In the meantime, we – John, Vern, Rob and I – were pretty much working alone, without any resources or authority.

As we were preparing for the day ahead, we were surprised to be greeted again by Larry Risser – we would soon learn that he has a habit of popping in unexpectedly. With him was Wirachai Songmetta, the deputy chief of the Royal Thai Police Force, whose first greeting was, 'I know what you did yesterday.'

Thinking he was having a dig about Wednesday night's chaotic trip into the cave, I remained silent and braced myself for further comments. Instead, he was coming to thank us for saving the water workers. 'It would not have been good for the psyche of the Thai people if there'd been deaths in the cave on top of everything else.' At last, someone important was recognizing what was going on. Maybe this was progress.

The policemen began detailing their plan to intensify their search on Doi Luang Nang Non for another entrance into the cave. They'd be focusing their search on the mountain's flanks, hundreds of metres above the Tham Luang river passage. Vern and Rob had found several potholes up there in the past, but none had showed signs of connecting with the cave. On top of that, we knew that the river in Tham Luang didn't originate from Doi Luang Nang Non directly above, but from streams that sink into the flanks of the mountain in valleys to the north and south. Regardless, Vern and Rob agreed to join the policemen's team. Neither of them would be able to join the dives that John and I were doing, and I knew that they wanted to be useful doing something.

Our next meeting that morning was with the US military,[4] who had arrived in Thailand very early on Thursday morning. The arrival of the Americans had been fraught with rumours, most of them based on Hollywood depictions, which they quickly had to dispel when they arrived. Among the more humorous was when the Thais asked the Americans – in all seriousness – if they had access to a satellite that could see through the mountain. I knew the men were pararescuers (PJs) and I was eager to speak with them, to get their impressions of the rescue operation. I'd seen them around the rescue compound already and had spoken to Major Charles Hodges[5] briefly by telephone the previous evening. Hodges, their commanding officer, had suggested we meet that evening, which seemed like a good idea until I learned that they were staying at a hotel nearly an hour away.

'What about 0600 tomorrow?' Hodges suggested next. I had no intention of waking for a 6 a.m. meeting and I had a good excuse, because we could only get on site when Tom and Bas took us there.

'Our transport isn't arriving until eight thirty,' I told him. 'Let's meet at nine.'

At 9 a.m. sharp on Friday, the Americans strode purposefully into our gear room. Before they had stopped moving, Major Hodges asked, 'Is there a Richard Stanton here?' As I introduced myself, Hodges told me, with apparent displeasure, that he'd been on the end of a chain of messages from the British government, informing him that John and I would not fall under the Americans' jurisdiction. It had never occurred to me that he would think we did.

'That didn't come from me,' I told him.

There was an awkward moment as he accepted this information, but it was quickly passed by as I recognized one of the Americans. Jamie Brisbin had been part of a cave-diving expedition I'd been involved with in Australia ten years earlier, and we quickly reacquainted ourselves. Because of his previous experience, Jamie had been brought along as their subject-matter expert. Next, we met Master Sergeant Derek Anderson, who was Hodges' executive operational officer and tactician on the ground. Derek would become our point person with the Americans, and we spoke several times per day throughout the remainder of the mission.

As a group of logistical experts and tacticians, the Americans were exactly the people who needed to be on site, and I very quickly came to appreciate their value. Their expertise was in assessment and planning, and they brought a sense of order to the scene that had previously been absent. Ben Svasti Thomson, the British Honorary Consul for Northern Thailand, had been accurate in his previous evening's email when he had suggested that the Americans could be a bridge between the Thais and Brits. Not only did they act in this capacity, but they managed to liaise between the different Thai groups – civilian, police and military authorities – that we had been having such difficulty navigating.

Hodges listened closely as we filled him in on everything that had been happening. 'We can't get a decent compressor.' 'There are people who are talking absolute nonsense being taken seriously.' (He had already seen this for himself, when he'd been asked about his satellites.) 'We never quite know whether we're going to be stopped from entering the cave by the SEALs.' And finally, 'We can't operate successfully in this chaotic environment. It just won't work.'

'I know it won't,' Hodges said. 'My job here is to make sure you can do yours.' They had identified John and me as the experts and knew that they could be most effective by setting up an environment where we were able to do our work. Their presence and trust in us became a critical component of the rescue's success. Before the meeting was over, Hodges asked the question that was on everyone's mind. 'Do you think it's going to be possible to rescue them?'

'I don't think it's likely,' I answered honestly. 'Right now, the cave is impassable beyond Chamber 3. There's a pretty good chance they're already dead, and even if they aren't . . .'

Hodges nodded and completed my thought. 'Time is running out.'

They hung around for a few minutes, chatting, and they told us about how they had entered Tham Luang in the very early hours of Thursday. Derek hadn't enjoyed the experience very much. 'We're not designed for being in caves, are we?' he laughed, hinting at their well-built, stocky physiques.

A few minutes later, as they were leaving, I overheard Derek tell Hodges, 'Sir, I really like these guys.' The feeling quickly became mutual.

We entered the cave early on Friday afternoon, not surprised to learn that Ben was already inside. I saw Ben's partner Bruce standing in line behind a group of SEALs who were waiting to dive through the first sump. When I approached him, Bruce told us that

Ben had gone through on his own. John and I overtook the others and went ahead, quickly passing through, while noting that the flow was much stronger than it had been the previous day.

At the far side, we watched in horror as a bunch of SEALs struggled awkwardly with a bag of thick rope. They were attempting to lay a hand line, to help pull themselves against the current. With a sense of dread, I recognized their inexperienced movements as those of people who were completely unfamiliar with these conditions. They were being thrown about and knocked over by the water, and my worried glance went from them to the live electricity cables. I hoped that somebody would get them out of the water before there was a disaster. This was not the place to be learning how to cave.

John and I were preparing to dive through Rob's archway – which would be even deeper underwater than it had been the previous day – when Ben was washed out by the force of the current. John grabbed hold of him and directed him to where we were standing in chest-deep water. 'How did it go?' we asked him. Gasping for breath and looking a bit flustered, Ben told us that he'd laid 100 metres of line. Then he went on to tell us, 'I found the current reversed. It spun me around.' Ben claimed the cave had been pulling him in, so he'd retreated.

I gave John a sideward glance and knew that he was thinking the same thing as I, but we both stayed quiet and listened to his tale. We knew it couldn't be true that the current had reversed. No doubt he had indeed been spun around by the violent swirls of water that we'd observed the previous day; I felt sure he was simply disorientated. We couldn't work out why he was operating there alone – it was really bold. I presumed he'd gone ahead of the SEALs while they were laying the hand lines because he had been able to progress more capably. In any event, given the extreme conditions, there seemed little point in us trying to go any further. We wouldn't have achieved anything more. We left as a team, with John and me carrying out some of Ben's equipment, and Ben reported to the commander that the cave was too dangerous for further diving today. Then we arrived back at our gear room, where we were alarmed to find men carrying our things out of the room.

What is going on now?

Apparently, the neighbouring room had had to be evacuated after a plumbing incident, and everything within it had been relocated to our room while we had been inside the cave. Now that the problem was fixed, the Thai Army were emptying our room of everything, indiscriminately. When I stopped them from carrying out any more of our gear, they seemed surprised by the interruption. This is when Derek and Major Hodges came to see us.

They had just spoken with Captain Anand Surawan, a deputy commander of the Thai Navy SEALs. The Americans had been concerned (as we had been) that the pump workers' absence had gone unnoticed for a full day. When Hodges suggested a method for keeping track of everyone coming and going from the cave to prevent a recurrence of yesterday's loss, Anand's response had taken them by surprise. 'He categorically denied that the rescue of the pump workers had occurred,' Derek told us. 'He said it never happened. He insisted no one was rescued from Tham Luang yesterday.' Derek asked if we'd be willing to speak with Anand to get it cleared up. We agreed, and they set off to find him.

While we waited for their return, John and I went through our equipment, because apparently security was something else we would need to be concerned about.

'Do you get the feeling we're fighting an uphill battle here?' I muttered sourly.

John was as frustrated as I was. 'We're unwanted by the SEALs, struggling to get any help or resources, plus the situation is hopeless.

We're only being used here as a token force.' I knew he was correct – even the Americans were beginning to discuss their staged withdrawal – and I went to speak with Ben Svasti Thomson on the phone, to discuss the same possibility for us.

Like John, I didn't see much good in staying there, but I had no pressing reason for getting back to England. While John had his business to take care of, I was happily retired. What's more, Amp had just arrived. After speaking with Ben Svasti Thomson, I went down to meet her as scheduled at the food drop-off station. As I greeted her, I remembered an offhand comment she had made in England after Jonathan had told her about some of the rescues that I'd participated in. 'I would like to see something like that,' she had told me. Now here I was, at her doorstep, for a rescue which she was about to play a role in.

Be careful what you wish for.

While I was greeting Amp, a drama was unfolding back at the cave. Only the SEALs were inside when something happened that led to someone being brought out on a stretcher. The authorities said it wasn't an electric shock – they claimed the diver had been poisoned and fallen ill – but at the same time, somebody ran up to our room and told John urgently, 'Are you thinking about going in the cave? Because if you are, don't. There's live electricity, and some-body has received a shock.'

When I returned, John told me what had happened. 'Vern did say that the water was tingly,' I laughed. 'Now they have fried seal.'

We were laughing, but both thinking the same thing: 'They're going to kill themselves.' They weren't engaging with the risks of diving in a swiftwater overhead environment. Much as they had done to Vern, the SEALs had disassociated themselves from us and were not interested in hearing anything we had to say, so I spoke with Brian Davidson, the British Ambassador in Bangkok, trying to impart my concerns. 'The SEALs are very brave, but they're also taking needless risks in an environment they clearly know nothing about . . . I can't go up to a group of 120 special forces and tell them they're incompetent . . . Is there any way you might convey this safety warning through diplomatic channels, via someone higher up?'

He promised he'd try.

As the story of the rescue had been spreading across the globe, the number of photographers and reporters had been doubling each of the days we had been there. By Friday we were hearing our story echoing back to us.

'British divers join mission to save football team from Thai cave'

'Pumps overwhelmed as downpour hampers cave rescue'

'US military joins search for boys' soccer team missing in Thailand cave'

'Rising water stops divers searching for missing boys'

'"Come home": Thailand clings to hope for boys trapped in caves'

Despite our best efforts to avoid media attention, John and I had become accustomed to the surge of reporters and the flash of cameras as we walked in and out of the cave. Over the years, I've become pretty skilled at switching off and keeping an emotionless front, but John usually doesn't bother trying to hide how he is feeling. On Friday afternoon, when we had been walking through the park compound after our aborted dive attempt, I whispered to him as we approached the media pack, 'Neutral face, John, neutral face!' I was worried his countenance would be a giveaway that we thought the boys were all dead, and I didn't want to be asked that direct question in front of cameras. There wouldn't be an easy way of answering it.[6]

We'd been described as 'stony-faced Brits' by one British newspaper, and our presence had led to the common question 'What the hell are these grumpy British pensioners doing there?' Everyone seemed to ignore the fact that John is ten years my junior and a fit endurance athlete; he'd somehow ended up classed with me.

Age and physique aside, I'm sure that we did stand out a bit in our T-shirts, shorts and Wellington boots – especially when seen surrounded by the uniformed members of the American and Thai militaries. In hindsight, we've agreed that, had we worn a common, official-looking item of clothing,[7] we would have been perceived as having some authority. We'd look more like rescuers, and less like middle-aged trainspotters. None of this was helped by John and me constantly being caught shaking water out of our wellies, with our legs cocked up to the side, as we left the cave. We looked like dogs marking our territory.

Most troubling to John was the attention that my wing was gaining, just as he'd feared. On one internet forum, somebody pointed out in horror that some ignorant fool 'with a car tyre strapped to his back' had been seen walking into the cave, looking like a Teenage Mutant Ninja Turtle. 'Get that man off-site and let the experts in.' Somebody else quickly pointed out, 'Er, I believe that's Rick Stanton. I think you'll find he is the expert.'

I didn't let it bother me; in fact, I kind of enjoyed the criticism. I had constructed the wing myself using an inner tube, bungee and webbing. In spite of its appearance, I knew that the inner-tube wing was the right tool for this job and I wore it with pride. At least I'd managed to keep my reading specs with me and hadn't needed to resort to my pinhole lens technique in front of the cameras. On the other hand, John was completely blind without his glasses and had to walk through the compound with his clown-like yellow mask on all the time, because he was dependent on their prescription lenses. I'm sure publicists would have preferred to have more photogenic faces on the heroes of the Great Thailand Cave Rescue.

Aware of our deficiencies, I approached Captain Jessica Tait, the US Air Force officer who was acting as media liaison officer for the 353rd Special Ops Group. I had seen her speaking with the press on site and asked her if she'd guide John, Rob and me in this area. 'We need a quick lesson,' I told her. She laughed and gave us an hour-long tutorial on dealing with the media – how to answer questions tactfully or twist the question around to what you want to say, that kind of thing. We wanted to be prepared for the seemingly inevitable time when we'd have to answer questions that had unpleasant answers.

As Amp walked with the three of us to our room at the resort, I saw the ubiquitous flies gathered on the screen door. They were always there when we returned, waiting to enter the room when we walked in. Maybe they were being attracted by the smell emanating from the room. 'More flies won't make much of a difference,' I thought as I reached to open the door. The room had been filled with flies since our first night there. Amp stepped ahead of us and tapped on the screen, causing the flies to scatter, before opening the door. John and I looked at each other as we followed Amp into the room. *Oh. That's how you're supposed to do it.*

Inside the room, Amp wrinkled her nose at the manly odour, before commenting on how hot and stuffy the room was. 'We never bothered to figure out the air conditioning,' I admitted. She shook her head, found the remote and had it operating straightaway. 'Are you sure you know what you're doing?' she asked us. I'm not sure if it was meant playfully or if she was truly concerned.

Amp and I moved my things into our new room, which she had

already arranged for the two of us to share. John would finally have his own bed. I knew that nothing was going to happen the next day and I just wanted to get away from everything, so Amp and I went out into town, to a bar and restaurant for some food. When we returned to the resort in the evening, I set to work with my nightly emails. The constant discussions with my friends and colleagues in England continued to provide a much-needed reality check at the end of each day.

I recounted for them the 'shocking' incident that had occurred earlier (they wisely ignored my attempt at humour) and reminded them that the SEALs were untrained to dive there in the first place. I sounded like a broken record, but I didn't think I was overstating our concern, and it didn't seem like the time or place to mince words. I wish there had been somebody on the ground in Thailand who had listened to our warning.

Nightly Correspondence:
Friday, 29 June 2018

From: Richard Stanton
To: Bill Whitehouse

Apparently the British embassy conveyed a message to the US counterpart saying that we were to be independent and not under their control.
This has caused a bit of an incident, now resolved.

From: Bill Whitehouse
To: Richard Stanton, Ben Svasti Thomson

I had an e-mail from Ben saying that attempts were being made to help get better organization in place. Glad the US/UK issue has been resolved. We wouldn't want Mr Trump twittering unfavourably about us. Does the US contingent include cave divers?

Well done with getting out the four trapped rescuers.

Heard this morning that the Thai PM was visiting the site – hopefully that might help with things.

From: Ben Svasti Thomson
To: Bill Whitehouse, Richard Stanton

I have talked to senior officials about this but I have to admit that their response was not great but they will have taken parts onboard.

I have been liaising with the US to see if they can also do something to improve coordination.

There is overwhelming support and admiration for yourselves and the British team from the general public.

So keep up the good work and soldier on.

Saturday, 30 June 2018

Saturday was a bit of a rest day for us. In the morning, we had another meeting with Larry and Wirichai, who had learned of our intention to leave and had turned up to persuade us to stay on. 'People are looking up to you,' Wirichai said. 'It wouldn't be good for morale if you leave the scene.' This was echoed by Weerasak, the Tourism and Sport Minister, who called me on my mobile a little while later. I told him that we were probably there until Monday. 'We'll see how the situation looks then.' If things changed in the next two days, then of course we would stay.

John and I went to the cave entrance for a look around. The water was still very high but had stopped rising.

In Chamber 1 we were met by Ben, who had been making claims that he had dived 2.5 kilometres into the cave. We thought this would have been impossible (and we now know that it would have meant that he'd dived 200 metres beyond the boy's location). The assertion seemed harmless at first, but it began attracting a lot of attention when he shared it publicly on social media. We began fearing that the mixed messages about the diving conditions and progress being made would cause confusion that would ultimately hurt the operation. I knew he'd already had an altercation on the topic with Vern and I didn't want to cause further strain, so when I met Ben, I merely shook his hand and told him, 'Well done for getting 2.5 kilometres.' We were then told that the SEALs had halted all further diving.

As we exited, we walked past the gargantuan pumps that were spraying water out from the cave. Thankfully, these pumps distracted attention from us, so we weren't barraged with questions from reporters. That distraction might be the only purpose those pumps were serving.

From the outset of the operation, pump workers at Tham Luang had been engaging in a colossal exercise to lower the water levels deeper inside the cave – first with the diesel pump located near Monk's Junction, then with the electrical pumps in the third chamber that Surapin and the others had been working on. Now there were larger industrial pumps installed in the entrance chamber to lower the water that had gathered there.

There were critical problems with this plan, which nobody seemed to be acknowledging. Namely, pumping water downstream of the third chamber would have little – if any – effect on the water that was pooled further back inside the cave, where we would be looking for the boys. Their notion of pumping all of the water out of the cave, so the boys could simply walk out, was next to impossible.

Go back to the analogy of the long hose running through your garden and emptying into a bowl on the ground. You can extract as much water as you like from the bowl; it's not going to have any effect on the quantity of water that is flowing through the hose pipe, nor will it affect the water that has collected in the low-lying sections. The only thing affecting the water flowing in the pipe is the person pouring the water in at the top. Furthermore, even if the bowl was pumped dry, there would always be water remaining in the lower parts of the bends. The only way to drain the cave completely would be to place pumps at the base of each sump . . . and to stop the forecast monsoon.

After entering Tham Luang from its source (the streams that sink on the mountain), the water unites into a streamway that flows through the cave to the entrance chamber, where it naturally drains away through a small cleft at one end of the chamber. During periods of heavy rainfall – e.g. the monsoon – this natural drainage cleft is overwhelmed, and a lake forms in the entrance chamber. Large pumps had been placed at this entrance chamber lake, and the evacuated water gushed dramatically from pipes outside the cave, close to the press area, quickly becoming a common clip in video footage during the cave rescue. I could think of only one reason for placing a 90-degree elbow on the pipe end and directing the fountain of water into the air: it looks good on news reports.

The symbolic gushing of water from the cave was used as a testament that progress was being made, that something was being done. In reality, a series of small, fast-flowing cascades exists immediately upstream of the entrance chamber. No amount of pumping from the entrance lake could have any impact on the water levels above those cascades; it would be like attempting to reduce the water in Lake Erie with pumps placed at the base of Niagara Falls.

After naturally draining through the cleft in the entrance chamber, the water from Tham Luang continues through the mountain and eventually resurges 2 kilometres away, just below Sai Thong cave. Another 'water removal' effort was being made there, to drain the water from Tham Luang's resurgence.[8] On Saturday, after we were banned from diving, Vernon drove us there to show us the area that was being used as the base for these water-draining operations.

A JCB had been used to clear boulders from the resurgence, to facilitate more rapid draining of water. Close by, three giant diesel pumps were used to allow this water to bypass a narrow restriction that had been caused by a bridge over the drainage channel. On level ground not far away, a series of boreholes had been driven into the underground aquifer; from these, water was spewing out. Although a lot of water was being moved at this elevation, the operations were having zero effect on the water that lay inside the cave 2 kilometres away and 20 metres higher.

The amount of water being shifted by those three pumps was an impressive display of man's attempt to control nature . . . but where was all of that pumped water being drained?

Sadly, the displaced water at Sai Thong was being diverted into rivers which led onto the plains in front of the mountain, which resulted in hundreds of acres of nearby rice fields being flooded, thus destroying the local farmers' source of income. When we drove past the flooded fields, we had no clue about its meaning, of the sacrifice that was being made.

The local community has, deservedly, become famous for the way it banded together during the rescue, willing to sacrifice their own time and resources for any opportunity to help save the boys.

Anyone who had anything to offer came to the makeshift village that formed on the mountain, providing what comforts and necessities they could for everyone involved in the rescue mission. Food, laundry, even haircuts were given freely by the Thai locals. Everybody became a part of the rescue, even those who never set foot inside Tham Luang. The rice workers who sacrificed their yearly crop for the chance of contributing to the efforts inside the cave were just another example of the selflessness displayed.

After our impromptu driving tour around the mountain, our group returned to the resort for dinner. Spending the day away from the cave had made me aware of how drained I'd become, and the single day of rest was leaving John and me feeling rejuvenated. Amp's presence helped, and it had been a convivial outing for all of us. To top off the day, Larry came to the resort in the evening with some beers, which were a welcome sight, as I'd been missing my local pub. (John never drinks alcohol, which left more for Rob and me.)

Perhaps aided by the beer, Larry summoned the courage to finally ask us the question that had been weighing heavily on his mind. 'Tell me straight,' he implored. 'Do you think the boys are still alive?' Uncharacteristically for us, John, Rob and I all responded in unison, without hesitating or even looking to each other for confirmation.

'No.'

He wasn't expecting such an immediate and blunt response from us, and his eyes welled up with tears. I felt a bit guilty then for being so direct. After he'd left, the three of us spoke even more frankly to each other.

'It's a good thing I hadn't answered what I was really imagining,' I said to John and Rob, knowing that they shared my same taste for using dark humour to provide some levity during very grim times. 'I think they've all drowned, like a basketful of puppies thrown into a canal.' They winced at the image.

I then turned to John with an old joke that he and I often use when we're discussing the potential existence of a cave that had not yet been discovered.

'It's Schrödinger's football team.'

Nightly Correspondence:
Saturday, 30 June 2018

From: Richard Stanton
To: Bill Whitehouse, Ben Svasti Thomson

We have all four simultaneously stated our opinion that the 13 lads are probably no longer alive. Given the nature of the conditions nothing more can be done from a diving point of view.
Furthermore it is now becoming clear that there is no cooperation between the police side of things (under whom we appear to be successfully operating), and the military operation (with whom we have had clashes).
That is apart from the US military personnel who are realistic, professional and excellent. I believe they will shortly be making a phased withdrawal. Don't believe the stories of rock melting lasers! The nature of the scene on site is rapidly changing. It is now becoming more of a military operation, most volunteers have been kicked off site and security locked down. You may think this is a good thing but there is a more sinister feel and our intention is to evacuate all of our equipment down to our off site accommodation first thing tomorrow morning before our room is requisitioned and gear tampered with or lost.

From: Bill Whitehouse
To: Ben Svasti Thomson, Richard Stanton

Worrying news, but I suppose the signs have been there for a while. Whatever you decide to do, Rick, will have our support – just keep me posted on events so we can be ready to act appropriately as and when necessary.

From: Emma Porter, secretary of the British Cave Rescue Council
To: Rick Stanton

Can you confirm that diving beyond the Third Chamber is now impossible due to a mix of flow strengths, debris and visibility?

From: Rick Stanton
To: Emma Porter

We have not managed to dive beyond the 3rd chamber ourselves. On the first occasion when we planned to, we were rudely interrupted by the four trapped Thai rescue workers so were obliged to dive them out before they were casualties.

5.
Making Progress

'You looked like you were floating across the floor.'

When I began cave diving, I jumped in head-first without looking back or even looking around much to see what else might be out there. I didn't care if there were any 'normal' things I was missing out on, because I was living the life I wanted to live.

For much of my early adulthood I had no car, no career, no relationships and no permanent home. Those years were spent either living on the dole or working in tedious office jobs and going to caves in my free time. I owned the basic caving and diving equipment I needed, I was always able to hitch a ride, and I was learning how to select future exploration projects. My life was lacking for nothing. I saw my friends who had settled down – Ian Rolland and Steve Joyce, among others – and I didn't envy them or their lives at all. So, in October of 1984, while I was at a cave hut in the Mendips with Steve for a weekend of caving, I was a bit surprised to find that, for once, my interest was deflected away from caves. I suddenly found my life veering into a world of domesticity, which was uncharted territory for me.

Her name is Angela Timms, and we met because of a ruptured eardrum I'd sustained during a whitewater kayaking incident.

On Friday night at the Cerberus Speleological Society's caving hut, there was quite a group gathered in preparation for the weekend of caving. Drinking beer, planning weekend trips, talking with fellow cavers – all the typical activities. For this one, though, my injury was keeping me from enjoying myself fully, as the pain in my ear was only getting worse. Throughout the night, as I was chatting with others, I felt the occasional twinge from my eardrum, which would cause a small muscle contraction on the side of my face. Despite my distracted state, I did notice an attractive blonde woman whom I hadn't seen before. That was Angela. I wasn't much good at talking to people, and I was particularly bad at talking to women, so I kept my distance and watched her from across the hut.

What I didn't know was that she had been invited along by Steve, specifically because he wanted to introduce her to another one of his friends, thinking they might hit it off. Perhaps they would have, but before Steve had the chance to introduce them, Angela couldn't help but notice the tall, thin guy on the side of the room who kept looking over and seeming to wink at her rather oddly. That was me. She came over and introduced herself.

I don't remember many details from our meeting that night, but I do know that we spent the remainder of the weekend caving together. We were caving in groups, and I made sure to always be in the group with her. She was quite a good caver – fit and comfortable in the caves – and I was having a good time. At the end of Saturday's trip, after emerging from the caves wet and muddy, I even thought I saw Angela eyeing me as we changed from our caving gear.[1] We sent cards through the mail that week, arranging to see each other again. Our first date was set up via postcard. The following weekend, when we met to go caving, it was just the two of us; from that weekend, that was it. We were pretty much set in stone after that. Despite this being my first relationship, it all happened very naturally and smoothly.

At the beginning, I was working in an excruciatingly dull job in a

London patent office and living back with my family during the week for the easy commute into the city. Soon I began spending all of my free weekends with Angela and within a year, I'd resigned from my London job and moved into her home in Coventry. Caving was still the central focus of my life, but I was beginning to establish a bit of the balance that I had seen in others. Those were some of the best years of my life, but I knew that I still had to figure out what I was going to do for a career, and I was at a bit of a loss there.

A lot of people seem to be drawn to an area of study at a young age, but I had no interests pushing me towards any particular career. I just knew that I wouldn't last for very long in a bullshit job where the work was tedious and pointless. I'd need to do something that I found worthwhile. A flexible schedule that allowed plenty of time for caving trips was another absolute necessity. I thought of only one possibility that ticked all the boxes, and it happened to be the same job my father had performed during the war: firefighter. I already knew a disproportionate number of cavers who worked as firefighters,[2] so I figured there was something about the job that was appealing. These people were all similar-minded to me, so if they could hack it, I was sure I could. The job seemed to be challenging and engaging; it kept them fit; and, most crucially, it left them with enough time to spend caving.

I applied to work with the West Midlands Fire Service in 1987, not long after moving to Coventry with Angie. Before being accepted, I had to go through a series of interviews and physical tests that were all part of their selection process. The final test consisted of carrying a heavy drum of water around and finding our way through a pitch-black basement with tunnels, while wearing a breathing apparatus cylinder on our back. Many of the candidates found this to be the most challenging test. I moved through the test with ease, probably as well suited for this activity as anyone could be.[3] I happily passed through and in 1989 was formally selected as a recruit for the incoming Blue Watch at Coventry Central Station, even earning the coveted 'Silver Axe', which is awarded to each course's top recruit. I quickly got into the top physical shape of my life, which I knew would pay off during longer caving excursions. Maybe now I'd be able to match Ian's pace.

I excelled at the job requirements but had no interest in applying for promotions or in any way rising above the minimum responsibilities of the job. Any excess energy I had was still devoted to caving, and there was little room for any other pursuits. Fortunately, the station shift work consisted of a four days on/four days off schedule, so I was able to take advantage of the long breaks to pursue caving projects at home and abroad. When my watch returned to the station for a working shift, we'd exchange tales about how we had spent our days off, and my colleagues learned pretty quickly that my stories were usually quite different from theirs.

While my colleagues traded stories of their fiddle job or redecorating their house, mine went more like: 'I went into a cave, searching for bits of a diver who had died seventeen years ago. My mate found the skull, I found a foot.'[4] I'd gone on a foot recovery. At the time I didn't find any of this unusual, but looking back, I wonder what the others must have really thought about the quiet new guy.

$\oplus$ $\oplus$ $\oplus$

I've often been asked what it was about caves that drew me in, and I haven't always had a satisfactory answer. There was the appeal of exploration . . . but why caves?

I do appreciate their hidden nature. Unlike a mountain's summit, which can be seen and measured before it is ever ascended, a cave is unseen, and its details are unknown. An explorer can never be certain what a cave will do until they're there, inside it, seeing it first-hand. This is what makes exploration and discovery of new cave passage so appealing to me. Early on, I also appreciated how the diagram of a cave showed the path of water flowing underground. I liked the idea of mapping a cave, connecting points, adding to its story. When I was first learning about the cave systems of England with the university club, I'd always been most interested in those systems whose maps were left unfinished, maps that held clues for further exploration. For me, there is nothing more exciting than finding a master cave and being instantly propelled to see it through to the end.

In 1991, after spending a few years focusing on my new domesticated life in Coventry while going on the occasional big trip abroad, I suddenly found myself confronted with a new exploration project right at home, in the Yorkshire Dales. Gingling Hole was a challenging cave on Fountains Fell that ended when a 62-metre shaft plummeted straight into the sump pool. This sump lay a considerable distance from the water's resurgence at Brants Gill Head and, crucially, it was perched at a higher elevation. As with Notts Pot, this was a clear signal to me that much unexplored dry cave must lie between the two.

Kitting up and preparing for the ensuing dive was a challenge, and a test of balance, as I straddled the pool on awkward footholds while donning my diving equipment. The two walls I'd just used to brace myself against while kitting up continued straight down into the water; I stepped off and dropped into the sump. As I was descending between the two submerged walls, through a rift which became so narrow in places it was impassable, I searched both walls to find the way on. I could never descend in a straight line because the protrusions and restrictions were in different places, so I'd have to keep adjusting my path to try different routes, like I was moving through a vertical maze. I knew that if I lost my orientation, I would become stuck in a narrow fissure between the walls.

On my first dive, I found a horizontal passage leading off at the bottom, which I identified as the way on. On a second dive, I was able to pass through the sump to find myself in a gloomy low section of dry cave. I had not expected to pass the sump so quickly, so I had not brought my wellies along with me on this trip. I removed my gear and set off into the virgin cave wearing only neoprene socks on my feet. The tunnel soon opened into a gallery of the master cave where all of the underground streams of the area drained, followed by 3 kilometres of dry passage. My socks were shredded by the end, but my cold feet didn't lessen the enjoyment of walking alone through a space where no other person had ever set foot.

On my way home that evening, I stopped in multiple caving huts, eager to report what I had found, before ending at Greenclose. Years and years later, a friend who had been at one of those huts told me, 'I'll never forget when you came back from that Gingling trip and you looked like you were floating across the floor.'

I couldn't be more pleased with the continued, steady progress I was making. Gingling Hole was a really big project in Yorkshire, similar to Notts in many respects, but in every way it was scaled up a bit. Notts Pot had been a short walk across a fell, some ten pitches to get down – relatively straightforward – and then a moderate sump followed by a big passage to explore. Gingling Hole was a longer walk on a more remote hill, with more difficult access to a much harder cave that was less frequented. The sump was much more difficult, with lots and lots of big passage . . . and this time I was alone. It was like another tier in my progression, taking small steps forward to tackle big projects and reach a larger goal.

As we had done following the discovery of Notts 2, the

breakthrough dive of Gingling Hole was followed by many subsequent trips with friends, in which we pushed and surveyed nearly 6 kilometres of new passage. I felt that the discovery I'd made in Gingling Hole was more important than the one in Notts, but it didn't achieve anywhere near as much attention from the caving community. Most people chose not to go there, as it wasn't so nice to carry cylinders, so it didn't generate the momentum that Notts Pot had, or the infectious group dynamic. I didn't mind, though. By the time my friends and I completed the follow-up trips, my attention had already been drawn elsewhere.

Later that year, I visited the caves of southern France for the first time. I'd travelled to Spain for a week of caving with Steve and Dani, only to find the weather was wretched. The caves were flooded, undiveable, so we dejectedly got into our car for the return drive to the UK. Somewhere along the way, in an attempt to salvage what we could from this trip, somebody suggested we take a detour to check out the caves of the Dordogne and the Lot. And so it was almost by accident that I began my fascination with the caves there.

The area between the Pyrenees mountains and the Loire River valley is the most concentrated cave-diving area of Europe, containing many underwater caves that have been the target of exploration for decades. After arriving in the region, I cajoled Steve to head straight for a cave we'd heard about called Emergence du Ressel. The entrance to the Ressel lay on the bed of the River Celé, but without guide books or maps we didn't have any clear plan for finding its exact location. By some stroke of brilliance (or luck), Steve was able to recall some photographs he'd seen during a presentation.

'There's a bend in the road,' he said, trying to envision the photographs. 'There's a tree that hangs over the river right above the cave's entrance.' As desperate as it sounded to us, it was enough for Steve. He was able to recognize the location when he saw it, based entirely on his memory of those two photographs. (This was particularly impressive because Steve isn't typically known for his navigational prowess.)

Getting out of the car, I stood on the bank of the Celé and watched the water ripple from the cave's entrance. Within minutes, I was dressed in my diving gear and making my way into the Ressel. I knew it had been previously explored, but still I savoured the feeling of finding my way through a cave I'd never been inside before, discovering its layout for myself as I went along. It was a really pleasant dive – the water was clear and warm. I wasn't used to making pleasant dives; this was a revelation. Eager to see more of the region, we went on to dive in other local caves that week: Saint Sauveur, Fontaine de St George (which is the main resurgence from the popular tourist cave Gouffre de Padirac) and Pou Meyssen. I was impressed with them all, and knew that I would like to return for more dives.

Thoroughly pleased with the unexpected turn of events our trip had taken, I couldn't help but take a rare introspective moment to appreciate how well things were going in life. I was thirty years old and already living with a partner, working in a job I didn't hate and able to spend time in some of the world's best caves with good friends to go with. During my twelve years of caving, I had already done an impressive bit of exploration, and the caves I'd just seen in France were leaving me with ideas for future projects.

Life was good.

'We have a two-day window to achieve something.'

Sunday, 1 July 2018, Thailand

On Sunday morning, I received a text message from Ben Rey-menants, reporting that the currents in Tham Luang had reduced and forward progress was now possible. Ben, his diving partner Maksym Polejaka,[5] and the SEALs had managed to progress beyond Chamber 3 for the first time since Wednesday's evacuation.

All along, John and I had been saying that our knowledge of cave diving made us aware of the risks, which allowed us to proceed safely. In truth, that knowledge had worked against us on Saturday, when we'd readily accepted that the abhorrent conditions would prevent us from ever diving there again. The SEALs – without our precon-ceived ideas that the cave would be undiveable – had lived up to their motto, 'Never give up', by persevering and continuing attempts to dive. Ben and Maksym had led the diving efforts, partly out of con-cern for the SEALs' safety. They reasoned that if they were diving, the less-experienced SEALs wouldn't feel the need to go into the danger zone themselves.

In his text message, Ben suggested we rejoin the pathfinding mission. John and I were still sceptical that it was even possible, but we headed back to the cave and prepared to dive. We needed to fill our cylinders, so I went with Amp to try to find some petrol for the motor that runs the compressor. John and I had been finding it impossible to get our hands on any gasoline while we were there, but I was desperate and had no choice but to try again. Amp and I walked down to the military's gazebo, where, unsurprisingly, we were given the typical runaround.

They told us there was no gasoline. I told them that there must be some somewhere because the compressor had been running on it. Just as I was about to give up, a man stepped over from the neighbouring gazebo. He looked like a civilian initially, an elderly man, but then I noticed he was wearing the same blue shirt, yellow bandana and blue cap that I'd seen on Governor Narongsak.

'What did I hear you need?' he asked.

'Gasoline.'

'There's gasoline right over there,' he said. He walked behind the military gazebo, picked up a can of gasoline and handed it to me. I stared in disbelief. This was the first time since I'd been there that a problem had been solved so efficiently.

Who on earth was this guy that could get this done so quickly?

There had been a two-day break in the rain, so we expected there to be a decrease in current, but the water levels had dropped much more rapidly than we'd dared think possible. After diving to Chamber 3, we saw the large space was now being used to store supplies, with rows of 11-litre aluminium cylinders standing along one side. Getting them all inside must have been quite a mammoth effort for the SEALs, and I was quite impressed. Some of them had even set up camp there, despite being less than thirty minutes from the entrance. John and I walked from the muddy side, across the dividing rock, to the sandy plateau where we'd found Surapin and the pump workers taking shelter from the rising water. The water had receded a good 3 metres since the day of their rescue. When we reached the upstream sump, I noticed a still pool with just a few ripples of current, instead of the boils of pulsing water we'd seen there before.

We could hardly believe how drastically things had changed. Ben's description had been accurate.

As we stood there, two SEALs emerged from the sump, each wearing a single cylinder on his back and shivering from the time spent underwater.[6] The Thais watched John and me as we got into our side-mounted diving gear, which was quite different from theirs. They looked particularly intrigued by the snoopy loops that we used to hold things in place. (They liked the elastic bands cut from inner tubes so much that we left some for them after our dives.) We noticed that some of them were filming us with their phones as we kitted up, but they didn't say anything until we began clipping our line reels to our harnesses.

'We've been using these.' One of the SEALs – his name was Jay and he seemed to be the one in charge[7] – approached us, holding out a couple of rice sacks. Each sack contained 200 metres of rope that was at least 9mm thick and made of nylon. Cave divers typically use thin cord[8] to lay line, but the thicker rope being offered would be useful for people who were pulling themselves along against the current and less likely to cause an entanglement hazard. Ben had thought of using rope on Friday and had borrowed some of John's[9] from our gear room, to give the SEALs an idea of what they needed to procure. The requested rope had arrived on Saturday, and that's what they'd begun using.

At first John was reluctant to accept the sacks from Jay, but for once I thought we needed to conform with the Thais' plan. 'I think we should do what they request,' I urged John. 'Besides, we're going to need a hauling rope.'

Knowing the bags would be quite unmanageable to dive with, John and I only took one each. Eager to finally be diving beyond Chamber 3, we finished kitting up and went into the sump, following the line laid by Ben and the SEALs. The sump upstream of Chamber 3 was jumbled with hoses and cables, and I could hear the whir of pumps operating. For a moment I hoped I didn't get sucked in.

The line situation was quite confusing, but we had been given a good description and were able to navigate through to a clear, single guide line. Further on, this line had been laid through a narrow fissure close to the inclined ceiling, instead of lower down in the passage where the cave was more open. It was a classic line trap that would prove to be problematic during the rescue.[10]

John and I got through the clutter easily enough, passed the air pocket that was named Chamber 4, continued to where the SEALs had tied off their line and began extending that towards Monk's Junction. Excited to finally be marking our way onwards, we took turns in the lead. To my surprise, we soon surfaced in a canal passage that was at least 100 metres long. Vern had predicted that most of the cave beyond Chamber 3 would be sumped, but for once he had been wrong.

As we continued moving forwards and extending the line, we encountered more of these canal passages where we could remove our regulator and swim along the surface to conserve the gas in our cylinders. Without having to stop to discuss the implications of the airspaces we were passing through, John and I both understood what this meant. The cave back here was at the water level, so there would be lots of dry spaces. This left hope that the boys could have found sanctuary when they'd become trapped, instead of being overwhelmed by the flood. This was a turning point. For the first time since we'd arrived, we were considering the possibility that they might still be alive.

Our day's target was Monk's Junction. There was a 100-metre stretch heading due north just before the junction, so when our navigational compasses indicated we were heading north, we knew we were close. At the Junction we noted the change that was caused by the incoming water of Monk's Series, the inlet stream. The water here was both warmer and clearer – for the first time I could see as far as my fins – but these conditions faded quickly as we continued along a section of rope that had been laid down by the SEALs before the passage had flooded. When we reached its end – where it was tied to a wall in an air pocket – we turned around. We had little of our rope left and we'd reached a landmark, so this was as good a place as any to finish for the day.

The next landmark we would be looking for was the area Vern had spoken of, the one he had called Pattaya Beach, which was just over 500 metres further south. It had always been Vern's hope that the boys would be found there. Having seen the unexpected and fortuitous amount of canal passage beyond Chamber 4, John and I were now feeling that same hope.

The Wild Boars might be alive.

With these thoughts of the boys' survival came an enormous sense of responsibility. There would be no more talk of going home until this project was seen through to its end.

When we surfaced back in Chamber 3 and reported our progress to the SEALs, they were visibly pleased and excited. They even helped us out of the water, taking our fins and cylinders from us to lighten our burden. For the first time since arriving, I felt like we'd made a connection with them, like we were working together. It seemed like everyone knew that something significant had happened, or was about to happen.

Nightly Correspondence:
Sunday, 1 July 2018

From: Rick Stanton
To: Bill Whitehouse

JV and I reached the Monks junction so there is now 800m of continuous rope beyond 3rd chamber.
500m to reach Pattaya beach from there.
Much more airspaces than expected so passage beyond 350m is mainly canals with many short dives. Water dropping, 2 m vis at one point.
We have a two day window to achieve something.

From: Bill Whitehouse
To: Richard Stanton, Ben Svasti Thomson

If you successfully find the missing 13 alive will you have the capacity to dive them all out without more cave divers to reinforce those currently involved?

From: Ben Svasti Thomson
To: Bill Whitehouse, Richard Stanton

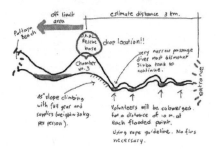

An urgent notice has been put up today for strong divers to help with logistics and ferrying tanks to advance camp

Notes from Rick:

The 'Estimated Distance' of 3km was more like 800m.
Also, who's vetting? They could have got anyone, all sorts of wannabes who didn't know what they were doing.
But at least beyond Chamber 3 was deemed off-limits to them, so I guess it didn't matter.

Monday, 2 July 2018

Something was different.

As soon as I woke on Monday, I could sense the change in both myself and John. For the first time since arriving, we had a clear objective and purpose for the day. We were aiming to reach Pattaya Beach, the site Vern had identified as the boys' best hope for survival. We were hoping to find the boys alive, but there was still every possibility that they had been swept away and drowned, so we were preparing to find them dead. Whatever had befallen them, it seemed likely we'd be finding them today. Dead or alive.

We reached Chamber 3 and began kitting up silently. With 200 metres in each of the sacks of rope we were carrying, plus 200 metres in John's small drum of 4mm line, we would have plenty to reach Pattaya Beach on this dive. As we were getting into our diving gear, Jay approached us again, this time with a request. He had a GoPro camera with him and he asked us if we would record parts of our journey to assist them; he was specifically interested in the area around Monk's Junction. John stepped forward and accepted the camera from Jay, tucking it into one of his pockets.[11]

We were now familiar with the cave up to Monk's Junction, so that segment of the dive went smoothly and quickly. From there, we followed the line Ben had installed earlier in the morning, reaching its end after 115 metres, which was sooner than expected. There, we found it connected to a 20-metre section of black tape that was pushed into the mud at the side of the passage, where it was impossible to pass. This was where the SEALs had become stuck on Monday the 24th and therefore marked the limit of their search. We simply moved to the right and continued along the main passage, into the flow, like a salmon making its way upstream.

Nobody searching for the boys had been further than this, making it very likely that we'd be finding something before our dive ended. As we continued to encounter short, air-filled canal passages separating the sumps, I developed the habit of removing my mask to breathe in through my nose, knowing that a change in odour would provide a definitive clue of human presence.

During the dives, John did most of the line-laying, because he was fitter and faster at fighting against the current. This task kept him close to the wall. My role was to tension or secure the line where needed, and also, with the line as a reference point, I could reach off to the side and blindly feel around. I couldn't see anything, and at any moment I expected my fingers would collide with a submerged body. If I found one, I knew there would likely be a number of them.

Throughout my career as a firefighter, we were constantly doing breathing apparatus drills, where we'd go into a darkened room wearing all of our heavy breathing apparatus and have to find the 'casualties' that had been placed inside. I saw these drills as a game and I was really good at them. I would always go in and find everybody early on, often ruining the whole exercise. I was reminded of those drills during this search, and I was trying to approach it the same way. Go into a darkened room and find the casualties.

As my hands searched the cave, I thought of that classic scene in *Jaws*, when a diver is searching a shipwreck and the face of a bloated corpse appears inside, floating past a window. Whenever I see that scene, the suspense puts me on edge and it absolutely makes me jump. Yet there I was, facing a similar prospect in reality, and I was totally accepting of it. Completely calm. I felt no nervous suspense.

I glanced down at my compass and saw that we were now heading east. From the survey, we knew that Pattaya Beach lay on the only bit of passage where we'd be heading east. We passed through this section and turned south again. Bollocks. I caught up with John and tapped him on the fins to get his attention. I pointed to my compass, indicating that we had gone past Pattaya Beach. We turned and went back, we actually retraced our steps, looking for the airspace where the boys would have been. We only found one tiny air bell, in the corner of the passage. We stopped and had a quick discussion.

'What the fuck is Vern going on about? There's nowhere here that would have survived the floods of Thursday and Friday.' This was absolutely Pattaya Beach, and the boys were clearly not there.[12] We were confused, but also aware that the further upstream we were going, the more likely it was that they could have been alive. If they were dead, their bodies would have washed downstream, and we would have already encountered them.

We'd used up all of the thicker bagged rope, so we switched over to John's line. We had both just finished the first third of our gas supply, which meant that it was time to turn the dive, but neither of us were ready to turn back yet. We knew the journey out would be easier, going with the current, so we chose to continue. We'd go to the end of John's line.

It was an uncharacteristically long way to the next airspace, but finally I glanced up to see the familiar glimmer that signals the meeting of air and water. I felt the change in pressure in my eardrums as I began to rise, then I watched the line of water against the lens of my mask slowly fall as my head rose above the surface. Floating beside John, I sensed the vastness of the space. Taking the regulator from my mouth, I looked around, with my head torch providing illumination. We were in an arched passage that opened up ahead of us. My light was absorbed into the darkness of that space, with nothing to reflect it back. We'd need to swim through to investigate. John held out his reel, which was nearly empty.

'Let's just go through to the end of this canal and turn back,' he said, and I agreed. We weren't going to dive another sump, but we'd go through this canal. That was the intention. We swam through it a bit until the water was shallower. We stopped where we could see a side passage going up and around a muddy ramp.

I rested on my fins while John looked for a place to tie off the end of his line. I remembered the Snickers bar in my pocket, and I thought I'd have a snack before we started our exit from the cave. It was then that I realized I hadn't yet breathed in the air to check for odour, as I'd been doing in the other air passages. I lifted my mask.

We'd found the Wild Boars.

6.
A Force of Nature

'There's an old adage: You can always tell who's the right
person for the team when the further they get from the
entrance of the cave, the bigger the smile gets on their
face. It takes a certain kind of personality.'
Dr Bill Stone, trying to describe the right stuff
necessary for a deep caver[1]

'Only one torch?' Duncan asked me sceptically, gesturing to my helmet, which was relatively light on lighting devices. I glanced at his
helmet, which was laden with torches. I peered down at the sump,
whose water was absolutely thick with mud and impossible to see
through. Finally, I looked at Duncan and shrugged.

'When the water is this muddy, it doesn't matter how many lights
you wear,' I told him pragmatically. 'You can't see anything
anyway.'

He laughed at my logic but didn't disagree.

After listening to Ian's stories of caving with Duncan Price for a
few years, I finally had the pleasure of meeting him personally in
March of 1990. Duncan was beginning a job in Coventry, and when
Ian learned that Duncan would be in my city, he was adamant that
we would have to meet. Having a fellow explorer right there in Coventry with me would be a novel experience, so I was happy to meet
with him. Following a bit of discussion, we decided to go to P8, a

short sporting cave in the Derbyshire Peak District, which was the closest caving region to us. This would be a relatively easy trip, giving us a chance to become acquainted socially while measuring up each other's skills. I knew that Duncan was a member of the Cave Diving Group and I knew of his past projects and exploration, but the fact that Ian was personally vouching for him was his most impressive credential. If Ian liked caving with him, I expected that I would as well, and I was correct.

I think he liked caving with me, too, even though he initially thought some of my choices were a bit odd. My equipment wasn't the only thing he questioned about me that day; he still makes fun of the fact that I was wearing my jumper tucked into my trousers when I'd arrived at his house. 'Perhaps to hold them up?' he'd wondered bemusedly. (Thirty years later, I consider Duncan to be one of my good friends, and I can always count on him to take the earliest opportunity to insert a joke about the size of my nose.)[2]

Having sussed each other out as worthwhile caving partners, we planned our next trip for the following weekend (which happened to be April Fool's Day). It was going to be a long day in Agen Allwedd, with Ian joining us. Ian and I quickly fell back into sync with each other; our caving styles were so similar that we had even taken to cutting down on our equipment by sharing what we could between us. Duncan didn't comment while Ian and I split a pair of fins between us to get through the sumps – using only one each – but I could see him watching with amusement. The joke was on him, though, when he learned that having two fins put him at the disadvantage: we made him carry the bag of climbing gear through the sumps that day.[3]

A few months later, Ian moved away to Leuchars, a small seaside town in Scotland, where he'd been relocated by the Royal Air Force. I knew he wouldn't be available for much caving, so it was timely that Duncan had arrived in Coventry when he did. Duncan and Ian had met while working in the caves of the Llangattock escarpment in South Wales, and it was here that Duncan and I continued caving.[4] These were favourites of Duncan's at the time, and he would always be found digging at something in there.

In addition to caving nearly weekly, Duncan and I were always socializing. Angela and I went barn dancing at a social club with him and his wife; there were many nights spent at the pub; and I even saw him during my working hours. Duncan worked as an industrial research chemist, and they were always starting fires. Their alarm was going off so frequently that it became a joke among my watch. If we hadn't been called to Duncan's lab for two weeks, we knew that something must be wrong there.

Ian's good-natured personality, impressive stamina and strong work ethic, which had impressed me so easily, had not gone unnoticed by others. Although the seemingly non-competitive world of cave diving can become quite competitive when exploration is involved, he was never seen as a threat. Instead, he was recognized as somebody who was truly as enthusiastic and committed when working on someone else's project as he was when leading his own, and he quickly rose through the ranks of Britain's cave-diving community. When he was just past twenty years old, Ian had joined Rob Parker's 1985 exploration of Wookey Hole, and it was during this project that he first met Dr Bill Stone.

Stone, an American explorer, had become consumed with the vast Sistema Huautla in Oaxaca, Mexico. After completing his 1984 expedition inside Peña Colorada cave, Stone had set his sights on the sump in San Agustín, at the system's other end. That sump lay 1,325 metres beneath the surface and had not yet been passed; it became Stone's white whale.[5]

After returning to the US following the Peña Colorada expedition, Stone spent the next nine years developing a back-mounted, fully redundant, closed-circuit rebreather to be used for the San Agustín mission. Instead of breathing from cylinders on an open-circuit system that releases wasteful bubbles, in a closed-circuit rebreather the diver's exhaled breaths are recirculated around the system; after being scrubbed clean of exhaled carbon dioxide, oxygen is added to fuel the diver's metabolism. No bubbles are released, so no oxygen is wasted, making the system more efficient.[6] This recycling of gas drastically reduces the number of cylinders that need to be carried on a dive, and would make the San Agustín project possible. At the end of 1993, Stone finally felt he and his CIS-Lunar rebreather were ready to begin. With Ian already on board, Stone formed a team of forty-four cavers and divers who committed to spending months on the project in Mexico.

I had first learned of Bill Stone when I saw Rob Parker give a presentation at the 1984 national caving conference, describing his Peña Colorada exploration. I was hugely influenced by the ambition and innovation of the project and had dreamed of someday going on a Bill Stone expedition. In the decade that had passed since, I'd followed his progress with interest but had never become directly involved. When he'd been assembling his team for the 1994 project, my name had been put forward by both Ian and Rob, but I'd been unable to join. There was no way I could have taken leave from work for the four months that were required (one month in Florida to receive training on the rebreather, three months in Mexico to work on the project). The fire service had already let me know where my priorities should lie, earlier in the year, when I had told them that I might be called away during a shift because there was an overdue cave diver in P8. In no uncertain terms, the divisional commander had reminded me: 'Stanton, you're here to be a firefighter, not to rescue people from caves!'

Not wanting to miss out completely on an opportunity to progress into this new realm of cave diving, I planned to make a short visit to Stone's cave in March of 1994. The last time I'd seen Ian was in 1992 – on a very successful caving trip in Thailand with the Army Caving Association, where we'd explored some large flood-prone river caves – and I was looking forward to catching up with my friend as much as I was looking forward to seeing the project in action and finally meeting Bill Stone.

Another cause for celebration, Ian's thirtieth birthday would be passing while he was in Mexico. Before I left Coventry, Duncan handed me a birthday card with the instructions to pass it along to Ian with a big hug. Mexico was promising to be a great adventure, and I knew I'd have some good stories when I returned to the fire station.

I travelled to Mexico in March with Paul Whybro and Mark Madden, both members of the Northern Pennine Club. None of the cavers were present when we got to the houses they'd rented in the village, so we took advantage of the opportunity to rummage through the contents of their gear room. I was curious to see what they'd brought with them and I was surprised by what we found. Instead of being selective with his equipment – bringing only what would be needed, as we would have done – Stone seemed to have just brought everything along with him, with no sense of logistical purpose. This was the antithesis of Ian's spartan approach, and I could imagine what he had been thinking. On my first cursory glance around the shed, I spied a bag of forty-plus drysuit overpressure valves, two breadmakers and even an orange Sked rescue stretcher standing against a wall.

We made ourselves comfortable, slept off our jet lag, and in the morning we made our way down San Agustín. Despite its size, the cave wasn't technically difficult by our standards, so we had quite a good trip moving down through the pitches and through the sumps on our way to meet up with Stone's group. Before long we were at Camp 3. I looked around the camp with wonder, taking in the vast array of equipment and food lying around, and a circle of square boulders making up the communal sitting area. This campsite was an extension of the tackle room on the surface – anything you might possibly need – and I smiled with the realization that Ian had somehow found himself camping in the style of the Rock Steady Crew.

As we were still taking it all in, I saw that I was standing near Dr Bill Stone. We introduced ourselves, pleased to finally be meeting in person, and he then introduced us to the other team members who were there at the camp: Barbara am Ende, Don Broussard and Jim Brown. Missing at camp were Ian and his partner on this project, Kenny Broad; the two of them were camping further down, at the edge of the sump. After we'd met the members of the team, Bill poured us a drink: a concoction of Tang orange-flavoured drink, to which he added pure ethanol. Over tin mugs of potent cave-made Tang, Bill and Barbara filled us in on their exploration up to that point.

The team had arrived at the San Agustín sump a few days earlier and had set up Camp 5 on its edge. Ian had made the first dive into the sump, with the other divers going in turn. Camp 5, at the foot of a crashing waterfall and suspended over the sump, was 'not the most comfortable camp', so after a few days, the team had elected to return to Camp 3 for a rest. Not long after settling back at Camp 3, Kenny and Ian were itching to dive and announced that they were going back down to the sump. The two of them were still down there now, tonight.

I wondered what additional progress they were making and I was eager to see the sump for myself. Mark, Paul and I had originally only planned a day trip inside, but around midnight, after a number of rounds of Tang, Bill pointed out that they had plenty of food and sleeping bags down there, so we might as well camp with them. For the first time in a cave, I fell asleep slightly intoxicated and comfortable. 'So this is what life is like in the Hard Rock Café,' I thought as I was dozing off, aware that Ian was down at his camp, which would be much more like the Restaurant at the End of the Universe.

Two hours later, I was awakened by the distinctive sounds of someone walking purposefully towards our camp, the noise of their metal SRT equipment reverberating around the chamber. The person was making no attempt at being quiet, as you would expect of someone arriving in the middle of the night. With a growing sense of dread, I recognized the sounds of urgency. *Something has gone wrong.* Knowing that Ian and Kenny were the only two camping below, I rose from my sleeping bag as others in the camp also began shaking themselves awake. I switched on a light, and my heart dropped a bit when I saw a man I didn't know standing there. It had to be Kenny, and I could see from the look on his face that my fears were about to be confirmed.

Ian had not returned from his last dive.

We all sat around on the stone circle as Kenny talked of the progress they had made that day, Sunday, 27 March. At 8 a.m. Ian had dived first, making steady progress to the south. On Kenny's subsequent dive, he had finally broken through the sump at 430 metres, surfacing in a chamber that was 20 metres high and wide. Without leaving the water, Kenny had returned to Camp 5 with his exciting news. After hearing Kenny's report, Ian had excitedly put his diving gear back on and set off for his second dive of the day. Before going under, Ian left Kenny with the instruction, 'If I'm not back by

10 p.m., call out the cavalry.' He was telling Kenny to wait six hours for a dive that would have taken no more than three, allowing himself plenty of time for exploration beyond the sump. Kenny watched as Ian swam away and then he waited, with rising anxiety as the hours ticked by. At 7 p.m., he began assembling the second rebreather rig they had with them at the camp. At 10 p.m., with still no sign of Ian, Kenny had set off to raise the alarm at Camp 3.

Kenny wanted us to go down to the sump immediately, as did I. If Ian was in trouble, we had to help. Stone was thinking more practically, though, pointing out that we needed a few hours of rest before mounting what would likely be a difficult rescue or recovery mission. Ian was either dead in the water or alive in the dry passage beyond, Stone rationalized. Either way, an additional few hours wouldn't change the outcome. As we sat in a circle on the slabs of rock, Don Broussard reminded the team of Ian's diabetes,[7] musing that this condition could have played a role in his delay. A spare emergency pack with syringes and first-aid equipment, chocolate bars and a space blanket had been left at a depot two hours up in the cave. I volunteered to fetch it first thing in the morning, after first getting the sleep that had been prescribed by Stone.

Of course, I barely slept. I don't imagine any of us did. In the morning, I ascended to get the emergency kit and then raced back down to catch up with the others. Beyond the third camp, I found myself in a streamway with lots of small drops and I noted the change in the cave. Instead of being a big borehole cave like the rest of San Agustín, this section was more like a Yorkshire pothole – narrower, with cascades, and atmospheric – dropping down a few hundred metres.

When I joined the others at Camp 5, I saw it was even more grim than had been described, and I couldn't believe anybody had volunteered to spend a single night there. Bill hadn't been exaggerating when he'd described it as being 'suspended over the sump.' With no flat ground, he had constructed two platforms hovering over the sump pool: a nylon floor stretched tautly across a framework of aluminium poles, fixed with bolts drilled into the rock wall. The chamber was filled with the thundering roar of the waterfall as it crashed down, and everything was soaked by the spraying mist.

By the time I arrived, the spare rebreather had been fully assembled, and Kenny was nearly kitted up. Since he alone had travelled through the sump in its entirety, he would be the one diving to search for Ian, and he was looking understandably unhappy about what he might find. Bill had spoken the night before about the close bond that Ian and Kenny had formed while working together, and I didn't envy the position Kenny was in. Although I'd recovered bodies from caves, I'd never had to go in after a friend, and I could see from the defeated look on his face that Kenny hadn't prepared for this.

Just as he was about to slip under the water, he looked up at our faces, hoping for some words of encouragement or moral support. What he heard instead was Jim Brown's call, 'You'd better be prepared to find his corpse!' Unbelievable. I reeled at his lack of tact, and Kenny looked crestfallen as he set off.

Forty minutes later, much sooner than I'd hoped, he returned. We all knew the truth before he surfaced and spoke the words, 'Ian's dead.' After he'd surfaced beyond the sump, Kenny had followed footprints across a sandbar to the next sump pool. There, three metres beneath the surface, was Ian's body – lying on the floor, resting on his side, with the mouthpiece of his rebreather out of his mouth.

We listened to Kenny's report and held a brief discussion. Mark and Barbara exited the cave to summon help and to assign somebody the unenviable task of phoning Erica, Ian's wife. Bill was making plans to dive and retrieve Ian's body, but he would wait until the following day to begin what was going to be a protracted recovery mission. Not wanting to spend the night at Camp 5, I ascended to Camp 3 with Paul and Jim. The next morning, after years of planning and preparation, Bill finally achieved his goal of diving through the San Agustín sump, but surely not under the circumstances he'd imagined. His dive lasted two hours; when he returned, he was towing Ian's body alongside him.

We pulled Ian's body, still burdened by 60 kilos of diving equipment, onto the lower of the two platforms. I hadn't seen him for two years, and to be honest I hardly recognized him. He didn't look how I'd remembered him, and I had a hard time connecting this body, this face, with the Ian I knew. As we began systematically removing the pieces of kit, I reached down to rotate Ian's hood so that his face was covered, just as I recalled Watto doing to David Anderson in Rowten Pot. I just remember thinking, 'This isn't Ian any more. This is just his body. Ian's gone.' We were all standing there, staring at the body.

'Well, now what do we do?' Bill asked. 'How are we going to move him without a stretcher?' I switched off thoughts of Ian and dealt with the task at hand. Before leaving Britain, Paul and I had spent a day rehearsing rope rescue and hauling techniques, mindful of the fact that we were going down one of the deepest caves in the world. The day had left us well-practised and confident, on the off-chance – not on the assumption – that we'd be needing it. We were prepared to take on the recovery.

'This is what we do for a living,' I told Bill. 'Paul and I are firefighters.'

We began moving the body back up through the cave, getting as far as Camp 3 that day, needing twelve hours for a journey that would typically take two. Since Paul and I had something of a practised system between the two of us, Bill just let us get on with leading all of the rope work. The job was made significantly harder without a stretcher, but we soldiered on awkwardly through the many pitches and traverses, sometimes wrestling with the dead weight of his limp corpse.

Decomposition had begun, with fluid leaking from every opening in his wetsuit, and as the recovery progressed, the smell worsened. In the most gruesome bit, I was alone with his body at the top of a very awkward shaft. It was my task to transfer him sideways while the others hauled his weight. The simplest way I could see to achieve this was to make him do a somersault, turning his body upside-down and then sitting him on my lap before I could pass him across. When he was upside-down, all of the body fluid went into the hood; then when I sat him on my lap, it all came out. This yellow-red liquid spilled out from around his collar, pouring down the back of my neck and into my own suit.[8]

This was by far the most ridiculously gruesome thing I'd ever had to cope with and, surprisingly, that made the whole thing a bit easier for me. I knew I had two choices: I could be horrified and throw up, or just try to see the ridiculousness and laugh. Sticking with my tried and tested method of sick humour – which I'd ably practised with the fire service – I went with the latter and carried on.

At camp that night, with Ian's body lying close by, Stone made a suggestion. 'To make hauling easier, we should dismember him and carry his limbs separately.' I briefly imagined someone having to carry a tackle bag with four dismembered limbs jutting out of it, but didn't otherwise engage with this suggestion. While most people would be appalled by the thought, I considered it rationally. 'It wouldn't make the overall weight any less,' I pointed out, 'and it would certainly be a lot more gruesome.' I'm not sure if he agreed with me, but the suggestion wasn't raised again.

The next day, Mark came back down with the Sked stretcher I'd seen in the shed (the same type we'd later use in Thailand), and this made the process easier. We were also helped by the passage being much bigger and less awkward from there on out.

By the time we were back on the ground outside the cave another two days later, six British cavers had arrived from their own expedition in the town of Cuetzalan. They'd travelled across on buses, still wearing their caving gear, to join us for an impromptu wake in the village. Despite the physical, mental and emotional exhaustion that was overcoming the San Agustín team, we all stayed awake drinking and talking late into the night. The person who sat across from me was named Big Nose (insert joke from Duncan here), and we had a good conversation. John Palmer by birth, he worked as an intensive care nurse, which I think is how we started talking. I'd never met him before, but by luck he was just what I needed right then, really empathetic.[9]

I'd arrived in this village six days earlier, prepared to set off on what was expected to be a fun and easy ten-hour jaunt underground, but what instead had turned into a five-day nightmare. Now that I was out of the cave, it was hard to believe what had just happened inside.

$$\oplus \qquad \oplus \qquad \oplus$$

'How was your trip?'

Back in Coventry a few days later, I arrived at the fire station for my shift. My colleagues knew to expect a good story from me when I returned from a trip, but they were shocked by the one I was about to tell them.

'Not good,' I replied. 'My close friend died, and I had to bring his body out of a cave.'

Later investigations – an attempt to find a reason – show that the rebreather had been functioning properly and Ian had plenty of gas remaining at the time of his death.[10] His computer showed that all had been going well, when he'd suddenly descended to the floor of the sump and hadn't moved again. Don's assertion that his diabetes could have been a factor is the most widely accepted theory. Following days of strenuous exertion, poor sleep, insufficient food intake and suffering with mild diarrhoea, Ian had most likely become hypoglycaemic and lost consciousness while in the water.

I had never had any experience with diabetes and I didn't understand the danger that a sudden attack of hypoglycaemia can cause, but a few days after arriving home I witnessed one such attack firsthand. While pouring my beer, a barman at my local pub suddenly began swaying erratically before collapsing to the ground, taking my beer with him. The manager calmly walked over, lifted his head, and helped him to drink down a few sips of lemonade. The easily digested sugars in the drink quickly kicked in, and the barman came right back to his senses. The utter senselessness of Ian's death took hold of me while I watched the barman get back to serving my drink.

That was all it took to revive him. Something so simple.

Ian's funeral was held at the RAF base in Leuchars the following week, with some cavers and lots of military personnel in attendance. I heard people consoling themselves and each other by saying, 'At least he died doing what he loved.' I've always been troubled when I hear people say that. I would hate to die while I was doing anything I loved, because a death then would mean that I hadn't reached the end. I hadn't finished. If I'm doing something I love, why would I want my death to cut it short? If I had to pick, I guess I'd want to die while I'm doing something that I despise, like completing a tax return, cutting the grass or – heaven forbid – decorating. People could then say, 'Well, at least death got him out of doing something that he hated.' Surely that's much better.

Ian had been doing something he'd loved when he'd died, but it wasn't where he was happiest. Whereas I'd devoted my life to exploration, Ian was a family man first. His family was everything to him, which was evident to anyone who had even a passing contact with him. Leonie, Carly and Connor are his children, and he carried their pictures with him everywhere. He had already begun talking about the adventures he would have with them someday, once they were old enough. Impatient to start these adventures, he'd even begun diving with Connor's teddy bear fastened to his diving equipment. 'If the bear gets bent, that's when I'll know I'm really in trouble,' Ian would joke.

Connor's bear had been attached to Ian's helmet during his final dive in San Agustín.

More than two decades later, a cave diver in his father's footsteps, Connor would see this sump first-hand, on an expedition led by Chris Jewell and alongside Jason Mallinson.

'They're all alive.'

Monday, 2 July 2018, Thailand
The Preparation Phase

As the boys descended into view, I quickly started counting, hoping I'd arrive at the number thirteen. I heard voices from the ledge saying, 'Thank you' over and over again, repeating the two words until they filled the darkness. Then John's voice cut through, clearly and loudly, as he called up to them.

'How many of you?' I imagined that was his Scout Leader voice, the one he used to round up the group when he took his pack of young Scouts on caving trips. Now, more than ever, I was grateful for John's experience with children.

I finished my headcount and blurted out, 'They're all alive,' just as one of the boys answered John in English: 'Thirteen.'

John: 'Thirteen? Brilliant!'

Boy: 'Yeah, yeah.' The group spoke to each other in Thai, and then the one, Adul, called back down to us.

'Will we go outside?'

John: 'No, no. Not today. There's two of us. You have to dive. We are coming. It's OK. Many people are coming.' We still didn't know what was going to happen, of course, but we wanted to reassure them. I joined in, telling them: 'Many, many people. We are the first.'

Adul: 'What day?'

'Tomorrow,' I answered, assuming that he was asking when the others would be coming in for them. I didn't know this to be true, but what else could I answer?

'No, no,' John corrected me. He thought they were asking

something different. '"What day is it?"' We had to stop and think. In all of the madness, we'd lost track too.

'Umm . . . Monday.' After a pause John clarified, wanting them to understand how much time had passed for them in the darkness. 'But one week . . . and Monday.' He held up both hands to show ten fingers. 'You have been here ten days. Ten days. You are very strong. Very strong.'

The boys spoke to each other. They were all hunched on the muddy ramp that rose from the water ahead of us then extended upwards behind them and around a corner of rock. We had begun to feel a bit silly standing in water up to our necks and calling up to them – plus we were curious to see what their space was like – so we had a short discussion between us and came to an agreement. 'Let's go up.'

John motioned them to back away from the water's edge, where they had crowded and were blocking our way. 'OK, move back. We come.'

Adul spoke his next words quietly. 'We hungry.' To emphasize his point, he lifted his shirt to show his emaciated torso, and the other boys followed suit. I had already noticed their thin legs; they were like sticks, instead of the strong footballers' legs you'd expect.

John's voice softened, 'I know. I know, I understand.' They'd been ten days with no food. I couldn't imagine the scope of their hunger. 'I can't go four hours without feeling peckish,' I thought to myself, and with that thought came the memory of the Snickers bar tucked in the thigh pocket of my wetsuit.

Oh, no. I suddenly felt a panic that the boys would see the chocolate bar. I knew I couldn't give it to them – one small dose of sugar could do more harm than good for them here – and I also knew that seeing it would be unnecessary torture. I was suddenly overcome with the fear of it being discovered, and I pushed it down further in the pocket. As I was talking with the boys, I kept feeling the bar pressed against my leg, and I imagined it was inching upwards in my pocket, trying to reveal itself to the starving boys.

As the boys began to shuffle backwards up their ramp, John and I climbed out of the water. I made a comment to John as we were regaining our footing on dry land. 'This is the most amazing timing.' I still couldn't quite believe that we were there, with the boys we had been sent to look for a week earlier. If we had turned back at Pattaya Beach, or if John hadn't grabbed another reel from our gear room this morning, or if Ben hadn't done his part with the line that morning . . . If all of those pieces hadn't been in place, we'd be heading back out of the cave at that moment, disappointed. But all of those things had happened, and there we were, climbing onto the muddy ledge that had been the boys' home for the past ten days.

Trying to climb.

The thing is, embarrassingly, I was struggling to get up the ledge to the boys. When John had gone up first, the water had poured out from his wellies, leaving the ramp like a slippery slide. He was up there now and having a look around while I was still below, trying to gain foot purchase on the lubricated 45-degree incline that led to their camp. While I was struggling, I could hear the boys' questions for John. When will they be saved? What will happen next?

'Navy SEALs will come tomorrow,' I heard John answer optimistically, as I finally began making my way up the slippery slope. 'With food and doctor and everything.'

I'd gone about 5 metres up the ramp when I lost my footing and felt myself slip. Like a child at a water park, I slid back down and splashed into the water below.

'That looked fun.' I heard John's comment from above as I swore under my breath.

The boys above watched silently, shocked, too respectful to laugh at my awkwardness. There these boys were, for ten days waiting to be rescued, and two middle-aged westerners show up who don't even speak their language. One of them has a rubber ring on his back, looking like he can't swim, and now he can't even climb up the muddy ramp. *Some heroes.*

While I was struggling, John was trying to film the team. He gathered them all together as a group, then stepped back, paused and called down to me. 'My lights are quite shit, Rick. Come over here with yours.' I laughed. Mine wouldn't be much better.

While John continued filming, I wanted to examine the full extent of their living quarters. One of the boys deftly scrambled upwards to guide me, while I continued to slip and slide on the muddy slope. Realizing that I needed help, he came back, motioning with his hands towards my feet, which were still clad in their rubber wellies. I under-stood what he was trying to tell me. *Take off those ridiculous boots and use your bare feet, as we've been doing. You'll get better grip with your toes.* I smiled and nodded at him, but stubbornly continued my struggles.

Once I reached the top of the ramp, where the boy was waiting for me patiently, he pointed to an alcove that extended off at the back. I didn't know what I was looking at initially but soon realized. They had been digging. The boy mimed the action of digging to freedom, the huge smile on his face relaying his pride. They were 2,300 metres inside the cave and trying to dig themselves out.

Meanwhile, John was leading group activities and giving instruc-tions to the boys. John handed over his pad of waterproof paper and a pencil to the boy (Dom),[11] who appeared to be acting as their leader, instructing him to write a note to be taken out. Next, he began recording the boys individually, lingering on each face for a few seconds. This would give a clear record of the boys, along with their physical and mental states, to act as proof for the authorities as well as reassurance for the families. Finally, he roused the team to cheer on the groups of rescuers who were working outside. 'Give a big cheer to the rescuers from England! . . . America! . . . China! . . . Thailand!' The Wild Boars raised their collective fists after each country was named and cheered on their effort with a hearty cry. 'YEAH!' (Unfortunately, John named Thailand last, and I wonder if that's why these later portions of the video were never released to the media.)

After a bit more time passed, we needed to leave. 'We have to go, to tell your families you're all OK.' I wasn't sure if I was trying to convince them, or myself.

'I promise I'll be back tomorrow,' John said. I wasn't sure I'd ever heard John make a promise before. I knew that he, too, was finding it difficult to leave them there. We didn't know their lights situation, so we each took a torch off of our helmets and gave it to them. We didn't want to leave them empty-handed.

The boys lined up to hug us, one by one, before we made our way back down their ramp. This was unexpected, as I understand that hugs are not common among Thai people; they are not given as freely, as meaninglessly, as we give them in the West. Seeing the boys standing in line like this, waiting to say goodbye, made me feel the weight of what we were doing. *We're leaving them in here.* We had no choice, but it felt unreal to me.

Out of sight from the boys, John and I were silent as we kitted up. Normally we'd be talking, but neither of us said a word. I took advantage of this silence to finally eat my Snickers bar. John's words to them lingered in the silence between us. 'I promise I'll be back tomorrow,' he had said, but the truth is that we didn't know if we'd ever see them again. With one big rainstorm, we'd never get back to them. The water would rise again, as quickly as it had fallen on Saturday.

The initial triumph, excitement and relief of finding the boys had been replaced by a leaden weight of dread as we became aware of the enormous responsibility on us. It was just a massive, unbearable weight. It felt like an impossible task to get them out, and I had no idea how it could be done. We glided along, with the current whisking us out, as our thoughts continued to churn.

Just before we ducked beneath the surface to begin our dive out, our gazes met, and I know he was already thinking the same thing.

How on earth are we ever going to get them out?

Less than two hours after leaving the boys, we surfaced inside Chamber 3 with our news. Two SEALs were waiting by the water, and, without pausing, I blurted out to them. 'We've found the boys. They're all alive.'

After our previous dive, when we'd returned with news of our progress, the SEALs had been happy to see us and had helped us with our kit as we climbed the ramp out of the sump. Not this time. As soon as we'd spoken, the SEALs took off running to spread the news to the others in the chamber. Soon, there was a crowd of about fifteen SEALs huddled and talking excitedly among themselves. We walked over to them, and John handed over the camera he'd used to film the boys. 'Here is your proof, we've filmed them all . . . There's now a continuous line running from here to where they are.'

The SEALs wanted to reach the boys immediately, and the oldest man there – a retired SEAL named Chenyatta, who was in his early sixties – wanted to be included on that mission. He seemed to be crestfallen when his colleagues told him that it would be impossible and he dejectedly left with us. As we were climbing through the boulders leading upwards to Chamber 2, his pressure gauge got caught on something and snagged his forward progression. Instead of retreating to free himself, he just started thrashing about. Seeing this made me happy with the SEALs' decision to keep him from diving.[12]

RICK STANTON

There was another SEAL leaving the cave with us, and I believed him to be the one carrying the GoPro camera. I'd already begun to feel nervous that we had handed over the camera so quickly. It had become clear to me that the military were the ones with power, the ones who wanted to be controlling this situation, and I became worried that the camera wouldn't be safe in their hands.

'We need to keep pace with this guy,' I told John. I wanted to be present with the authorities when they received the evidence so that I could urge them to share the news with caution. We weren't certain we'd ever get back to see the boys again, so that video could be the last interaction anyone had with them, the last time they were seen alive.

The four of us arrived at the cave's entrance thirty minutes after leaving Chamber 3, and I immediately knew that controlling the spread of the news would be impossible. Days earlier, a fibre-optic cable had been run to Chamber 3 to allow wi-fi connectivity for the SEALs who were stationed there; I'd seen them using this wi-fi connection to follow the World Cup games. After receiving our video footage, one of the SEALs had uploaded our video and shared it with the authorities, who had immediately released it to the global media. Before we'd even left the cave, the news had already been shared around the world.

Tom, Bas and Amp greeted us in Chamber 1 with broad smiles on their faces. There was a swarm of others waiting for us there as well – all of them smiling, laughing, crying tears of joy. A seemingly endless line of people formed, wanting to shake our hands and clap us on the back to thank us for a job well done as we walked away from the cave.

They were acting like the boys were saved, which of course they weren't.

They were acting like we'd already rescued the boys, but of course we hadn't.

I was already deeply lost in my thoughts and largely unaware of what was going on around me. Before we could walk past the SEALs' camp, we were sat down for a thirty-minute informal debriefing session. Finally, we insisted we had to go back to our room to get changed, then we'd be back for a more formal meeting.

We got to our gear room, and after a few moments I reached for my phone. I found a couple of text messages and emails sitting there already, friends who wanted to congratulate us on the boys' discovery. My head began to spin. How did they know? How did they know it was us? It was too much to process, on top of everything else. As I stood there, phone in hand, another text message came through from my friend Dan – the Morris Dancer who had driven me to Heathrow the week before.

'Good one mate, nice to have a rescue instead of a recovery.'

I looked at those words for a moment, surrounded by the cheering crowd, debating how to answer, if even to answer at all.

We headed back to the SEALs' area of the rescue base. As we were approaching, we met with Ben, who congratulated us. 'Now the hard work starts,' he said, accurately enough. I think he joined us as we entered the SEALs' area, but as we sat down at the table, Ben faded into the crowd that had gathered round.

The debrief was being chaired by the SEALs' commander, Rear Admiral Arpakorn Yuukongkaew. We four Brits were seated on one side of the table, with four Thai SEALs on the opposite side (Arpakorn, Commander Pinyo, and the two high-ranking retired SEALs Pook and Chenyatta). US Air Force Captain Mitch Torrel was at one end of the table, and the Australian Major Alex Rubin[13] was at the

RICK STANTON

other end. The meeting was being held between those gathered at the table, while dozens of others were crowded around us and filming with their mobile phones.

I began by discussing the dive, saying again that the line had been installed, and briefly detailing the conditions of the cave. Before I was able to explain fully how gnarly the dive had been, I was cut off. They were keener to hear our assessment of the boys' physical and psychological states. 'They're all fine,' was the best medical description we could come up with. 'The smallest ones and the coach appeared to be the weakest . . . Every one of them was in remarkably good spirits.' (This was mostly true, although the smallest ones – Titan and Mark – had been overcome and cried at one point.)

Arpakorn spoke next. 'Thank you for being pathfinders,' he said before telling us that we would no longer be diving, and the SEALs would take over. 'You and John will now act in an advisory capacity.' I tried to hide my shock as this news sunk in. I didn't bother to argue. It seemed hugely unlikely that they would be able to execute a successful rescue – even if I gave them the best advice, which I didn't yet have. I sat back and bided my time, knowing that we wouldn't be turning our backs on the boys. We had seen the skill sets of everybody else there, and we knew that we were the boys' only hope for survival.

The SEALs then announced that they were sending in a team immediately, without any detailed consultation with us; I thought it seemed a bit impulsive. Throughout the meeting, there had been frantic background preparations going on all around us. It was like watching a navy preparing to go to war. Everyone there seemed to have a common purpose, everyone was engaged.

Maybe Ben hadn't heard that we had been moved to an advisory role and that the SEALs were already planning to send their team in, because suddenly, out of the sea of faces surrounding us, I heard Ben's voice from the crowd. 'We need to go and save the boys now. I've got a stretcher and can get some masks.'

John tried to reason with him. 'Slow down, we've only just found them. We're not rushing to get them tonight. For the time being, they're fine. We need to come up with a plan.'

'How do you know they're fine?' Ben shot back. 'Are you medically trained?' He carried on talking rapidly, and we couldn't make sense of anything he was saying. John told him to speak more slowly and coherently. As Ben became more excited, talking about his plan to get moving immediately, some of his Thai friends stepped up and gently led him away from the crowd. That was the last we saw of him for a week, and he took no further part in the rescue. After this interruption, the meeting continued as if nothing had happened.

The Thais were already moving forward with their plan. Before the end of the night, four or five new, efficient compressors – *where did they come from?* – were being run, filling countless shiny new cylinders. The team of SEALs went into the cave at around 2 a.m., just as we were leaving.

Back at the resort, I found myself looking again at Dan's message. 'Good one mate, nice to have a rescue instead of a recovery.' Should I just leave it? In the end, the outcome would speak for itself. But I wanted him to understand the reality. I wanted somebody to understand. Finally, I replied with a correction.

'We found them, not rescued them. They're probably not getting out alive.'

PART THREE
Practice

7.
Spirit of Adventure

What the fuck am I doing here? I thought to myself. *This is ridiculous. Only a week ago there was an absolute epic here, and I'm about to re-create it if I'm not careful.*

Today, I pride myself on my ability to identify and manage risks, but this hasn't always been the case. Though careful in my planning, I may have omitted the risk-assessment portion when I was young. I was never an adrenaline junky or thrill-seeker; I just wanted to keep going forwards on a task until I couldn't any more. I didn't always stop to consider how dangerous something might be.

The first time that I remember stopping myself from doing something because I realized it was dangerous was the occasion of my friend Alien's accident inside Notts Pot.

Alien (Andrew Goddard) and I had been doing a ton of caving together; some people even called us brothers. During the winter of 1995–6, we were trying to find a dry entrance to Notts 2, the magnificent piece of cave that Barry and I had discovered by diving. A vertical shaft had been found that led directly upwards from a side branch off the main streamway, and it seemed to be heading directly towards a possible entrance, connected with a lime kiln on the surface. Its featureless walls were unclimbable, so we needed to ascend by drilling a series of steel expansion bolts into the rock. It made a good project within a project.

On the day of his accident, I was diving with Dave Morris[1] while Alien was climbing the shaft with Martin Holroyd. About 30 metres up, Alien drove a bolt into a bit of rock, which then broke free as soon as he put his weight onto it. He fell, smashing his arm in the process and was left with an open fracture. They were a long way in and had quite an involved journey to get out. It was a remote place for such an injury.

Knowing they couldn't wait for help, Martin helped Alien down the inlet passage to the streamway. When Dave and I finished our dive, we made our way back to rejoin the others and found no one there. Instead, we saw rope lying on the floor in a tangled heap, and there was blood everywhere. We followed the trail of blood to the sump, and there was Alien, sitting on the ground, covered in blood, with his bone visible out of his arm. Between the three of us, we managed to get Alien back through the cave – first kitting up and diving through the sump, then switching to SRT and climbing the pitches. It was a right epic.

A week later, knowing that the ropes had to be reinstalled and wanting to continue the project, I went alone into Notts. I just went back there, not thinking twice. This is how I was at the time. I walked across the fell on my own, went down the cave and through the sump to where the ropes were still lying, caked with dried blood. I climbed 30 metres above the floor, installing the ropes with a self-lifeline, until I reached the spot where Alien had fallen. I eyed the loose rock where he had driven his bolt, saw that there were more loose rocks above me and finally I stopped.

This was when I questioned the decision-making process that had taken me back there alone. In a move that was unlike me at the time, I retreated from the cave, leaving the job unfinished. When he heard I was looking for a new caving partner, Jonathan Sims suggested someone I might want to team up with.

Jason Mallinson had followed a similar sort of learning curve as I had: taking up caving at university, quietly doing his own thing and making steady progress. He'd started with dry caving and now was teaching himself to dive. Without any preliminary getting-to-know-each-other trips, we went straight to the sharp end, climbing the shaft in Notts Pot to finish the job. I had described the cave up to Notts 2 as being 'involved' – a full-on multidisciplinary trip – and Jason wanted to see the famed streamway, so he was keen. Based on his reputation, I suspected he wouldn't have trouble, and I was pleased to see that he moved through both the dry cave and the sump skilfully.

We climbed the vertical shaft – I was in the lead – and as we reached the point where Alien had fallen, I saw the loose rocks that would have to be removed before we could continue. I began pulling the rocks to get them out of the way, letting them drop down the pitch. Jason was below me, tucked into an alcove that acted as a sentry box, as the rocks whizzed by him. There were rocks falling everywhere, flying past his head – they could have hurt him quite badly – but he wasn't bothered at all, and that was significant for me. I knew this was somebody who was never going to complain.

And that is Jason. He complains about a lot of shit, but he gets through the hard stuff without moaning about it. He just gets things done, without being bothered by the difficulty of the work involved. He was exactly the person I wanted to work with on the next project I had in mind: the Emergence du Ressel.

Since first visiting the caves of southern France in 1991 with Steve and Dani, I'd been following exploration of the region's many large caves and I'd quickly become familiar with the work of two explorers. The Swiss Olivier Isler and the German Jochen Hasenmayer both pursued intense exploration in the French caves, while constantly expanding their skills and equipment to complete the dives they'd planned. As I was learning and growing as a cave diver, I closely followed their progress and their methods, using them as guides for my own.

Jochen Hasenmayer was a pioneer of using mixed gases (specifically, adding helium to nitrogen and oxygen to make trimix) to increase his depth capabilities and duration while avoiding oxygen toxicity, nitrogen narcosis and decompression injuries. From studying his dive profiles, I began to work out how different gas blends and decompression schedules could be used to safely complete more technical dives. Hasenmayer's dives taught me about the logistics of using mixed gases for deep dives, but it was Olivier Isler who truly sparked a fire inside me, giving me a glimpse of what was possible with the right equipment.

In 1981, during his ongoing exploration of Doux de Coly in the Dordogne, Isler had travelled 3,100 metres on a single dive, using standard open-circuit diving equipment. In 1984, when my friend Clive Westlake had told me about the dive, my reaction had been immediate: 'That's not possible.' Travelling for 3 kilometres at an average depth of −50 metres was inconceivable to me then, when I was still diving with two 7-litre steel cylinders filled with air. Determined to understand how it had been done, I quickly began learning about Isler's huge role in the development and advancement of equipment used for technical diving.[2]

A diver's gas supply sets the limit on their dive, therefore most advances in diving equipment are focused towards extending the dive's range (depth, time and penetration) while conserving gas. The two most significant advancements towards this goal were the dive-propulsion vehicle (DPV) and the rebreather. A DPV, also known as a scooter, is a propeller driven by a battery-powered motor, encased in a pressure-resistant watertight hull. A traditional scooter is less than a metre long, and the diver is towed behind, hanging on to a tether. Isler's heavily modified long-range DPV was a massive long torpedo that he rode on, lying on top with a saddle between his legs to push him along.

In the late 1980s, at the same time that Bill Stone was working on his CIS-Lunar, Isler teamed up with engineer Alain Ronjat to develop his own semi-closed-circuit rebreather. Named RI 2000, the rebreather was used to reach a penetration distance of 4 kilometres inside Doux de Coly in 1991.

I admired Isler's determination and innovation. He was driven to reach the end of a sump, regardless of the depth or distance. If the equipment to make the dive possible hadn't yet been developed, he developed it himself. He showed that, in exploration, the only thing holding a person back was the limit of their imagination and their determination to see a project through to its end. I've never held personal heroes as such, but watching Isler's progression was an inspiration to me, and I recognize that I modelled my cave diving after his.

When I'd first visited the Ressel in 1991, I hadn't gone in very far. That same year, Olivier Isler had been the first to pass the cave's extended first sump, finally surfacing after 2 kilometres. Isler had been breathing mixed gases on a triple-rebreather configuration (two mounted on his back and one on his chest) and using two large Aquazepp scooters (one as a primary, the other as back-up) so he didn't have to swim. Most crucially, he'd had to make multiple stops during his ascent in the sump, possibly the first time a diver had completed internal decompression while still proceeding into a cave. Until then, nobody was doing such long dives that they had to decompress while they were still going in. His one dive had been a pioneering game changer, breaking a lot of psychological barriers.

Further cave lay waiting after the sump, but Isler had not continued. He'd needed a team of people to put him into his equipment on the riverbed at the cave's entrance, and the weight of it meant that he wasn't able to get out of it on his own inside the cave. To me it was ridiculous that he wasn't autonomous. He'd made such an amazingly technical approach as an explorer but then was unable to de-kit and get out of the water to explore further. It was all wrong.

After his dive, Isler had stated that passing the sump in the Ressel could not be done without the use of multiple rebreathers and he was convinced that his exploration was unlikely to be extended. I disagreed with both of his assertions. I was certain the sump could be dived open-circuit and that I could adapt the equipment in a way that would allow me to continue exploration beyond the sump. This cave became my new focus. I'd recognized all of the elements I sought in a project: multiple sump diving in an enticing cave that was still unfinished and beyond the reach of most people. This project would involve a long and steep learning curve leading up to some long and deep dives, but the potential for exploration was huge, and I knew it would be worth the investment.

I knew this wasn't a project I could do alone. When I told Jason what I was planning to do and asked if he'd be interested, he immediately joined the project, and we got to work.

I studied photographs of Isler on his dives, trying to learn about his equipment and techniques. I read everything I could find. Then, in May of 1996, I had the chance to see it first-hand when I was invited to join the support team for Markus Schafheutle and Philip Lawo, who were attempting a long-range survey dive in the Ressel.[3] I arrived in France as an eager student, thirsty for the opportunity to learn new methods and procedures, and I watched everything they were doing.

Instead of filling their cylinders with air, they boosted helium into the compressor to make trimix gas. Instead of finning along slowly and laboriously, they each used two Aquazepp scooters to propel themselves. Instead of decompressing while submerged in water and breathing from their cylinders, they used a structure called a habitat to rest inside, partially de-kitted and breathing more comfortably. I could see the value in everything that Markus and Philip were using, but I could also see their existing design flaws. The divers were overloaded by all of their equipment, just as Isler had been in 1991. They each had six 20-litre cylinders (four on their back plus one on each side). They were so burdened by their equipment that they couldn't even get their fins on once they were kitted up. 'What if a fin drops off underwater?' I thought incredulously as I helped them into their fins.[4]

In the water, things only looked worse. Their scooters were off-balance and only just rideable. The configuration of the four monstrous cylinders on their backs was a huge strain on their bodies – even while underwater, where it created unnecessary drag – and was even more difficult to manoeuvre above water, as it weighed over 120 kilos. I instantly dismissed it as being impractical and offered a suggestion. 'I think I can do this better.'

They looked sceptical but told me to have a go.

British cave diving uses a side-mounted system, and by then I'd also done quite a bit of back-mounted diving,[5] so I amalgamated the two. With twin cylinders on my back, I put the other four at my sides, using elastic bungee cord to hold them in tight and close to me – two at each side. It was like being surrounded by cylinders. My configuration was more modular, and I never had to wear more than two on my back at a time. It was more streamlined and had better trim.

I'd never even seen a 20-litre cylinder before this trip and had never dived with more than three cylinders at one time, yet I nonchalantly kitted up by myself – putting on my own fins – and set off with six 20-litre cylinders. It was a pivotal moment, and I was excited about the possibilities this would open up. The Germans were also convinced; I don't think they ever went back to four back-mounted cylinders.

Back in the UK, Alien and I were the first CDG members to buy scooters.[6] There's hardly room to move in most British caves, and certainly no need for scooters, so everyone in the CDG ridiculed our purchases. 'What on earth do you want them for?' they asked. 'You'll never use them.' I wasn't focused on British caves, though. I hadn't told anybody what I was planning, or where I would be using the scooters. I always preferred to wait and say, 'This is what we've done,' instead of, 'This is what we're about to do.'

This is when I teamed up with Jason, and we spent all of 1997 practising hard, slowly and steadily acquiring skills and experience. With the help of the Germans, we obtained 20-litre cylinders. We practised mixing gases, then gained experience diving to increasing depths on trimix to learn our decompression schedules. There were no dive computers back then, so I had decompression tables from a DOS-based program printed out on sheets of laminated A4 paper[7] – different permutations for how long we'd be in each section. We bought new scooters, and I even organized a training trip to Florida, which was funded through a grant from the National Lottery. (When my colleagues at the fire station were paying into their weekly lottery syndicate, I'd tease them – and not only because I'm against gambling in principle. 'You do realize that by buying lottery tickets, you're subsidizing my diving hobby.' They weren't amused.)

We made countless trips to flooded quarries in the UK with the sole purpose of becoming familiar with our new kit. Many days were spent at Stoney Cove quarry, repeatedly dumping our cylinders and clipping them back on, until we worked out all of the kinks and had our optimum configuration down. One day, partly in jest, I'd said to somebody, 'I reckon I could wear fourteen cylinders.' When

I was taken up on the challenge, a group of us went to Stoney Cove to see if I could do it. I managed it – with two cylinders on the scooter, four on my back, two on each side, and four clipped onto my waist. It wasn't practical, but it worked.[8]

I spent most of 1997 planning for the Ressel with the same single-minded focus I use on any big exploration project I'm undertaking, thinking about nothing but the problem and the preparation. Every spare moment was spent diving, training or testing new equipment. When I was at home, I was absorbed with planning or researching. The only time I was not preoccupied with it all was when I was working. I considered that my downtime.

After fourteen years, my relationship with Angela was already under strain, as we had begun to grow apart. Her interest in caving had lessened as mine had grown. Recently, she'd been spending her free time pursuing her newer pursuit of long-distance cycling, something that didn't interest me at all. It was inevitable that the relationship would end, and I wasn't surprised when it did, but it was a shame. No relationship I've had since has lasted one-fifth of the time I spent with Angie. Coincidentally, we split up in the exact same month as my first trip to the Ressel with Jason. While most people would have been preoccupied with their break-up, I was only focused on the Ressel. Not only did I neglect our relationship, I didn't even give the break-up the attention it deserved. At least I'm consistent.

I think that true exploration requires a single-minded focus that doesn't leave room for much else. An explorer has to be selfish with their energy and attention, unwilling to let anything distract them from their goal. It's not something you can commit to halfway, not if you want to be successful, and that takes its toll. I don't know of any explorers who weren't later described as being a bit anti-social, and that includes myself.

Newly single in March of 1998, I went to the Ressel with Jason,[9] where we'd be making our first attempt to pass the sump open-circuit. This would also be our first time using a habitat for underwater decompression. I'd seen the expensive custom-built domes, made from quality materials and complete with seats to rest on, that were used by the Germans. Rob Parker and Bill Stone had used similarly extravagant contraptions in Florida. At the other end of the spectrum, American cave divers like Sheck Exley and Tom Morris – the good old boys – were decompressing inside upturned cattle water troughs. The latter style was much more aligned with mine, and that was the concept Jason and I went for.

One day in France, we spotted a plastic waste bin on the side of the road. It was one of the industrial-sized ones you find behind shops and restaurants, plenty large enough for the two of us to fit inside. We went back for it in the middle of the night, with Richard Hudson driving the getaway van. During the haste of the midnight raid, we didn't take time to look inside the bin and when we inspected our loot, we discovered it was laden with feathers, chicken heads, and poultry innards. Unperturbed, we cleaned it out and took it into the Ressel, wedging it under the roof at a depth of about 6 metres. We were quite pleased with our habi-bin – as we named it – and continued to use it for the next couple of years. (We would say that we'd been sponsored by the local municipality – which was sort of true, although they weren't aware of it.)

Beset by mishaps and combined with unusually poor conditions on this trip, our attempt to pass the sump was unsuccessful, but by the time we left France, the cat was out of the bag. Everyone in Britain knew what we were attempting to do and everyone thought we were punching way above our weight. We were trying to compete with the top cave diver in Europe – Isler, whose diving ability was way beyond ours – and we were doing it on his home turf. Despite the obvious prowess we'd shown in the UK caves, this was a huge step-change, and most people thought it was doomed to fail.

Never ones to be deterred by the scepticism of others, we stayed focused on our goal and returned to the Ressel in May for another attempt. This time we were not alone there. Two Germans — Reinhard Buchaly and his dive partner Sandro Madeo — had also set their sights on the Ressel. Reinhard was a millionaire dental practice owner, with all the top toys, all the top equipment. They had the best rebreathers, all the scooters and cylinders they could ever need — all neatly lined up in uniform rows. We watched them erecting folding tables to configure their top-of-the-line equipment, while Jason and I dumped our eclectic mix of second-hand and borrowed equipment onto our tarps on the ground.

We were there for over ten days just to set up this one dive, using siege tactics for an expedition-style assault on the cave. I was forced to devise a convoluted scheme for juggling the use of my scooters, neither of which had the range to get me all the way through. My Mako was limited to a depth of −55 metres (which would be reached 900 metres into the sump), then I'd have to switch to my second scooter, a Predator, which was rated for greater depths. Our dive plan had its complexities, and we were trying things that hadn't been done before, but I was confident it would work. We'd done what we could to shift the odds in our favour.

We had to leave stage cylinders at several points in the sump — extra supplies of gas to ensure we didn't run out. We had a thirteen-cylinder plan, where we'd wear six at a time and carry another couple on our scooters. There was one cylinder depot at 900 metres, another at 1,300 metres. We moved from cylinder dump to cylinder dump, and eventually on the last one we went all the way through to the end. We put enough gas in the cave that we'd have redundant cylinders for decompression. This was crucial. Even if something went wrong at the far end, we'd still be able to get to the surface beyond the sump.

Eventually, after some equipment mishaps, we managed to get ourselves into a place where we were ready to go. Reinhard heard us talking and he knew we were close to departing, so he stayed up all night working on his equipment. He was desperate to beat us into the cave.[10] They dived early in the morning and returned to the camp late that evening, beaming with pride. Not only had they passed the sump, but Sandro had been able to de-kit and leave the sump for further exploration. Sandro told us that the dry cave ended at a boulder choke,[11] a mere 15 metres from the sump.

'That was it,' he said confidently. 'It ends there.' While they were certain that they'd reached the end of the Ressel – even going so far as to make such claims on internet caving forums – Jason and I kept setting up for our dive, without paying them mind. We weren't convinced that they'd reached the end, and anyway we wanted to see it for ourselves. A day or two after their dive, Jason and I went in on ours.

I entered the water first, knowing that Jason would follow a bit behind me. The maximum depth of the sump is −81 metres; after descending to this depth (the sump's elbow), the cave begins to ascend again. I rose through a vertical shaft, then the cave levelled off for a bit before rising again, and I soon reached a second vertical shaft, where I would be completing most of my decompression. During the four hours I spent there, I kept expecting to see Jason approach, but he never arrived.

People have often asked me what I was thinking and feeling during that time, when Jason failed to arrive. 'Were you worried?' 'Were you tempted to turn back to look for him?' Nobody ever seems satisfied with my answer, which is, 'No, not really.' I was surprised he didn't show up, but I wouldn't say I was worried about him. Something must have gone wrong, but I trusted he would take care of it. I knew that he wouldn't expect me to wait or to go back looking for him. By the time I'd got back to him, there was nothing I could have done anyway.

After I finished decompressing, I went on.

Five and a half hours after setting off on the dive that I had spent more than two years preparing for, I spotted the reflection of the water's surface just ahead of me. I'd done it, the way I'd planned. The feelings of satisfaction and accomplishment were euphoric, and I regretted Jason not being there to enjoy the achievement. Beyond the sump, I began taking off my gear and set off to explore Sandro's boulder choke. 'This is the end,' he'd said. From a distance it did look like it might be blocked, but he clearly hadn't investigated it, because I practically walked straight through.

On the other side, there were 100 metres of open passage in front of me. I'd started to work up a sweat, so I removed my dry-suit before continuing down the passage wearing only my thermal undersuit. When I arrived at a lake, I removed the undersuit and entered the water and swam around the perimeter of the lake to investigate. Finding no onward passage, I knew that this was a second sump. The cave would be continuing underwater, but further exploration would have to wait for the next trip – another dive, more planning. I climbed out of the just-discovered sump with a grin on my face that nobody could see, then began the long process of leaving the cave, excited to tell the others what I'd found.

Back at the campsite, Jason told me what had happened on his dive. First, he'd had some trouble in the staging areas, which had left him behind schedule; then, during the dive, he was very much out of trim. After having a lot of difficulty in the vertical shaft – at one point he'd performed an underwater somersault, which isn't as fun as it sounds – Jason had wisely decided to turn the dive. Outside the cave, he'd found that our support team had already left for camp, not expecting anyone to return for hours. Exhausted from his dive, Jason had had no choice but to walk back to the campsite, in bare feet no less.

The group of us stayed up late, talking and laughing, fuelled with excitement by our discovery and the cave's ongoing potential. Somebody mentioned Reinhard, and how all of his expensive top-of-the-line equipment had not helped him in the end. I scanned our mismatched supply of battered and borrowed equipment, our refuse-bin habitat, and I commented on our victory: 'The spirit of adventure has triumphed over technical supremacy.' The team laughed, then another diver added: 'Yes, and that is how we won the war.'

Within hours of our dive, someone added a postscript to Reinhard's internet post, announcing that I had just passed his end. The news spread quickly through the caving forums, with cave divers everywhere excited by our discovery. Things changed for us after that. Although we had already made names for ourselves within the small world of British caving, this accomplishment was our introduction to the world stage. Our names became known internationally as the ones who passed the Ressel's sump on open-circuit equipment, using only the kit we had thrown together and with a group of friends as support. I'm especially proud that we persevered and showed that our British sump-diving techniques could be expanded to accomplish anything.

Back home in Coventry, Angela had been letting me stay in her house until I found a new place of my own. Jason and I were planning to go to France in August, so I didn't spend much time looking.

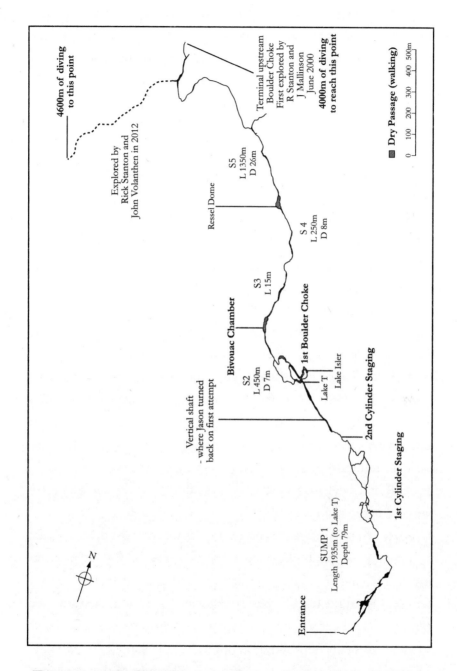

Emergence du Ressel

In July, not long after getting back from our big dive in France, I moved out of Angela's and into a house just down the road from her. (This is where I still live today. For what it's worth, it was already fairly run-down when I moved into it.)

Immediately after moving into my new house, I set to work preparing for our next trip to the Ressel. Before I'd even purchased furniture and fully unpacked, the neighbours could hear my compressors running through the day. They'd first thought I was mowing the lawn, but quickly realized my lawn wasn't big and shouldn't be taking so long. (As they came to know me better over the years, they would realize how unlikely it was for me to ever be mowing my lawn.)

Our trips to France were so gear-intensive that we borrowed a large four-wheel trailer to tow behind my Land Rover for transporting it all.[12] Before our trip in August, Jason came to my house to help pack the trailer, and my neighbour, watching us load it, commented on how harmoniously we worked together, without ever exchanging a word. 'The two of you moved around each other, fitting things into the trailer, it's like the whole thing had been choreographed.' I knew what she was talking about. That ability to work in sync, without communicating, is what makes a great dive partner. Unfortunately, Jason and I didn't always get along as smoothly on the surface, when we could communicate.

After arriving in France and setting up for our next dive, we went to a nearby nightclub. We were intent on spending the night drinking and having fun, but we ended up having an altercation over a female. Out of the blue, he punched me in the face and then stormed off. Two days later we dived together – me with an unsightly black eye and him still not talking. Nobody on the support team could believe that we were going to go through with the dive that depended on complete trust in each other, but we never considered not diving.

We knew that we needed to work together, and we were too determined to let anything affect the project.

I dived first into the unknown second sump, with Jason to follow a couple of hours behind me. Luckily the Ressel's second sump was short and shallow; I passed through and reached a nice area beyond it, then waited for Jason. When he arrived, it was his turn to take the lead, and he reached Sump 5.

We were kitting up to dive out through the first sump at about four in the morning, having been on the go since early in the morning of the day before. We were utterly exhausted and drained, a far from ideal state for a deep dive through the interminable sump that still lay between us and the exit. We were trying to kit up slowly and deliberately, but we were half asleep. When we finally surfaced in the River Celé, more than twenty-four hours after beginning, we were falling over from exhaustion. This was madness, and it was clear that there would have to be a change.

In the future, we'll be camping in there.

1998 had already been quite a year for me. Angela and I had split up, I'd completed three significant exploratory dives in the Ressel and I'd moved into a new house. Before the year ended, Jason and I were recruited as lead divers on Bill Stone's ambitious next project, Wakulla 2 in Florida. Stone's project had the objectives of continuing development of his CIS-Lunar rebreather (Mk-V), while testing a new digital mapping device. However intent we had been on diving the Ressel on open-circuit, Jason and I did appreciate that closed-circuit rebreather technology was the future of cave diving. We knew that Wakulla 2 would provide the perfect opportunity to gain knowledge, so we accepted Stone's invitation.

In September of 1998 – a few months before the project was set to begin – Jason and I flew to Florida for a week-long trip to focus on learning the rebreather. Richard Pyle took us through various troubleshooting scenarios to illustrate and prepare us for the dangers that come with using a rebreather. He stressed that most accidents are caused from lack of oxygen being delivered to the diver – a user error that would debilitate a diver within seconds. Never one to take anyone at their word, I guess Jason felt the need to put this assertion to the test.

While on a training dive in the entrance lake of Madison Blue spring, I became aware that I was suddenly alone in the water. I surfaced to see what was amiss and discovered Jason floating on the water's surface, having turned a quite alarming shade of blue. He was still breathing, but just. As divers rushed to him, I heard somebody scream the instructions to call for an ambulance. When I reached him, Jill Heinerth (a Canadian diver and explorer who would be joining us as a lead diver at Wakulla 2) was leaning over him, checking his pulse and breathing rates while providing assurances. 'Hang in there, Jason. Help is on the way. An ambulance will be here soon.'

I could see that Jason was starting to come around and to hurry the process I provoked him a bit. 'Don't worry, Jason. The paramedics will be here soon. They'll cut you out of your drysuit.' The threat had its desired effect. Jason's body immediately stiffened, and his eyes widened.

'No they fucking won't,' he proclaimed. I smiled, quite pleased with myself for bringing him back to life, while Jill looked at me, bewildered.

'He's fine,' I assured her.

A few months later, we began our diving at Wakulla Springs, where Jason and I made incremental steps in the duration of our dives, until we were spending nearly five hours at a depth of −90 metres, with the corresponding sixteen hours of decompression.

Those dives were hugely important for breaking psychological barriers. Once we did that, the Ressel paled into insignificance, and it increased our comfort for longer, deeper dives in the future. There was nowhere in Europe where we could have gained that sort of experience.

As our time spent in the cave system increased, Bill returned to his idea of using dual rebreathers for redundancy. Jason and I were given the task of taking apart two rebreathers before reconfiguring them as a single package, which allowed me to spend time examining the inner workings of the machine. When we finished, I had a more solid understanding of the components and I was left convinced that changes needed to be made. Stone's rebreather was too technology-driven and too bulky. If I was ever going to progress to a dual system, I'd be using a modular approach, as had proved successful in the Ressel.

I'd already begun imagining adaptations I would make, visualizing the simplified and streamlined rebreather I'd like to use. I'd even been taking engineering classes in the evening. Working from some crude sketches I'd put together after returning from Florida, I began designing a rebreather that I would build to my specifications and capability to assemble.

Jason and I went back to the Ressel in 1999, and this time we were alongside Reinhard. Jason wasn't very happy about it – and it turned out to be a mistake – but Reinhard didn't have anyone to dive with, and I thought we might benefit from his gear. This time, remembering how we had reached the limit of our endurance during the previous trip, we knew we'd be camping inside. It would be the first time that I – or anyone – had camped beyond such a long and technical sump, and I'd acquired a canister to use for carrying our stuff through. (I called this my camping trailer, and it's the same one I took to Tham Luang with me.)

We encountered an unexpected problem with the atmosphere in the chamber where we were camping. At one point we measured 16 per cent oxygen at the campsite – down from the 21 per cent oxygen that is normally present in breathing air. The corresponding increase in CO_2 had us panting and out-of-breath the whole time. Reinhard was clearly out of his comfort zone camping there in the first place, and the poor atmosphere didn't help. Jason, on the other hand, was so happy at our camp that he didn't even want to leave.

'Right,' I told him in the morning when it was time to go and he was still in his sleeping bag. 'You do what you want, but I'm leaving.'

⊕   ⊕   ⊕

Around this time, I attended Chris Cooke's wedding – he'd been a fellow caver at university, then my flatmate after I'd left university. There was a girl there from Aston's caving club; she was with her two teenaged children. I hadn't seen her in nearly twenty years and to be honest, I barely recognized her. She looked too normal.

'What have you been doing with yourself?' she asked me.

'Exactly the same thing,' I told her.

'That's amazing!' She sounded impressed – she'd known how passionate about caving I'd been at university – but I saw it differently.

Not really. It's quite sad, I thought to myself. *Twenty years later, and not much has changed.*

In spite of my successes with exploration and the wider acclaim we'd received from our work in the Ressel, I still felt like I didn't quite fit in with most people who were living more traditional lives. My feelings of accomplishment were strictly reserved for caving.

I'd begun receiving invitations to speak at local diving shows and conventions. I had to force myself to do this in the beginning and I didn't enjoy it, but eventually I became more comfortable speaking in front of others. From the time I was a child, I'd always been painfully shy, but I felt more confident when I was talking about diving, since it was something that I loved doing so much. Compared to all of the times and places where I felt like an outsider and couldn't relate to anybody, these dive shows were places where I always felt comfortable. I knew I was with like-minded people. My first ever presentation was to the North Warwickshire BSAC diving club in the late 1990s, and this was the start of my willingness to share my experiences and overcome my shyness.

Perhaps it's unsurprising, then, that a disproportionate number of my friends have been met at these events. At a dive show in Birmingham in early 2000, I'd finished giving my presentation about the Ressel dives when a woman raised her hand from the front row with an unusual question.

'How can I get on one of these expeditions?' she'd asked, eagerly.

I shrugged. 'What are you doing in July?' And like that, Helen Rider, a cave diver, became one of my very dear friends and joined our support team on our next trip to the Ressel. When we returned in 2000, for what would be the final year of our project, I was there with my girlfriend Abigail, whom I'd met at a caving hut earlier in the year.

(It's also a running joke that I've found most of my girlfriends at either dive shows or caving huts. I blame this partly on the fact that I'd gone to boys' schools until I was eighteen, then I'd attended a technical university where it seemed like the men outnumbered the women three to one. At university, I'd taken up a male-dominated hobby, which had led into a male-dominated job. It's not my fault that I don't understand women.)

We didn't have a large support team that year; it was pretty much Abigail and Helen. After we'd set up the dive, Helen had to go back home, leaving Abigail alone on the surface for the two days we'd be gone.

Before Jason and I set off on our dive, I handed Abigail a piece of paper that said something like, 'If I don't come out, ring this number . . .' I don't even recall whose number I'd given; there probably wasn't anybody in Europe who could have dived far enough to help us. I think Abigail had already been a bit worried about being left alone on the surface – *what if something went wrong?* – and being given that slip of paper certainly didn't help settle her nerves.

This year was different because we'd each managed to borrow rebreathers from friends. We hadn't fully transitioned our thinking to closed-circuit, though, so we kept to our tried-and-tested logistics plan. Inside the Ressel, the dive went smoothly, but we found the air beyond the sump was even worse than it had been the previous year. Setting up to camp, we struggled to get our gas stoves alight because of the low oxygen. Finally, we had to put them in a hollow in the rocks and then squirt Nitrox[13] in there to get enough oxygen to get them going.

We got to the upstream end of the cave on that dive, reaching the end at a boulder choke in Sump 5, a total of more than 4 kilometres of diving. After everything I've done, I still consider the Emergence du Ressel to be a personal favourite cave, and one of the most meaningful for me. It even got us mentioned in British diving magazines, bringing us to prominence among divers outside the caving world for the first time.

With the Ressel project completed, I set my focus on cobbling together a functioning rebreather. I knew that my rebreather needed to allow passage through tight restrictions, so it couldn't be worn on my back. The only viable alternative was my chest. Years earlier, I'd found a bucket of rudimentary rebreather mouthpieces in an Army Surplus store; on the off-chance that I might someday need it, I'd purchased one for £2.50, which was a fraction of their normal price. (I should have bought the whole bucket.) The display panel for the oxygen was the only electronic component, and it was held at eye level with a wire coat hanger – my low-tech version of a heads-up display. Within a few weeks – during which most of my time was spent fettling endlessly with each of the components – the rebreather was built. In contrast to the automated CIS-Lunar, which I found to be cumbersome and overly complicated with electronics and sensors, my rebreather was fully manual and mechanical. The diver was in control instead of the machine. Most crucially, it was modular. With a bit of pride and a nod to Isler's rebreather, I named mine the RS2000.

Cost of CIS-Lunar: approximately £8,000.

Cost of the parts I used to build the RS2000: approximately £200.

Before long, Jason had built his own rebreather as well, and we began using them in earnest on our dives. In 2003, when Bill Stone asked us to join another of his projects – this one at Cueva Chevé, one of the deepest caves in the Americas, with potential to be the deepest in the world – he first insisted that we use his rebreathers. We refused and told him we'd be using our own. Not only were ours more rugged, they were one-quarter the weight and one-third the volume of Stone's gargantuan machines. Stone warily eyed our machines – fitted as they were with inner tubes and coat hangers – and insisted that he didn't want us 'diving with those death traps' on his project. We didn't bother arguing, or even answering. Jason and I were the ones who'd be pushing the sump, and we'd dive our own equipment. Knowing this wasn't something he could control, Stone let the matter drop.

The rebreathers worked perfectly, allowing Jason and me to become the first to pass through the targeted sump. The complicated route, which had foiled others, was clearly given away to me by the tell-tale signs of the gravel slope. We continued dry exploration for approximately 1,000 metres before arriving at two vertical descents, each of which was about 12 metres. We paused only briefly, before free-climbing down. When Stone was there later and saw the pitches for himself, he gave them the name 'Madmen's Falls', perhaps in consideration of what could have happened during our bold descent.

Later in the same expedition, we went on to dive the second sump, reaching the bottom of what was then the ninth-deepest cave in the world. Our homemade rebreathers had been tried and tested. Nobody ever questioned their use again.

These were some of my favourite times, the best bits of my life. Jason and I were just diving for ourselves, largely self-funded and not relying on corporate sponsorship[14] or anything. There was no pressure, and we were able to be creative with our resources and equipment. We were doing dives that were thought impossible, by throwing together borrowed or homemade equipment. It was all sort of a wing and a prayer at times, which made it more challenging, but also more rewarding. We were solving problems – proving ourselves and showing what we could do on our own – without help from anybody else. I was having a lot of fun.

'When the boys had been found, that was a magic moment. Big, euphoric lift experience. But then you think, in the know, "Hmm. Now what?" I think the Thai authorities were in the dilemma: "Yes, the boys are alive. They're in remarkably good spirits. If we try and rescue them by diving, we might kill them."'

Bill Whitehouse, vice chair of the British Cave Rescue Council

Tuesday, 3 July 2018, Thailand

In some ways, Tuesday morning feels like the beginning of a new chapter in my life. By the time I woke on the day following the boys' discovery, John's video footage had been seen by millions. Notes of congratulation poured in from friends around the world. Newspapers around the world were running cover stories with headlines such as 'Who Are the British Divers Who Found the Football Team?' Before long, reporters had traced and were attempting to interview our loved ones; they were showing up at our friends' and neighbours' homes to learn anything they could about us, wanting to understand what had led to us being the ones to find the boys.

I'd always said that my exploration of the Emergence du Ressel, with Jason, had 'thrust me onto an international stage' but I hadn't known what I was talking about. This is what it was like to be on an international stage. Reporters from news outlets I'd never heard of were writing to ask for an interview.[15] 'We know you're busy,' they all began, before continuing on to make their request, 'but could you just give us twenty minutes?' or 'We'd love to do a live interview, if possible.' It wasn't possible, of course. None of it was possible. *A live interview? Do they think we have nothing better to do right now than stop and give interviews?* If you added up all of the twenty-minute interviews . . . There wasn't enough time in the day.

I didn't even bother reading many of the requests; I didn't have time to engage with anything outside of Tham Luang. We hadn't gone to Thailand simply to find the boys; we had gone there to rescue them. 'Schrödinger's football team,' we had joked to ourselves a few days earlier, when the boys had only been a possibility. Now they were real. Even worse, they were counting on us. We had promised to go back for them, to get them out of the cave. I had never felt such overwhelming responsibility for another person's life.

Thirteen lives, depending on us.

Although we had officially been taken off the case, John and I never stopped feeling like the ones who would ultimately be responsible for the rescue of the Wild Boars. We, alone, had been in their shelter with them. The team had welcomed us in and asked us for help. We had made them a promise and we weren't going to turn our backs on them. 'This is why I don't make promises,' I thought to myself wryly as I woke and scanned through the messages that were filling my inboxes.

I've always been a proponent of creative problem-solving and thinking outside the box, so I enjoyed reading some of the wild ideas that were pouring in from people – strangers – who wanted to help. Many of their ideas were things we had already ruled out, but some of the solutions were quite inventive. Entirely impractical and implausible, but inventive nevertheless. I shared some of them with John as we waited for Tom and Bas to pick us up.

'Could you put a waterproof smartphone in front of the eyes of the children when they need to dive in sections where there is no visibility at all?'

'. . . make a small kind of sub for getting these kids out. Just one capsule with an air bottle that a cave scuba diver could lead?'

'. . . send in a modified steel cylinder (mini-sub) that has the integrity to withstand the pressure changes . . . and scooter them out? With guide lines, they could pulley them out.'

'. . . use a plastic tunnel of good length in those passages too difficult for the boys? Greased on the inside, one or two boys get in on their side. The tunnel is closed behind them, and air is pumped inside.'

'What if you have a very long chain . . . attach each boy, space them apart, and then use a winch to pull them all out.'

Though these ideas were creative, there were many reasons why they would be difficult to set up and impractical to use in the cave. Anything holding the boys (e.g. a 'mini-sub') would need to have a life-support system attached to allow constant breathing and off-gassing. The capsule would need to withstand collisions against jagged rock. A tunnel or tube to provide passage would be impossible to build to the specifications of the cave . . . not to mention the task of installing such a tube through 1.6 kilometres of cave to reach the boys' haven . . . not to mention the fact that one leak would lead to a flood and everyone drowning. I called this the 'sausage skin idea', because that's how it would have looked if it had all gone wrong.

The strangers' ideas, extended with good intentions, highlighted the gap in understanding between those who were 'in the know' and those who weren't. People unfamiliar with underwater cave environments couldn't imagine the problems involved or the dangers present. Unable to fathom all of the different things that made this rescue so difficult, they thought it was just a matter of going in and bringing them out, while keeping them calm during the journey. On the other hand, people who were familiar with caves and cave diving – those who were 'in the know' – had a very clear understanding of the dangers involved. Those people had an idea of what would be required of the divers and the boys, and they couldn't imagine that a successful rescue would be possible.

I later found out that the exception to this was a small group of friends and cave divers who knew me personally. Those people were all certain that I'd find a way to get it done. Andy Eavis, chairman of the British Caving Association, had said very early during the search, quite boldly during a live interview, 'I predict it will be Rick and John that find the boys.' Other friends – fellow cavers back home – have said that they never felt very worried about us, or the boys, in the days to come. They trusted we'd have it under control.

By Tuesday morning, I had already sent out messages to Jason Mallinson and Chris Jewell in the UK, asking them to be on stand-by. We still hadn't figured out a plan that could work, but it was clear that we needed more people there who understood the risks involved, and we wanted them to be ready.

Another stranger's message came in as Tom and Bas pulled up to the resort in their truck.

'I've been praying for you and John. Please read Acts 12, about the angels removing Peter from the inner prison. I believe you can teach those boys and get them out. They can do it! I believe you and John will have supernatural help too. You will all be fine. God is in on this. He will help – no fear.'

'Oh, good news, John,' I said as he climbed into the truck behind Tom. 'We don't have to worry; we will have supernatural help. We will all be fine.'

He looked at me. 'Just get in the truck.'

We arrived at Tham Luang, where we were suddenly being treated as VIPs. As the week had progressed, our parking situation had become increasingly tenuous, until finally we were walking to the rescue area from nearly a kilometre away.[16] But beginning on Tuesday, we never had any trouble parking right up close. I felt like we'd been promoted to managing director of a large company, gaining the prime parking spot.

The first people I wanted to talk to were the Americans. Although they wouldn't be able to aid with the rescue itself, they were experts with logistics and would prove helpful during the next few days' planning. Crucially, they had formed a working relationship with the SEALs, which John and I were struggling to do, so we were hoping they could help us to relay messages to the ones who were in charge. We spoke cave, they spoke military, and we needed the Americans to act as our babel fish.[17]

Before long, we were sitting in the gear room with Derek Anderson. We made small talk for a while, before Derek asked us what we were thinking about the rescue. John spoke candidly. 'This is good news, but I think we just opened Pandora's box. I don't know how we're going to get them out alive.'

Derek took in a breath and then began breaking things down, starting with the basics. We liked Derek a lot and knew that talking things through with him would be helpful. 'If the SEALs are going to insist on being the ones to bring them out, what would be their best chance for success? Can you think of anything that might work?'

Knowing that the SEALs' strengths lay in their numbers and resources, John and I speculated a plan that took advantage of those. 'They could put dozens of divers in the cave and relay the boys between them.' We both knew that this plan was impractical and unlikely to be successful for many reasons but we couldn't think of another way that the SEALs would be able to manage. Using a whiteboard, we mapped how this might look. When we had it drawn out, we saw that it relied on lots of elements being in the exact right place at the exact right time. There were far too many failure points. (Later, when Commander Pinyo came over and looked at this drawn-out plan, we watched his eyes glaze over as we explained it to him and walked him through the steps that would be involved. The plan was summarily ruled out.)

Next, Derek asked us what we would do if we were the ones in charge.

John and I had started to put together our own plan, which we weren't ready to share with Derek (or anybody) just yet. We had started with a few basic tenets, which would be the pivotal pieces to make or break any plan.

1) The plan needed to be simple, streamlined, as straightforward as possible. The cave itself – and the number of the people being rescued – presented its own share of complications. Anything we planned would need to be uncomplicated, minimizing any possible failure points; we'd use only as many people as necessary and as few as possible. Our basic tenet was always: keep it simple.

2) The boys' panic needed to be accounted for. This would be critical, which the rescue of the pump workers on Thursday had made abundantly clear. John and I never felt uncomfortable in the cave and would therefore portray confidence, but we knew without a doubt that trying to dive out with somebody who was panicked and fighting us would inevitably lead to somebody's death.

After Derek left, we had nothing to do. The Thais were still waiting to hear news from the team of SEALs that had been sent into the cave in the very early hours of that morning. From what I gathered, the SEALs had taken in some basic and very limited supplies (foil space blankets, iodine and only a few energy gel packs) but hadn't taken any food with them. Despite our being given an advisory role after finding the boys, the Thais didn't seek our advice before sending in their team of divers. I guess they figured that, since a bunch of middle-aged blokes had dived to the boys and back in five hours, they'd have no trouble.

Nearly ten hours had passed with still no sign of them, and we were told the Thais weren't going to do anything until the divers came out. In the meantime, nobody was speaking with us, and it didn't appear that anybody was moving forward with any plans. Out of sheer boredom and in a state of limbo while we waited, I decided to draw a map of the cave. I'm typically far too impatient to devote the time required for this, but I knew that a good map would be required for any further planning.

Gathered around a table with John and Tik, Amp and I spent the rest of the afternoon putting together a schematic hand-drawing of the cave. On a large sheet of Ao paper, I drew a grid and then free-handed the cave over that grid, using as reference the cave survey that was located in the park office. On top we had two overlays of plastic, which we could use for marking the map as we put together a plan. Once I'd finished, Amp labelled the map in both English and Thai. (My handwriting is terrible; even her English penmanship is more legible than mine.) I've got to say, it turned out quite well. Later, it was displayed prominently on a whiteboard in our gear room and became the primary resource used when planning the rescue.

With nothing being accomplished at the cave and the SEALs still inside when night fell, we left Tham Luang. Back at the resort, I resumed a conversation that had been ongoing between me and a cave-diving friend in Australia, Dr Richard Harris. The conversation had begun in the early days of the rescue when Harry (as he is known) wrote to express his interest in helping, if we needed him. Because he is accomplished as a cave diver and medical doctor, he thought his unique skill sets could be of use in the cave with the boys, should they need any medical support. He'd also been helpful in setting up cave-diving rescue protocols in Australia and felt that he was well suited for the mission.

From his first messages, Harry had impressed me by seeing through all of the commotion and identifying the key points to the rescue. I already knew him to be a clear thinker and clever strategist, and his messages had solidified that knowledge for me. Throughout the course of the week, he had become another sounding board for my thoughts, ideas and frustrations.

Thursday, 29 June 2018 –
Four Days Before the Boys' Discovery

Richard Harris:

Hi guys. Stay safe over there. I feel like I should be over there helping. If you manage to get to these guys they will likely need medical assistance and you will need a team of divers to take turns to baby sit them while an extraction plan comes together which may take some time. Craig and I are happy to provide any assistance to your team if required.

All the best, Harry

Rick Stanton:

Thanks for the offer of help, you've thought of the issues involved. Struggling to progress against the current and water unlikely to recede until end of monsoon season.

Friday, 30 June 2018

Rick Stanton:

We're here maintaining a presence to present a positive image that all is well. The circus here is so large and chaotic most have lost track of purpose.

Richard Harris:

Poor buggers . . . I feel v sad. Can't imagine how you guys must feel.

Rick Stanton:

We think the likely scenario is they fled a flood from the southern passage where they were headed. Encountered a sump at Monks junction halting their exit. Then it's whether they were able to retreat back upstream to possible sanctuary at Pattaya beach. I suspect not as there are U bends that would fill.

Richard Harris:

Might be kinder if they couldn't escape it.

Rick Stanton:

I agree.

Rick Stanton:

Things are gelling together. JV and I reached the Monks junction so there is now 800m of continuous rope beyond 3rd chamber.

Monday, 2 July 2018

Richard Harris:

Ben rang me . . . kids all alive! Wonderful news and congratulations!

8.
In My Element

Whereas British cave divers had always managed just fine by blundering along the floor during a dive, in the early 2000s there was a growing trend to dive with a buoyancy device. When I'd begun reaching greater depths and penetrations in the larger caves of the Lot, I'd been using a proper store-bought wing, but I knew that I'd need a different method in British caves. The trend in British caves was to use stand-alone buoyancy devices that could be taken off in the dry passages, but I thought they were a bit too small in volume and they didn't sit very well on the diver's back. I didn't like the ones I saw, so I chose to develop my own.

What could I use?

It would have to be simple, something that allowed gas to be added and removed, able to be worn with my side mount rig without adding drag. I've always enjoyed repurposing everyday items to fit my needs – or finding extra life in things that were set to be discarded. Duncan always says, 'Don't throw out your old worn-out equipment in front of Rick. He'll repurpose it, and you'll become sick of seeing him use it.'[1]

I glanced through the tubs of equipment pieces in my home and when I came across some sections of car inner tubes, I had a cunning plan.

For years, I'd walked past a motorbike and scooter shop in Coventry on my journey to work and never given it a glancing thought until now. One morning, on my way home, I stopped in. I paused for a moment after entering, as my eyes scanned the room to get a sense of the layout. 'Can I help you with anything?' the proprietor greeted me as I strode over to the tyre section.

'I know this sounds strange, but I need to try on some inner tubes.'

I spent the next twenty minutes or so attempting to find the optimum-sized tube. It not only had to fit on my back, but needed to have the right diameter, neither too narrow nor too wide. The ratio had to be perfect. I found the one I wanted and walked home, delighted with my purchase. Instead of sleeping after the night shift, I spent the rest of the day devising my homemade inner-tube wing, completing it with a sewn webbing harness and bungee elastic. I fitted a corrugated hose and inflation mouthpiece in place of the original valve.

I was eager to test it out on a dive, and I knew exactly which cave it would be suited for.

Gough's Cave, at the bottom of the Cheddar Gorge in the Mendip Hills, reaches depths of −60 metres. It had been explored into its third sump in the 1990s, which ends at a boulder choke. I'd had a lot of luck passing boulder chokes and I wanted to have a go at this one. Although the cave wasn't long or deep by current standards, the earlier expeditions had been massive affairs requiring support teams carrying cylinders and setting up camp inside. Using my new chest-mounted rebreather, I knew I'd be able to travel more lightly and make quicker work of it.

My new inner-tube wing wasn't the only new thing I'd be testing out at Gough's Cave; I'd also be diving with a new partner. When Duncan suggested I team up with someone he'd recently been diving with, I was open to the idea. Duncan told me that this man was relatively new to diving but had been caving since his teens as a Scout and was accomplished in just about every other outdoor activity. 'He's really good at everything, he's always running somewhere or climbing something.' Most crucially, Duncan said he was quick-thinking, naturally skilled and keen to progress quickly.

His name was John Volanthen.

One evening in late 2002, I met John for the first time at the entrance to the cave. We carried our gear in, planning to dive the following day. John, still diving open-circuit, would be supporting me as far as the third sump. I thought it would be an easy dive for him, and I looked forward to seeing how he did underwater. As always, I wanted to see him in the water to gauge his abilities before committing to more challenging projects. I'd be able to see easily enough if he was a true water person.

He was a complete natural in the water, and I was impressed with how well we dived together. We got along equally well out of the water, where he was eager to learn about the rebreather I was using. I already knew John worked with computers – Duncan had described him as a 'tech guru' – so I expected him to be critical of my manual systems. Instead, I could see that he was amused by the ways I had avoided using electronics whenever possible with the RS2000. As he looked it over and asked me questions, I could see his wheels turning and I suspected that we would get on well because he was another person who thought things through and liked building things. (I wasn't fully correct on the latter count. He does analyse everything to assess what he needs for a task, but his strength lies in sourcing available components, then tinkering with them until they fit his specification for what is required, instead of building parts from scratch.)

I answered all of his questions and the following day we set off into the cave, where I extended the line to an air bell further into the boulder choke. It was a good first dive for John and me to become acquainted, and we quickly began planning future dives. Before long, John went out and bought a rebreather of his own. He just went out and bought a commercial one, without knowing the first thing about rebreathers. A friend of ours was selling an Inspiration, and John told him he wanted to buy it.

'Right, do you want to look over it?'

'There's no point,' John said. 'I don't know what I'm looking for.' He was confident he'd be able to figure out how it worked, and he was correct. After gaining some practice on the rebreather by diving in the quarries and caves of the UK, he took it to the Ressel in 2003. Jason and I were camping inside, and John dived through the first sump. His first major dive on a rebreather was through a 2-kilometre sump.

I remembered when Duncan had first described John to me as being 'good at everything'. My first thought had been 'Jack of all trades, master of none?' and I'd worried that John wouldn't have the discipline to be a cave diver. I knew that I'd been wrong when I observed the single-minded focus he used while teaching himself how to use the rebreather.

That's how John is. While some people need to find the motivation to get started, John's natural state is action. When something sparks his curiosity, he gets to work, removes any obstacles that might stand in his way and keeps moving forward until he reaches his goal. John once said he had taken up cave diving because, 'I couldn't see a reason why not.'

On the surface he can be playful and surprisingly light-hearted – he's certainly less intense than either Jason or I – but he takes diving as seriously as I do, considering every possible risk and planning for all possible contingencies before deciding on an action. I knew that I could trust him, and his attitude was a nice contrast to mine. He and I are both realists, but while I tend towards pessimism, I'd say

John is more optimistic. (Jason is neither one nor the other. He just gets on with it.)

When we returned from France, I told John about the cave in northern Italy that I had set my sights on recently. In 1990, Isler had been the first to dive through Cogol dei Veci's initial sump; he broke surface after 2,340 metres then turned back without exploring the dry cave that lay beyond. Cogol dei Veci was a repeat scenario of the Ressel, and once again the invitation for further exploration was impossible for me to ignore.

'There has to be dry passage there. No one's gone into it yet,' I told John one day after a dive, trying to gauge his interest. He was keen to take on the project, as I'd expected he'd be, and we planned a trip to Italy for February of 2004 to have a look.[2]

Our friend Marcus Taylor, a filmmaker, had asked if he could make a documentary of the Cogol dei Veci project, and for some reason we agreed to let him.[3] One evening in the autumn of 2003, when John and I were at Marcus' house discussing plans for the filming of the Cogol dives, Marcus asked if we had any other projects lined up. John and I looked at each other and shrugged. There wasn't much going on at the moment, in terms of caves that were waiting to be explored. Then I mentioned something that had been nagging at me for ages: Wookey Hole.

Wookey Hole Caves in Somerset are largely known as being a tourist destination. The site contains a historically important show-cave system with guided tours, costumed witches, souvenirs, an ice-cream shop, the works. For cave divers, though, Wookey Hole has much more significance, as it is widely considered to be the birthplace and home of British cave diving. Traditional hard-hat diving commenced there in 1933, and since then, the progress of exploration has pretty much matched the advance of diving technologies. In 1985, during the massive expedition project that included Ian Rolland and Bill Stone on his team, Rob Parker had explored beyond Chamber 25, where he'd reached a depth of −68 metres and established Britain's new record for depth inside a cave. His dive was also noteworthy for being the first use of trimix in Britain. Rob thought he had found the end there, in a tight gravel squeeze.

In the two decades since Rob's dive, several experienced divers hadn't even been able to reach the end of Rob's line. None had been able to go further. Since my first dive there in 1983 with Rob Harper, I'd revisited Wookey many times for fun 'tourist' dives but had never previously considered going to the end – both of which were very unusual for me.

I'd always accepted there was nothing further to be found, but because of the cave's history and importance I now wondered if there might be more beyond that gravel slope. When Marcus asked John and me about ideas for a next project, with no other answer coming to mind, I mentioned Wookey.

'There might be nothing there,' I said, 'but I'd like to see it for myself.'

'I can show it to you,' Marcus offered.

Cave-diving films must have been a rising trend in the early 2000s, because Gavin Newman had recently finished making his documentary *Wookey Exposed*, chronicling its fifty years of exploration. Marcus, being a fellow diver and filmmaker, happened to have an advanced copy of Gavin's film at his home. A few minutes later, John and I were watching footage of Gavin's dive to the very end of Wookey Hole.

Beyond Chamber 25, 'the floor meets the ceiling' in a cramped and gravelly squeeze with just enough room to fit one diver. Gavin spends a moment there, awkwardly turning his camera, determined 'to film what I came to see'.

This was also what I wanted to see, and I watched closely.

The camera panned from left to right and then back again, briefly revealing some flat arches on the right-hand wall. It was a very low, avalanche-prone space where the rock ceiling descended at a steep angle to meet the gravel floor. Rob's line reel disappeared into the gravel and continued onward.

'I can go no further,' Gavin says in the film as he turns to begin his exit, but I saw it differently. The gravel had shown me the way on.

'There! What was that?' I said suddenly, breaking the silence in Marcus' living room. I moved closer to the television set. 'Go back.'

Marcus rewound the video, and we watched it again. Particles of silt floated in front of the camera in the dark space. Even so, the way on jumped out at me. The silt deposits had given it away. To the right of the spot where Rob's line disappears, there was a mound before one arch, indicating a current had been moving through.

'Look at the gravel there,' I said to John.

He was nodding. 'Yes, I see it.'

'We need to go there.'

Gavin's video footage had made it clear that pushing Wookey would require moving through a slot that was quite tight, maybe 40cm high but with a moveable gravel floor. I would need a rebreather that was more compact and streamlined than my chest-mounted one and designed for use at greater depths. I began working on plans for a compact side-mounted rebreather that could be worn on my side, tucked against my ribcage, where it would not add much to my profile when diving. I let myself splurge a bit when assembling the components for this new rebreather, purchasing a proper mouthpiece and oxygen injection system. In total, I spent a few hundred pounds to build my side-mounted rebreather, which I named BOTS.

The acronym stands for 'Bit on the Side', which is British slang for a secondary lover or mistress.

The name had been teasingly suggested to me by my friend Natasha Mitchell, and I'd appreciated the irony of it. I had developed quite a crush on Tash while diving with her, but she had politely declined anything further. She'd contributed to its design in more ways than just naming it, as I'd begun designing the rebreather hoping to address the difficulty that she'd had while breathing the chest-mounted one. (I'd had the same difficulty and was keen to design one that breathed more easily.)

During the spring of 2004, I spent Monday evenings in the Coventry public swimming pool, testing out different parts of the BOTS in various stages of development and then going home to fettle with it some more. One night, when I was trying to figure out the best placement for the scrubber canister and counter-lung in relation to each other, I used a plastic Rowntree's Sweets jar to stand in for the scrubber canister I hadn't built yet. It was probably best that nobody was there to see that.

I went into Wookey on 1 June 2004, with a bunch of friends on the support team. We had the modest goal of reaching Rob Parker's end and just checking it out. Duncan was with me in Chamber 25; the small air pocket contained little more than a ridge to rest on before the final descent. With muddy walls sloping into murky water, this area has since been given the apt name 'The Lake of Gloom'. Sometimes I wonder why I devote so much of my time and energy to reaching such dismal places. I looked over at Duncan as he went into the sump, then followed behind him a few minutes later.

Duncan passed me on his ascent as I was descending, and soon I was there, at the enticing arch I'd spotted in Gavin's film. It looked like the mouth of a giant angler fish made of gravel. I went inside.

The cave turned a corner and continued dropping, then I had to turn sideways to go through another narrow slot. After passing through that, I found myself at a proper gravel squeeze.

A gravel squeeze typically indicates the way on – and usually with a big passage lying beyond it – but they are both a bane and a blessing. I've already had a few close calls where I'd gone forward into a squeeze, then thought I might not be able to get back out of it.

As I eyed the gravel squeeze in Wookey, I remembered a solo trip I'd made into P8, years earlier, when I'd been going as far as Sump 9. Passing Sump 8 had involved going through a gravel squeeze so tight that I'd had to unclip my cylinders, pushing one in front and clipping the other between my legs to drag it behind me. I'd got through the upward squeeze by digging with my hands, shovelling the gravel aside as I passed.

Later, when I'd arrived back at Sump 8 on my exit, I'd discovered that the gravel at the top of the sump had slumped down into the squeeze, leaving it nearly unpassable at the bottom, with a gap of 15 centimetres. I'd sat at the edge of the sump, looking down into a tube that went underwater and was nearly closed off by gravel, wondering what to do. This was the only way out. If I went in forwards – trying to excavate my way through – and failed, I would be stuck with my head underwater in a position from which I might never be able to back out. I knew that reversing up an inclined passage filled with gravel stones would never work. (Imagine trying to move forwards and down, through a tube filled with ball bearings. Then imagine trying to reverse – backwards and up – through the same tube.)

Finally, I'd gone in backwards – sliding down into the tube feet first, lying on my belly, pedalling and kicking with my feet to shift the gravel into the little spaces on either side of me. 'If this doesn't work,' I'd figured, 'at least I'll be facing in the better direction to get myself back out.'

It had worked. I'd got through.

Fortunately, the squeeze I was facing at Wookey wasn't nearly as precarious, and I was able to go through forwards. I first made sure there were no projections in the ceiling, then I went in, making a reverse breaststroke motion with my arms to set off an avalanche that would carry me through the squeeze.

I have a video of me digging my way through this squeeze, and it's really unnerving to watch. When I show it at speaking engagements, people always end up on the edge of their seat and holding their breath. My friend Leigh Bishop thinks this is such a riot that he watches the audience's reaction more closely than he watches me speaking. At the end, someone always asks something like, 'How do you know the cave will open up again?' or, 'How do you know you'll get through?' or, 'What happens if you get stuck??'

I had the same answer for all of those questions: 'You don't.'

The passage beyond the squeeze soon opened up and began ascending. *Well, that was surprisingly easy.* It was so surprising, in fact, that I hadn't bothered to take a line reel with me. I was breaking a cardinal rule of cave diving by going without a line, so I turned back. An hour after we'd passed each other, I surfaced back at the Lake of Gloom to see Duncan sitting in wait. I pulled the regulator as my mouth broke into a wide grin. 'I got through, and it's ascending.' The cave's profile up to this point suggested that once a sump's elbow was passed, the cave would ascend directly to a surface, and there was no reason to suspect this sump would be any different. I felt the now-familiar twinge of electric excitement that comes with exploration. I was sure that Wookey's Chamber 26 was within my grasp.

Late that night, when we were returning the key to the office, we were accosted by a gruff voice asking, 'Oi! What are you lot doing?' It was Gerry Cottle himself, the circus impresario who was the owner of Wookey Hole. Duncan and I were keen to tell him what we had found on our dive, knowing that he could gain from the publicity of our new exploration.

When we returned to dive the following week, John and I discovered that some of our equipment had been sabotaged. Another diver had been hoping to tackle the same problem by a different means, but I'd beaten him to it, and he was a bit disgruntled. *Apart from all of the logistical challenges of diving at Wookey 25, we now have this to deal with?*

We weren't deterred.

When we dived next, I was confident we'd break through into Chamber 26. My good friend Helen Rider waited on the surface with a bottle of champagne, expecting us to come back with exciting news, but things in the cave didn't go exactly as planned. John and I passed through the gravel squeeze to where the cave ascended, but after travelling upwards for a short distance, we found the route closed down. *Maybe Chamber 26 isn't so close . . .* The only other route lay horizontally, to a collapse feature with boulders blocking the way on, at a depth of −70 metres.

We were so dejected by this turn of events that we didn't even look around or investigate, we just turned and exited the cave. I was crestfallen. Caves often become impassable – I accept that – but I'm never satisfied until I understand the reasons and mechanics of it. Only then would I know if I could do something about it.

Despite my disappointment, I still joined Helen for champagne on the surface, of course.

On our next dive, John and I went back to understand what had happened to cause the boulder choke and worked out that, if we could move some boulders, we might be able to get through. This began the underwater digging portion of this project, which is not as easy as it might sound.

I don't usually involve myself with projects that require a lot of digging, but in the early 1990s, I'd teamed up with Duncan and others on a massive digging project in Daren Cilau. Barry Sudell and Steve Joyce had been there, and we ended up having a lot of fun, working for years to remove the rocks that were blocking an underwater cave entrance, Pwll-y-Cwm. A couple of times we had to use explosives to break up the larger boulders, and we had a winch to pull them out. It had been a fun project, with challenging work, and we'd eventually opened up an easy back door to the bottom end of Daren Cilau, where I'd been caving with Ian twelve years previously. This enabled us to easily explore further sections of passage, but we'd still been unable to make a connection with Aggy.

I felt sufficiently prepared for whatever digging would be required in Wookey.

Using crowbars and hammers, John and I dug away at this boulder choke over a few dives; at one point we used an air-filled lift bag to remove the keystone boulder. Finally, a small gap was revealed. John removed his chest-mounted rebreather to wriggle through, and I watched as he slid in. I could tell, from the speed with which he moved through and disappeared, that the space beyond was open. His light soon faded in the murky water, and then the murk closed in and I couldn't see anything.

He had taken a leaf out of my book by making a quick reconnaissance without a line. This was exceptionally bold for John, who is typically very methodical, but he'd clearly got caught up with exploration fever. Still, I knew he would not continue on very far, so after a minute had passed, I began to wonder where he had gone. Then I heard his voice, muffled as he spoke into the mouthpiece of the rebreather, from the other side of the boulders.

'Rick! Rick!' His voice sounded more annoyed than it was frightened, but there was a sense of urgency. Like me, John doesn't panic when things go wrong, but there is a vague sense of annoyance at the inconvenience. I understood what must have happened. He'd popped through the hole and gone forwards, then when he turned around to make his way back, he'd been confronted by a bunch of holes that all looked the same. He didn't know which one to go through.

I unclipped one of the lights from my helmet and reached my arm through the hole in the boulder choke, giving him a beacon to swim towards, while calling his name. A moment later, his rebreather came through the gap, extended ahead of him. I grabbed onto the unit and helped to guide it through, at one point pulling him by the mouthpiece.

John and I continued at Wookey the following year. By this time, it was clear that we were never going to find 26, so we adjusted our strategy. Trying to dive together now that we'd gone through the choke seemed pointless, and the logistics of putting two divers in there was too much, so for the 2005 season we began taking turns.

On his final dive, John stopped when he reached a particularly precarious-looking boulder choke, confident that he'd gone as far as he could. He handed it over to me to see if I could get further, and after diving I agreed with his assessment. The terminal boulder choke was stacked precariously and seemed ready to collapse. The route ahead – barely visible through crumbling rock – was dangerously uninviting, and this was already beyond two very technical sections. Heeding the words of Ernest Shackleton – 'Better a live donkey than a dead lion' – this is where the project ended. The gains didn't justify the risks, and we were both satisfied that we'd reached the end.

I, for one, will not be going back. Who knows what future generations of divers and equipment might achieve?

Over two seasons of exploration, we'd greatly extended the cave system's map, while setting (and then breaking) records for depth inside a British cave. Working at Wookey Hole greatly reminded me of the Notts Pot project, because it had been fun and involved a strong and enthusiastic team effort from a group of close friends.[4] I was also reminded of the words of warning John Cordingley had spoken to me years earlier. *'Savour this, Rick. You're only at the start of your diving career, but you're unlikely to experience a project quite like this again.'*

How wrong he'd been. Although I say that I don't cave for fun, I have found myself involved in numerous projects that I've enjoyed more than I expected I would, and Wookey was certainly one of those.

One member of our Wookey team was Gavin Newman himself, the man whose film had started it all. Quite aware that our ongoing exploration was quickly making his original film outdated, with its now-inaccurate claim that Rob Parker's 1985 trip had been to Wookey's end, Gavin insisted on filming our exploration as we extended the line.[5] He'd become an active member of the team, and as the cameras followed us around, with Gavin interviewing us to hear our stories, I felt more than ever like I was following in the footsteps of Geoff Yeadon, who had been followed by Sid Perou for the making of *The Underground Eiger*.

When I surfaced after my final five-hour dive to the end of Wookey, I spotted Gavin with his camera, chatting with others. I had been using the same cylinders for multiple dives and by the time I surfaced from this one, I was at the very end of my gas supply. I looked around for John, knowing he would be dumbfounded by how little gas I had remaining. Gavin saw me checking my gauge and he must have heard the comment I made to John. He walked over to me, camera rolling.

'Rick. How much gas have you got left?'

I laughed, a bit embarrassed at having been caught breaking another rule of cave diving. 'I've got some gas left,' I answered vaguely.

'"Some?"' he teased. 'Is that a technical diving term?'

'. . . Wherein "some" is . . .' I looked down again at my gauge, where the needle was lower than was sensible. 'Enough, but not plenty.'

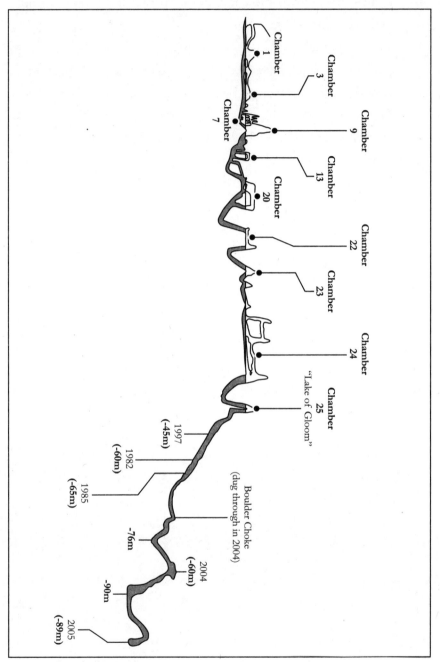

Wookey Hole Caves, Somerset

'Don't let the (unsurprising) incompetence
of the local authorities distract you
from trying to save the kids.'

Text message sent to me in
Thailand from Jonathan Sims

Wednesday, 4 July 2018, Thailand

When we returned to the site at 9 o'clock on Wednesday morning, Rear
Admiral Arpakorn and his staff officer Commander Pinyo[6] greeted us
with surprising news of the SEALs in the cave. We'd already known
that four had been sent in on Monday night; what we didn't know was
that, when they had not returned by late Tuesday morning, an additional three had gone in after them. After a day had passed with no
sign from any of them, they were all assumed to be lost. Arpakorn told
us that just before we'd arrived on Wednesday morning, three had
returned safely, with the other four remaining in Chamber 9. (We'd
learn much later that the three who'd emerged had been so exhausted,
they'd been taken straight to hospital.)

We had no clue what their plan had been, and I certainly couldn't
imagine why four had stayed inside, but I was relieved to learn that
one of the Thais with the boys was an Army medical doctor, Dr Pak
Loharnshoon. He, at least, could prove useful.

'Are they going to try to dive the boys out?' I asked.

'No,' Arpakorn told me. 'None of the SEALs will be bringing the
boys out. And from now on, no SEALs will be diving to their
location.'

OK, then, what is your plan? They had forbidden all other divers
from entering the cave, and now they had limited their own diving
efforts. What did that mean for the boys? Watching them walk away,

John pointed out an obvious fact that didn't appear to be bothering anybody else.

'He didn't mention food. It's been thirty-six hours since we saw them, and they've still had no food.' As incredible as it sounded, nobody seemed worried about feeding them. Other than the few gel packets that had been taken in with the first SEALs, nothing had been done to address the football team's malnutrition and impending starvation. We might have been forbidden from diving, but we weren't going to let that stop us from tackling a problem that everybody else seemed to be ignoring. There were now seventeen people in the cave, and surely the first step in saving them would be to feed them.

I wanted to take in all of the food we could carry. We didn't know how long they'd be in there. We didn't know when (or if) John and I would be able to get back into them again. We didn't know anything, really, except that the boys were in there, literally starving to death. We had promised to go back with food and we were already a day late. Forming a plan, we went to find Derek.

'How many MREs[7] do you have?' I asked him.

While Derek was gathering Army supplies for us to take to the boys, Arpakorn tracked us down. 'We don't know what to do,' he admitted, then asked us if we had any recommendations for them.

'Whatever plan you end up going with, you're going to need cylinders staged back there.' I had been telling the same thing to anybody who asked what they could be doing to help. For a diving rescue, we would need as many cylinders inside the cave as possible.

'Do you think they're setting us up for failure?' John and I wondered to each other after Arpakorn had walked away. We were relieved to be finally included in the planning of the rescue, but it also seemed a bit suspicious. I didn't expect that the Thais suddenly trusted us. It seemed more likely they'd acknowledged that they were incapable of rescuing the boys and didn't want the deaths to be on their hands. I didn't care if we were being used as their scapegoats, and neither did John, but we weren't stupid. We knew we had to protect ourselves.

I called Bill to tell him that more emphasis was being placed in our hands and we needed further government support, stressing our belief that the Thais had wanted to cut themselves loose before people started dying. Bill understood the dangers that could fall upon us if we became responsible for the deaths of Thai civilians. 'You're going to need political cover, diplomatic immunity, with full embassy support on site as soon as possible.'

Rob was scheduled on a flight returning to England that evening. He'd provided tremendous support and guidance in the early days, during the search phase, but now that the boys' lives depended on us being able to dive them out safely, he knew there wasn't anything more he could contribute, and he needed to get back to his work. We were going to miss his company and his humour. (At the airport, Rob was dreading being asked his prediction of how things would end. Following our lesson with Jessica Tait, he had his line prepared. If asked the six-million-dollar question, his prepared answer would be, 'I couldn't say.')

The last thing Rob did before he left was to help us pack the food for the boys. Derek had the Americans' supply of MREs brought to us at our room, and everyone on hand – Amp, Tik, Rob, Tom and Bas – all set to work packing them so they'd be suitable for diving.

Having done our share of overnight camping inside caves during expeditions, John and I were familiar with the techniques used to carry large amounts of gear through caves. The dry tube I had brought with me on the plane was quickly filled, and we had to use an additional three canvas military duffel bags to fit in enough supplies to last seventeen people for a week. In went 100 vacuum-packed meals, along with five flashlights with batteries, and space blankets. The MREs from Derek had come packed with toilet paper and cookies, which we discarded. Space was at a minimum, so we were taking only the essentials.

When news spread that we were taking things in for the boys, suddenly people began realizing things that 'needed' to go in. John was handed another camera to use for filming in Chamber 9. Derek provided us with an electronic gas analyser, used to measure the oxygen level inside the chamber. Commander Pinyo handed over a bubble-wrapped package containing a device – 'The satellites will pick this up, and it will help us locate exactly where they are.' Now, clearly John and I don't know everything about military equipment, but it seemed very unlikely that something so small would be able to transmit through rock. We took it anyway, squeezing it into the over-filled dry tube. It turned out to be a small satellite phone.

We were also given a sheet of paper with a handwritten message, which I had Amp translate. Among other things, the note gave an order: the four SEALs were to remain with the boys. I took this as a sign that the men had gone in without any coherent instructions, and it left me wondering why they were there. *Why are they adding to the burden of mouths to feed?*

Finally, Amp handed me a small package that contained a supply of beaded bracelets, one for each of the boys. 'They were blessed by a Buddhist monk, who has asked you to take them inside for the boys to wear.'

I took the package and tossed it onto the ground. 'We're not taking those.'

'Rick!' exclaimed Amp. She quickly picked up the bracelets and forced them into my hands. 'You don't see the value of them,' she argued, 'but the boys will.'

Ben Svasti Thomson had just arrived on site in response to Bill's request for embassy support, and when I wouldn't budge, Amp went off to find him, hoping he would understand. Ben immediately took Amp's side and told me that the bracelets, blessed as they were by the monk, held immense spiritual value. 'They will certainly boost the boys' morale.'

I wordlessly took the bracelets from Amp and packed them into a dry tube. It was time to dive.

After we'd finished packing the bags in our gear room, Mitch, Jamie and some others helped us to carry them to the lake at the entrance chamber, where we played around with the duffel bags' weighting. The goal was for the bags to hover in the water (neither floating nor sinking), while also staying horizontally level (or trim). If the MREs had been heavy, it would have been an epic, but luckily the MREs floated, so we could just add ballast to make a neutral pack. Much to the Americans' amusement, we solved the ballast problem by just shoving sand and rock into the bags to get it right. Finally, figuring it was as good as it was going to be, we headed in.

While scrabbling up the muddy slope leading to the divide in the third chamber, I was struggling under the weight of the dry tube and duffel bag, along with my diving equipment. A typically thin-framed young SEAL appeared at my side, picked up the bag and tube and carried them effortlessly up the incline. Watching the young man – I could theoretically have been his grandfather – was a harsh reminder that I was wildly out of place among all of the young, fit military men.

I fared better in the water; my dry tube was streamlined and easily followed behind me. The duffel bags, on the other hand, were a nightmare to handle, and John had two with him. We both knew that this wasn't going to be an easy dive, but we'd have to make do. We were hoping that this would be the last time we'd have to make such a trip. A week's worth of supplies was going in, and I wasn't prepared to consider the possibility that the boys would still be inside longer than that.

As expected, the dive was an epic, and we struggled with the large, bulky bags. John's two were clipped to his harness; one was heavy at the nose, the other at the tail. The current, still strong, was pulling the bags away from him as they trailed behind. Before even reaching Sam Yaek, he doubted whether he'd be able to get both bags to the ninth chamber. The bags were adding so much drag that John – an ultramarathon runner – was getting tired.

'We're not dropping one,' I told him when he was nearing his end. We stopped in one of the canals beyond the T-junction and strapped his two bags together, matching the light end of one with the heavy end of the other to create one unit that was better balanced. This helped a bit but not entirely. We had to make two trips through Chamber 7, the rocky section before the last sump, where the lowered water level now worked against us. On the day we'd found the boys, we'd simply swum over all of this. Having to walk through it now was much more awkward.

What this cave needs is more water, I thought to myself ironically as we laboured to get the bags across the long, dry chamber.

When we finally arrived in Chamber 9, everyone in the chamber looked relieved to see us.[8] Remembering the difficulty I had had scaling the muddy ramp on my first visit, we had come prepared. John retrieved a rope from his bag and threw its end up to one of the SEALs. Once this was done, he climbed up and used a sawn-off broom handle as a stake to anchor it.

After climbing the ramp, I noted the glum faces of the SEALs and Dr Pak; they initially seemed a bit lifeless and dispirited. In spite of that, the space was looking much more colourful and festive. The silver space blankets added some brightness to the otherwise drab scene, the SEALs had drawn their insignia into the rock walls and used their knives to cut out better sleeping platforms. They had done a good job making the place feel as homey as it possibly could.

The boys were happy to see us again. A couple of them were assigned to stock the pantry, creating for the first time a kitchen area in their living quarters. We expected them to tear into the bags immediately (as I would have done); instead they sat, showing amazing self-control by leaving the food untouched. It occurred to me that they were waiting for us to leave, not wanting to eat in front of us. Bearing this in mind, we didn't want to overstay our welcome, but we did have some tasks on our agenda.

First, we gave the bracelets to the boys and the SEALs, who accepted them gratefully and seemed very pleased to wear them. Next, John took time to film each of the boys again, with the goal of showing their families how healthy the boys were. His camera lingered on each of their faces as the boys spoke a message to comfort their family. Meanwhile, I used Derek's analyser to take a reading of the air quality inside the chamber.

Typical breathing air contains 21 per cent oxygen, and that is what we were expecting to find. I'd spent time camping inside chambers much smaller than this one, and I didn't think the air quality would have suffered much in the time the boys had spent there, but when I switched the device on, an alarm immediately began blaring and the digital display read 16 per cent. *That's not good.* I was more concerned with the carbon dioxide than the oxygen, but unfortunately the device didn't have the capability to measure that.[9] Wishing that I'd brought my own analyser in with me, I asked the boys if they had a headache, which is the classic sign of increased carbon dioxide. Dr Pak translated for me, and they all shook their heads. No headaches. That was a good sign, but not conclusive.

There's a uniform relationship between CO_2 and O_2, so if Derek's analyser was accurate – which it wasn't[10] – then the −5 per cent oxygen would mean +5 per cent CO_2. Breathing in that level of carbon dioxide would affect the central nervous system and eventually be fatal. I'd camped inside caves before where there was no gas exchange, so I'm used to high CO_2 atmospheres, and this didn't feel like any of those. The air in Chamber 9 was stale with odours and general mustiness – it was certainly no worse than our changing room on site – but this wasn't what high CO_2 air felt like, so I was never very concerned.

However, when we were back outside the cave, during our debrief with the Thais, we handed over our new GoPro footage and told them that the reported oxygen level inside the cave had been 16 per cent. Although I was extremely sceptical about the meter's reliability, I knew that I couldn't just ignore the reading. As expected, the Thais were alarmed by the implications and as soon as the press heard the report, news of the poor air quality inside the cave began circulating. The countdown clock began speeding up, just as John's video footage of the boys also travelled around the world.

John: 'What do you want to tell people outside?'

'Hi. I'm Tern. I'm in good health.'

'I'm Note. I'm healthy.'

'I'm Pong. I'm healthy.'

'I'm Bew. I'm healthy.'

'I'm Dom. I'm healthy.'

The boys were shown huddled together in the cave, wrapped in reflective space blankets. The video confirmed their health, their existence, just as people were realizing that they were in a potentially lethal environment. They had to get out of there, but how? It was clear that the Thai authorities wouldn't approve a plan that put lives in danger, and we began hearing the words 'zero-risk option' being put forward as if it was a formed plan, which of course it wasn't. The boys were safe where they were, for now. As soon as we put a mask on them and took them underwater, we'd be putting them into danger. There was no way to avoid it.

In the two days that had passed since the boys' presence in the cave had been discovered, a variety of ideas had been put into motion at Tham Luang: drilling, searching for a back door, teaching the boys to dive. At the same time, methods were being discussed to address the volume of water inside the cave. There was a new method being considered that showed promise: diverting the water from ever entering the cave.

The water diversion operation was an interesting one that was being led by Thanet Natisri, an American Thai whose known field of expertise was doing charitable work on groundwater recharge. He had first been involved in some of the earlier efforts, like drilling the groundwater boreholes; while working on the mountain, Vern had managed to impart to Thanet that the need to keep the water from entering the cave in the first place was more important than the need for pumping it out. (In our analogy, the most effective way to keep the water from filling the hose would be to prevent it from ever going down the funnel.) Thanet had understood this significance. He shifted his strategy and led the diversion activities when most of the other officials on site did not see its value. His work was well away from the 'action' of the rescue so was largely dismissed. Because his work would not directly save the boys, it wasn't considered a prestigious undertaking, yet it was the most effective one being done.

Everyone at Tham Luang was trying to think of a way to get the boys out of the cave without killing them in the process. In the meantime, nothing was happening inside Chamber 9, and the boys were fine. They were still there – alive, healthy, waiting and not in any immediate danger. They'd managed to get by on their own when they'd been largely in the dark. Now they had a doctor with them, as well as adequate lights and food. People had begun supposing, 'Why do we have to do something? What happens if we do nothing? If we just wait for the monsoons to pass, the water will drain from the mountain, the cave will empty, and the boys could just walk out.'

This plan of doing nothing had been gaining momentum and was soon accepted as the 'zero-risk option'. It wasn't without risk, of course. Anybody who can think more than two steps ahead would see the impossibility of keeping a group of men inside a cave for four to five months. Who was going to take in food, take out garbage, take in medication as needed, monitor air quality and water quality? What happens if one of them becomes sick or injured? What happens when the heavy rain returns, and divers can't get back to them any more? Once the monsoon started, nobody would be diving through to them again.[11]

We knew that the 'zero-risk' plan was garbage, and we also knew that the authorities would be reluctant to turn away from the 'least risky' plan, so I was relieved when the 16 per cent O_2 reading – inaccurate as I knew it to be – galvanized them into action. John and I had never been swayed from our conviction that we were the ones responsible for the boys, and so we had never stopped planning a diving rescue.

There were a few things that set John and me apart from the other rescuers on site, and these things are what gave us the ability to think more freely. We were untrained and unregulated, we had been given no rules to follow and nobody to answer to, and we were there by choice – divers by hobby and not profession. On paper, it seemed like we were utterly unqualified to helm the rescue – and possibly dangerous. But instead, our autonomy gave us the ability to be creative and find an innovative solution.

In 2014, there had been an accident in the Riesending cave in Germany, leaving a caver 1,000 metres deep and with a severe head trauma. It was widely accepted that he was likely to die from his injuries during a rescue attempt, and the professional rescue service was unwilling to take on board that responsibility and liability. They were effectively leaving him to die, to his own fate. Rolf Siegenthaler, a Swiss caver and volunteer rescue leader – a quiet, unassuming guy that I see at caving conferences– came forward, willing to take responsibility for the rescue. The professionals were content with this, the rescue was successful, and the guy is fine. I've never forgotten Rolf doing that, and I thought of him again at Tham Luang.

Making bold and passionate decisions is easier to do when it's not your job on the line, when you have nothing to lose.

Early in the evening, while fettling with equipment in our gear room, Derek asked to see us. We went to his gazebo and found him talking with Claus Rasmussen, an experienced Danish diver who worked for Ben as a diving instructor in southern Thailand. At Tham Luang, Claus was the leader of a group who would be known as 'the Euro Divers'. Derek told us that he wanted us to collaborate with them moving forwards, and I was sceptical at first but didn't argue. I had something else I wanted to talk with Derek about and I got straight to the point.

'The only way those boys are coming out is if we sedate them,' I told him, watching Derek's face for a reaction. Instead, I saw a look of surprise on John's face. I'm not sure he had expected me to voice our plan to Derek so soon. After announcing the idea, the only emotion on Derek's face was slightly raised eyebrows, and I could see him processing what I'd said. I already knew that I trusted Derek, and his training as a paramedic would make him more aware of the medical risks involved than I was. The fact that he hadn't flat-out discounted the plan – or fallen off the seat laughing – was promising. His response was calm and measured. 'Are you sure about this?'

Committed cavers are always practising different rescue techniques. Cave-diving rescues, in particular, have always been ongoing thoughts at the back of my mind, and I was always trying out new methods that might be used. Twenty-five years ago, maybe more, I had practised a drill where I was leading Martin Holroyd through a sumped cave in Yorkshire. He had a full-face mask on and was supposed to remain inactive, as if unconscious, as I led him along a line. It was not a smooth process. Martin was being jerked along unevenly, he didn't have the line as a point of reference (because I held it in my other hand), his face was often on the gravel floor; it was very disconcerting for him. Martin was a very experienced cave diver, in a cave he was familiar with, but he couldn't take it. He'd aborted the drill when he became too disorientated and concerned for his safety. That always sat with me.

'Absolutely. For us, this is non-negotiable.'

I began reminding Derek of the pump workers' panic-stricken responses during their rescue, and he nodded as I spoke. He knew what an epic that had been. Sedation would be the only way to prevent a panic response. Then, diving with an unconscious boy wouldn't be any more difficult than diving with those food packages had been. 'We'll bring them out one at a time, one diver with one boy all the way through the cave.'

'You'll never get permission for that,' was Derek's immediate response, and I was afraid that would be the end of it, but he wasn't discarding the idea. 'Wouldn't it be safer to have two divers with one boy? In case something goes wrong?'

He was proposing that the second person be there as back-up, serving no primary role or purpose in the rescue, but we knew that back-up wasn't needed. We were 100 per cent certain that we'd be able to get out. Once we were diving, the only thing that would stop us would be some sort of catastrophic medical event, like a heart attack or something. But even if we did die, there would be somebody coming up right behind us, other divers stationed in the chamber, plenty of equipment among them. There would be tons of back-up in the cave.

Furthermore, if a problem arose when the divers couldn't communicate with each other, there would be chaos. One diver wouldn't understand the problem the other diver was having and therefore wouldn't be able to help. John and I had already learned this during a body recovery, when two of us had been working together in a zero-vis cave, and it had been an epic. It's simpler and safer to have one person in control, one person who is responsible for everything that is happening, one person who is making all of the decisions.

Perhaps most crucially, doubling the number of divers making each trip would double the length of the entire operation, and we were already racing against the impending monsoon. The weather forecast indicated that the rain would begin by the end of the week.

Derek asked what we thought about the plan for leaving them inside. I answered him honestly, 'If they stay there, they're all going to die slowly.' The idea of letting them stay in the cave was unfathomable to me. The Thai authorities were treating it as the safest, risk-free option, but that was rubbish. They were removing risks from themselves, not from the boys. They were freeing themselves of the responsibility that comes with making a choice, and in the process condemning everyone in the cave to a slow, miserable death. The most likely scenario, in my opinion, would be that they would suffocate or starve. I didn't think the flood would ever reach the top of their ramp, so they wouldn't even be spared with a quick death by drowning.

Derek continued through the list of options that were being considered, wanting to hear why each was impractical.

Drilling? I knew people were wondering why a shaft wasn't drilled, as it had been done for the Chilean miners in 2010. The idea wasn't completely daft, but there were several reasons why it would never have worked in Tham Luang. The Chilean miners had been in a man-made, precisely mapped mine, and the drillers had known exactly the place they were aiming for; the Wild Boars were in a natural cave, and their precise location was unknown.[12] Furthermore, even if their location could be pinpointed, time and access considerations made drilling unfeasible.[13]

Searching for another entrance? Many volunteers were still searching the mountainside for another entrance to the cave, a 'back door' that may or may not even exist. We thought the existence of one was extremely unlikely, since none of the potholes that had been discovered were 'breathing' – they did not contain the tell-tale draught that would signal open cave passage. Furthermore, the area where they were searching was so far above Tham Luang, anything they found would have had to be one of the deepest caves in Thailand, in a region where there weren't any deep caves.

Teaching the boys to dive? Although the boys were already fair swimmers,[14] they didn't have the time to learn to dive. They lacked all of the background skills and knowledge and discipline. Cave diving requires years of training, and even that doesn't guarantee success.

The crucial component inside the cave was the water, so we discussed our thoughts on managing that element.

Pumping? I've explained about the source of the flooding and why the pumps would never be able to empty the cave.

Water diversion? For days, Thanet's team had been employing diversion techniques to control the surface water entering the caves. Although effective, these efforts would be overrun by the full onslaught of the monsoon that was forecast to begin on Monday. The arrival of the monsoon was the only thing we could be certain of, among all of the unknowns and variables. If the boys were still inside when the next rain began and the strong currents returned, any chance of a rescue would be erased. We wouldn't even be able to dive to them, much less guide them out safely.

We ended up right where we'd begun: diving the boys out under sedation, treating them as inert packages to be moved through the cave by an experienced diver. The only way they'd be coming out would be the way they went in. The forecasted heavy rain had been holding off, but it was a constant threat, and the beginning of the monsoon would mean the end of any rescue attempt. We were running out of time, so this had to be done as soon as possible.

Derek's next question told me that he was coming around to our plan.

'What would you call a success?' he asked.

'I can't see this being fully successful, but if we manage to get more than half out, that would be a pretty good success rate. Half alive is a hell of a lot better than all of them being dead.' Because we knew they would all die if we did nothing, John and I were focusing on the number we could save, instead of the number that might die in the process.

'Then surely getting just one out would be a success, wouldn't it?'

While that was technically true, we weren't going to process twelve consecutive deaths just to bring one out alive. On balance, I thought a success rate over 50 per cent would be considered acceptable, but this was an ethical debate that none of us were prepared to delve too far into.

Instead, we went back to discussing logistics. I made it clear to Derek that John and I operate under a rule of simplicity, and that we would want to keep the process as streamlined as possible. I returned to the point that Derek had taken issue with earlier. 'It has to be one diver, one child. There's no other way. Adding a second diver doesn't provide any benefit; all it does is increase the chances for things to go wrong.'

I paused before adding my final statement.

'We won't have any Thai divers working beyond Chamber 3.' The language barrier would add too much confusion, and, most importantly, if we had to flee a flood, we didn't want to be caught behind a load of Thai divers who weren't moving swiftly.

After listening in respectful silence and giving careful consideration to what we were discussing, Claus piped up, speaking on behalf of his team of Euro Divers. 'What can we do to help?' The Euro Divers had self-presented so, much like us, they were not responsible to anyone and were not included in the Thai's command hierarchy. I knew Claus and the Euro divers weren't sump divers, but something about his demeanour indicated that he could be trusted. He wanted to find a way to be useful but – knowing the limitations of his group – he deferred to us for instruction.

'Start going into the cave and get yourselves familiar with the passages. Improve the line where you can,' I replied, figuring out my answer as I spoke. 'And take in lots of cylinders. You'll never go wrong by taking in more cylinders.'

He nodded. 'We'll get started in the morning.'

A plan seemed to be forming, but we were still missing the most crucial element. I had rather pre-empted myself because I hadn't consulted about sedation with anyone who had any medical knowledge on that subject.

Richard Harris had been offering his help for days, and I was about to take him up on his offer in a way he wasn't expecting. More important than his skills as a cave diver, I needed him to work as an underground anaesthetist.

Wednesday, 4 July 2018

[12:52] **Richard Harris:**

Hi Rick, wondering if you are still on site. Would be great to get an update if you have any down time. Congrats again to you and John for the break through. Fingers crossed for the next bit.

[16:09] **Rick Stanton:**

There's stuff to talk about.
They're not being dived out by Thai navy.
No one will take charge and the military are defeated.

Richard Harris:

Really? What do you think about diving them out?

Rick Stanton:

Could you sedate someone and dive them out??

Richard Harris:

Sedation not an option.

[05/07/2018 01:09]

[Rick Stanton called Richard Harris]

9.
Calling Out the Cavalry

'I remember feeling overjoyed when Rick surfaced and
I saw his face. It was a great relief.'
Jonathan Sims, discussing his rescue
from a Mexican cave[1]

As with most extreme sports, the circle of cave explorers is quite small, with everyone separated from each other by only a few degrees. This had appealed to me at university, when I had first been welcomed into the caving club and had found a surrogate family among its members. As I continued to make my name known throughout an expanding circle of cavers (first in the UK and then internationally), I quickly discovered that everyone knows each other. This makes it easy to become well liked, or well hated, by everyone all at once. If you earn respect, word will travel, and you will be invited on future projects. If you act like an ass, your reputation will end up travelling further inside a cave than you ever will.

I've always tended to keep to myself, so I was able to quietly work at whatever I was doing without standing out. Although I've spent a lot of time working alone, I do appreciate that a few key connections, made early in my caving career, went on to have quite an impact on my life. The one that stands out as being particularly pivotal is my early friendship with Dani. His connection with the Army Caving Association had led to me being taken on some great trips early on, which had vastly expanded my experiences. This then led to my partnerships with Ian Rolland, Barry Suddell and the NPC, and Jonathan Sims, among others. Then I have Jonathan to thank for introducing me to Jason Mallinson . . . and, many years later, for introducing me to Amp. One thing leads to another.

I had remained grateful to the Army Caving Association for allowing me to tag along on their trips, back when I was young and not yet a mainstream caver. I had a lot of fun on those trips and learned more than my share about caving. Although we'd drifted apart over the years (Dani left the Army; I became active with the NPC and work), I always felt a bit indebted, aware that I owed a lot of my early learning to them. So, in February of 2004, when Jonathan Sims phoned me to ask for a favour on behalf of the Combined Services Caving Association,[2] I was more than happy to oblige.

Jonathan's request seemed simple enough: thirteen members (there seems to be an unlucky theme here with the number 13) of the CSCA were leaving for an expedition to Cuetzala in Mexico, and he wanted to put my name down as their emergency contact, in case Alpazat cave flooded, which it was known to do.[3] The only catch was that he also asked if he could include Jason's name with mine. His request made sense, of course: I wouldn't be much good alone, and Jonathan knew that Jason and I had been working together. He also knew that we each had experience inside the cave systems of the Cuetzalan area, as well as experience conducting rescues from caves. What made it awkward was that I hadn't seen Jason since he'd abruptly left just before a planned dive at Saint Georges, France, earlier the previous year.[4] Regardless, I told Jonathan to go ahead and put down both of our names, figuring that we would never be called. I knew Jonathan was an experienced caver, and he'd be travelling with other cavers into a relatively straightforward cave.

What could possibly go wrong?

I learned the answer to that question on Sunday, 21 March, when I returned from a weekend away to find about sixteen missed calls and messages waiting for me on my answering machine. The messages were from an Army major in London, who was telling me (with increasing urgency in his voice) that he needed to speak with me immediately.

The Army major gave me the specifics that were known: a sudden rainstorm; a flash flood; six men had been trapped in the cave for five or six days already. They were safe inside, but with the weather showing no sign of letting up any time soon, the military had finally decided that action needed to be taken to get them out. They'd looked through the expedition files and had found the note: 'In case of emergency, call Richard Stanton.'

I knew the experience would be an interesting challenge and I was pleased to have the chance to give something back to the Army Caving Association, so I told the major I'd make a few phone calls and come back to him. I hung up the phone and debated which would be less fun: calling work to tell them I'd not be in for the next few days (*'Stanton, you're here to be a fireman, not to go on cave rescues!'*), or calling Jason to tell him that I'd secretly volunteered him for a rescue mission and we were being called to Mexico.

Taking a deep breath, I dialled Jason's number first. 'Jason? I've signed us up for something.' I started hesitantly, not looking forward to how he would react to this. 'Sims is trapped beyond a sump in Mexico, and we're obliged to go there to rescue him.'

'He can fuck right off. I'm busy. I'm not going all that way to sort out that buffoon.' He hung up the phone.

Well, this was awkward.

I stood with my hand still resting on the receiver of the telephone, debating what I would say to the major, when the phone rang again. It was Jason, telling me he'd had a change of heart.

'All right, then,' Jason said gruffly. 'I suppose we can go. It might be interesting.'

With that done, I turned to the other phone call.

'I've been called to Mexico to rescue the Army from a cave,' I told the brigade duty officer. 'I can't imagine I'll be in for the next week.' It must have been the most innovative excuse ever given.

'OK, then,' he said, agreeably. He'd accepted this news surprisingly well, not requiring proof or anything.

The next day it was all over the television. My watch was sitting there at work when I popped up on the news bulletin. 'Oh. It wasn't an excuse, then.' Press began ringing the control switchboard, looking for information about 'the cave rescuer' and – because I'd always kept my head down – the operators had no idea who they were talking about. That soon changed, and from that point on, I was known at fire service headquarters as 'the Cave Man'.

I spent the rest of the day fielding calls from London while sorting through the diving gear piled in my living and dining rooms. I had never been involved with an international rescue before, but I knew enough about this type of cave to know which equipment I'd need. That part was easy, but I was stuck after that.

All of my clothes needed washing. When I looked in the mirror, my hair was dishevelled and unkempt. *Will I be speaking with government officials? Will there be press coverage?* I thought maybe I should prepare for the times I would need to look more presentable. My own washing machine had broken, and there wasn't time to go to the launderette in town, so I called Angie and explained what was going on.

'You're a mess,' she told me with a laugh before agreeing to help out. 'Bring the clothes over.'

After leaving my laundry with her, I stopped at the hairdresser for a trim. I was fielding calls from the Army major while in the hairdresser's chair. Sorting flights to Mexico, discussing logistics of the rescue. The hairdresser was looking at me like, *'What the fuck's he on about?'* (A few days later when it was all in the news, he made the connection.)

My priorities before leaving may seem narrow and uncharacteristically vain – appearance, hair, clothes – but I wasn't very concerned about the rescue itself. They were well-trained adults, in a mapped cave; I knew we'd get it done. Jason and I would, however, find ourselves unprepared for what happened outside the cave, where we were about to be given our first lesson on foreign diplomacy and international relations.

On the previous Monday, six of the thirteen men on the expedition had entered the cave for what was planned as a thirty-six-hour trip. Their purpose was recorded as being an 'official military expedition to support adventurous training'. In other words, they were there for fun. The men in the cave were: Jonathan, Simon Cornhill, Charles Milton, Toby Hamnett, Chris Mitchell and John Roe. Apart from Jonathan, I only knew John Roe personally. I'd first met him at Ian Rolland's funeral, and I knew he was now married to Ian's widow, Erica.

After agreeing to serve as their contingency plan, I had given Jonathan a simple instruction: to lay out a guide line throughout the section that would flood. I'd told him specifically to lay it on the floor and against a wall, so there were points of reference. Were anything to happen, a rescue would be significantly easier if there was already a line leading to their exact location.[5] They had also taken a Heyphone[6] (which allowed them to communicate with their colleagues outside the cave) and a radon monitor (to measure levels of the radioactive gas, which is sometimes naturally found in caves).

The men knew that the cave was prone to flooding, but this was traditionally the driest season of the year, and the forecast had looked clear. When the rain poured down unexpectedly and stranded them inside, they didn't panic. They were disciplined, and this was the exact sort of thing they had prepared for.

There was already an emergency camp set up on a dry ledge over the subterranean river, and they took shelter there. They had sleeping bags and dry clothes, cooking supplies, enough gas and food to last for four to five days and reserve carbide to power their acetylene lights. The first night spent trapped inside was stressful, and they stayed awake, listening to a series of loud crashes as the flash flood filled portions of the cave. After that, though, they became confident that their camp would remain safe from flooding. They began passing the time by playing games, using cards they'd made from a torn-up logbook and reading the two novels that had been brought in with them.

As far as things go, they were rather comfortable inside. The rain stopped on some days, and they watched the water descend, becoming hopeful that they'd be able to walk out; but then the rain returned, and the water would rise again. After a week of this, their food had nearly run out,[7] and the experience was beginning to take its toll mentally – in that they were fantastically bored. At the height of their boredom, the men came up with a plan to raise money for British Caving by posing naked, with bits of strategically placed caving gear, for a photograph that would later be printed in the *Sun* newspaper. Perhaps in an effort to shield the world from any further assaults resulting from their boredom, a call was made to London, and not long after that the phone at my home began ringing.

Meanwhile in Mexico, outside the cave, the proverbial shit was hitting the fan.

The Brits had entered Mexico as civilians, not as working military, and they had not bothered telling any government authorities about the trip they had planned in Alpazat. Not surprisingly, when Mexican authorities learned that members of the British military forces were trapped in one of their caves, they had become suspicious. Worried that an unauthorized military operation had been taking place on his land, Mexican President Vicente Fox spotted the opportunity to boost his failing popularity by demonstrating a show of strength, and he penned a terse letter to London, demanding an explanation.

'We are asking the British government to tell us whether these people are military personnel, and if they are, what they are doing there.'

The presence of a radon monitor in the cave fuelled additional rumours that the men were on a mission to search for uranium ore; this caused Energy Minister Felipe Calderón to dispatch nuclear research institute scientists to the cave. Prompting further suspicion, the Mexican government had acted on the request of British officials to keep press away from the cave during all of this. The Mexicans became increasingly uneasy about what was happening inside the cave.

The building frustrations finally erupted when Major Stephen Whitlock, the leader of the British expedition, refused to accept help from the Mexican volunteer rescue squads who had arrived, preferring to wait for the two British specialist divers that had been deployed. In response, the Mexican government promptly sent out Special Forces. An officer arrived with orders to enter the cave, collect the trapped men – at gunpoint if necessary – and place them under arrest.

'You've got your orders,' Whitlock said agreeably, 'and I'll help you comply with them as far as I can.' The Mexican officer didn't seem to fully understand that the men were trapped beyond a submerged section of tunnel, so Steve walked with him into the cave up to the muddy puddle where it was sumped. 'They're through there,' he said. 'I'll leave it with you.'

Jason and I had arrived in Mexico City and were spending the day running between various government offices in the capital city, trying to acquire written authorization and working visas to conduct the cave rescue. At one point we were told to wait in a room while our forms were being processed, and as we waited a woman came in to serve us tea. She spoke perfect English and began casually asking us questions about who we were and which military organization we were from. Jason and I looked at each other and laughed. *They're planting spies.* We always had someone tailing us and we suspected we were being watched the whole time. It was clear they thought we were something special and they were suspicious. They couldn't fathom that the British Army had sent two ordinary blokes to conduct a rescue of their men, while keeping everybody else out. They thought that we must be working for somebody and they were determined to figure it out. The more we claimed to be who we were, which was ordinary civilians, the more intrigued they were to find an alternative truth.

After spending a full day in Mexico City, we were finally loaded into a vehicle with our equipment,[8] to be driven to Cuetzualan.

Inside the cave, the men were preparing to leave their newly adopted home. They had already been told that Jason and I would carry spare diving gear into the cave with us to dive the men out, one at a time. The trapped men were cavers but not necessarily divers, so Jonathan had spent some time assessing their comfort with the idea. Most of them were fine and readily accepted the dive they would have to make, but Toby freely admitted that he was afraid of water. There were 170 metres of flooded cave separating them from the outside, so Jonathan knew he'd have to find some way to help Toby overcome his fear to prevent him from panicking.

He came up with the creative solution of filling a cooking pot with water, then having Toby practise breathing through his mouth while his nose was submerged. The idea is to desensitize the person to the feeling of water against their face and nose, thus decreasing the natural panic response that results.[9] This would be helpful for increasing his overall comfort in the water, and would be crucial in case his mask was knocked off during the dive. With repeated practice, the exercise had the desired effect, and Toby's panic subsided. The practice also helped by giving him something to concentrate on other than the impending journey out, while also building his confidence.

Jason and I finally arrived at Alpazat quite late in the evening, after enduring a perilous journey from Mexico City at the hands of an embassy driver who had clearly never driven outside the grid-locked streets of Mexico City. He'd raced through the small winding mountain passes in the fog and at night. *This will be the most dangerous part of the whole incident.* I held on for dear life through miles of dirt roads. We were deposited at our hotel quite late at night, grateful to have survived, and met Whitlock and his men in the bar. Despite having been on the go for over forty hours, we agreed to begin the rescue early the next morning.

In the morning, everybody got up early to prepare, while Jason and I had a lie-in . . . then they forgot to send a car for us, and we only just managed to catch a lift. When we finally arrived at Alpazat, we began kitting up on a platform on the side of the cave, while Whitlock used the Heyphone to inform the men that we were coming in. As we were getting changed, we saw an elderly military gentleman – maybe in his fifties – who was struggling to get up to our platform. Two other people finally grabbed his wrists and hauled him up. Jason and I watched this, laughing at him, until Steve nudged us to be quiet. 'Shhh,' he told us. 'That's the leader of the Special Forces.'

For the rescue, Jason and I were each wearing our own harness and side-mount cylinders, while also carrying in a spare set to be used by the men we'd take out. I was using my inner-tube wing; this would be its first rescue mission. We had masks for the men, even a full-face mask for anybody who chose to wear it. After receiving information about the men in the cave, in terms of their diving experience, we had risk-assessed all of them and formed a plan based on their competency. Two men were comfortable diving; we classed them as 'Expert'. Two of the men had tried diving once in a swimming pool; we called them 'Intermediate'. The last two men had never dived before (although one of them was a submariner who had spent more time underwater than we had), so they were the 'Beginners'. We'd begin with the Intermediates as practice, then go back to take the Beginners through, and leave the Experts for last.

'Someone round here owes me a pint,' Jason quipped as he lifted his mask and removed the regulator from his mouth. We'd surfaced beyond the sump to find the six men waiting for us. I climbed out and offered a disposable razor to the men. 'If you want a quick shave, it might help the mask seal to your face better,' I told them. All of the men waved the razor away, unconcerned, except for Toby, who grabbed it and began dragging it across his face and neck. I winced as I heard the razor scraping across his dry skin.

We spent a little while in there, having a look around the chamber and making small talk, before starting the process of taking them out. Jason and I were jovial, relaxed and casual, which immediately set their minds at rest. We didn't deliberately plan that, that's just how we were – that's how we felt about it – and our confidence calmed their nerves. One of the first questions they asked us was, 'Is there any outside interest in our plight?'

'No,' we said in unison. If Whitlock had elected not to tell his men that they were about to be detained and interrogated, Jason and I weren't going to.

Jason took Chris Mitchell through the sump first, and I was with John Roe. I appreciated the irony. I was with Ian when he died in Mexico and now I was rescuing John – Erica's second husband – from another cave in Mexico. I wondered if Erica hated the sound of my name by now.

Jonathan had placed a line where the floor met the wall, giving the men contact with the cave. We over-weighted them, so they just had to pull themselves along. We were able to stay side-by-side with our man for most of the way through the sump, but there was one tight space where we had to pass through single-file. The dive lasted thirteen minutes and was without incident. Once the men were safely on the near side of the sump, Jason and I dived back through, carrying the harness and cylinders back in for the next pair.

Jason went for Simon, while I approached Toby. 'Are you ready?' I asked him. He nodded and took the harness from me, then put on the mask. I'd explained to Toby that there was an air bell midway through the sump, where he'd be able to stop for air on the way out. This was a white lie – there was a bit of an air bell there, but not a place we'd be able to stop and rest – but I thought it might give him confidence and make the trip seem less daunting. This wasn't a quick duck-under, not something he could just barrel his way through in a panic. The dive was a bit involved, and he'd have to remain calm.

Thirteen minutes is a long time to have to hold your shit together.

A few times, I could sense rising panic in Toby and I paused to give him time to get his breathing under control. When we got to the restricted bit where we would have to go single-file, Toby was close to panic again. I knew he'd never make it through on his own, so I went in feet-first and pulled myself backward. This way, we were face-to-face and I held eye contact to keep reassuring him as he made his way through.

After that dive was done, Jason and I elected to top up the air in the spare set of cylinders that we were using for the men. This took an hour or two, during which one of the men filling the cylinders commented on how composed we were. Jason and I were standing around and having a laugh; this wasn't stressful at all for either of us. Once the spare cylinders were filled, we went back in for Jonathan and Charlie. Nine hours after beginning the rescue – and eight days after they'd first entered the cave – all of the men were together on the safe side of the sump.

Leaving the cave, we were suddenly surrounded by Mexican rescue workers, all in their uniforms, who joined us for the walk out, as if they had been involved in the rescue mission in some way. We heard the buzz of the crowd that was waiting for us, and before long we saw a mass of journalists crowding at the entrance, along with the Mexican military and UK embassy staff. The men who'd just been rescued were told they had an hour to pack all of their things and get in the military transport to be taken away.

At the hotel, as Mexican officials were loading the British military into their lorries, Jason and I made ourselves scarce for fear that we would be included in the group that was being taken away for detention. Jason spotted a suspicious-looking figure – he might have even been wearing a long overcoat – who clearly stood out from the rest of the crowd. 'We're definitely being shadowed,' he said, laughing. In an attempt to lose our tail, we slipped into the local bar and were seated at its only empty table, which happened to be directly underneath the wall-mounted television set.

As the evening passed, we were getting pissed while the news of the rescue was spreading around us. Suddenly, we noticed people in the bar watching the television, then looking down to us and then back up at the telly. We looked above us to see our faces plastered on the evening news; it was the footage that had just been taken outside the cave. The next thing, everyone in the bar was coming towards us, buying us drinks and asking for our autograph. I laughed when somebody asked me to sign a cast on their arm. So much for keeping a low profile.

When we flew from Mexico City the following day, we were met at the airport by the head of airport security – a man who was clearly ex-military, probably ex-Special Forces. As he was leading us through the airport, he kept asking us, 'Who are you really? Can you tell me who you are really working with?' Still, nobody could believe that we were civilians. They couldn't work out that Jason and I were just two cavers who were there on our own.

This is what we do for fun.

A few days after returning from Mexico, Jonathan Sims and caver John Taylor gathered at my home in Coventry to be interviewed by a reporter from the UK's *Sunday Telegraph* news magazine. (Jason, not surprisingly, had opted out of the interview.) I noticed the reporter, Amanda Mitchison, looking around my living room while she talked to us. She seemed as interested in the state of my home as in the cavers who were gathered inside it. When the article was printed, I laughed when I read her first lines: 'Rick Stanton . . . is not the most domesticated of men.' The irony here is that what she was seeing was my house in its finest state. Soon after moving in, I'd begun taking in lodgers to lighten the mortgage payments. They were usually students from Coventry University who were looking for inexpensive off-campus accommodation and only stayed for a term or so. In 2000, a Chinese student named Hana had moved in, and we'd instantly got along. She became a great friend and stayed all through her years at university; to this day, she credits me with helping her to learn the language. During her stay, she added a lot of nice touches that made the house feel more comfortable. After Hana moved out in 2004 and returned to China, I never bothered with another lodger, and the house quickly resumed its steady decline to its current state.

Amanda Mitchison would be appalled if she could see it now.

I hadn't told my family I was being interviewed, but my Aunt Bettie reads the *Telegraph*. When she collected the paper that weekend, she was first delighted by what she saw, but then horrified that I had been described as being undomesticated.

'That's disgraceful to write that about Richard!' she said. My cousin Sallie laughed and pointed out fairly, 'But it's true.'

Being trapped in a cave is something that you can't truly understand unless you've lived through it. After his experience in Alpazat, Jonathan has spoken a bit about what the experience had been like for them. They were all military men who had trained for just such an experience, and there was never a moment when they felt unprepared or in danger; even so, he described the moment they became trapped as being 'absolutely soul-destroying'. It is hard to sit with the knowledge that you're deep inside the earth and trapped there by water. There is no avoiding the uneasiness that comes when a force of nature takes control out of your hands.

Unlike most people hearing the news coming from Thailand, Jonathan was able to empathize with the Wild Boars from his own direct experience in such a situation. 'We were very hungry. We kept talking about what we were going to eat after we got rescued, to keep up our morale, and we told each other our life stories,' Jonathan remembered.[10] He was spot-on about this. I've always said that the boys played a role in their own survival in a few ways. First, by making the unusual but correct choice to retreat further into the cave, where they reached higher ground. Second, by maintaining their solidarity. They were a team, and they remained a team throughout their ordeal and indeed afterwards. Third, by their stoic acceptance of the rescue plan they were eventually presented with.

While John and I were in Thailand – just beginning to put that plan together – Jonathan, being someone who was 'in the know', appreciated how dangerous the mission would be. 'Our rescue [in Alpazat] was comparatively easy . . . a quite simple dive. Rescuing the children [in Tham Luang] will be really technically challenging, because there's a combination of swimming, walking and diving.'

Jonathan also knew that I was the person to do the job, that I wouldn't be bothered by the difficulty of the rescue. 'What I do hope is that they let Rick make the decisions, because he really knows what he's doing – and he never panics about anything. He's totally cool, calm and collected in a professional way. He will know from our rescue that getting the first one or two out, and then having that information relayed back, will have a big psychological impact on the rest.' He would prove to be correct about this as well, and we purposefully established this feedback loop when planning the first day's rescues.

Quite a few lessons were borrowed from the rescue in Mexico while planning the one in Thailand. John Roe, one of the men rescued from inside Alpazat, even had a direct connection with the Thailand rescue. When John and I were building our team and calling in more British cave divers to help us, one of the first names we thought of was Connor Roe. The biological son of Ian Rolland – and adopted son of John Roe – had become an accomplished cave diver, and I knew he would be an asset to the team. When we invited him to join the rescue team, he accepted without pause.

Erica must really hate hearing my name by now.

'I just want to warn you. You're going to dive to the
end of the cave. You're going to see these kids.
They're all looking healthy and happy and smiley.
Then, you're going to swim away, and they're probably
all going to die.'

Rick Stanton, to Dr Richard Harris[11]

Thursday, 5 July 2018, Thailand

John and I had continued putting things into place, preparing for a
diving rescue and forming a team for support, even though we had
never been given any official consent to take charge. UK divers
Jason Mallinson and Chris Jewell were already on their way. Following behind them on a later flight were Gary Mitchell and Mike
Clayton,[12] who were experienced rescue controllers[13] with the
BCRC. Following behind them, on a flight from Denmark, was
Martin Ellis, who spoke fluent Thai and had in-depth knowledge of
Tham Luang from previous exploration. The cavalry was arriving;
the plan was coming together; Derek and the US military were sup-
porting us and communicating with the Thai authorities; we were
just waiting for Thai approval to get started. And Harry. I had to get
Harry on board with the plan, and then we had to get him and Craig
to Thailand.

Getting Harry to Tham Luang would overcome the first major
hurdle. Once he was there, I knew he would see for himself what we
were up against and I wouldn't have to work very hard to convince
him. 'Could you sedate someone and dive them out?' I had asked
Harry on Wednesday evening after we'd discussed the plan with
Derek. Harry's reply had not been encouraging. 'Sedation not an
option.' This didn't put me off, though. Although this was his area of

expertise, I knew that he didn't appreciate the full scope of the situation at Tham Luang. I wasn't asking if sedation was ideal, because of course it wasn't. I just needed to know if it was possible.

I needed to know if he would do it.

I'd met Harry about eleven years earlier at the Pearse Resurgence, a deep cave on the north of New Zealand's Southern Island. When we met, I'd just been down to −77 metres in my homemade harness, with my homemade rebreather, and carrying a big lump of lead in the middle of my back. When he saw me come out of the cave, Harry had been amazed. He wasn't such an accomplished cave diver then and he couldn't believe the dive I'd just done with such shit equipment. I met him again two years later when we were diving Cocklebiddy cave, in the Nullabour plain of Australia. Craig Challen and Jamie Brisbin had also been on that project, Jamie as a support diver. I'd come to know and respect Harry well over the years, not only for the exploration he had completed in Australian caves, but also for his larger-than-life persona. At Tham Luang, both of those assets would be equally valuable.

I knew the plan to carry unconscious boys through an underwater cave was crazy. I knew that it seemed impossible. Of all the cave-diving anaesthetists I knew, Harry was the only one who would have the confidence and courage to take on the responsibility, and without him coming on board, the plan would never be successful. 'Sedation not an option,' he had told me, but he was wrong. Not only was it an option, I was convinced it was the best option.

I rang Harry on Thursday morning and was surprised when he answered my call while in the operating theatre. I trusted everything was going well on the table, and got straight to the point.

'You've sedated lots of children before, both in hospital theatres and at roadside accidents.'

'Yeah, sure,' he countered. 'Never inside a cave.'

'Look, we're not looking for the perfect solution,' I reminded him, 'only the best available one.' As I had done with Derek, I pointed out why all other options were impractical – Harry could see for himself why leaving them inside the cave would result in a 'medical nightmare' that would only delay their deaths – and we ended back at the idea of sedation. He was beginning to understand the impossible problem that we had to solve.

Harry was still sceptical and cautious, but hearing more information had softened his resolve. When he told me he would do some research, I knew he was relenting.

'I'm keen to come,' he told me, 'but I'm not promising anything.'

'Leave it with me,' I told him, trying to hide the excitement from my voice. 'I'll get you here.' I was convinced that the plan was going to move forwards. Once he was there, he'd never turn away.

After ending the call with Harry, I went straight off and found the Australian Army major who was supporting the team of Australian police divers. 'You have to get Harry and Craig here,' I told him and provided their information. While I had only been talking to Harry, I assumed as a matter of course that his dive buddy Craig Challen would be coming along as well. Craig is a cave diver who works as a veterinary surgeon, so they speak the same medical language; he was the perfect person for Harry to have alongside him. I appreciated the value of having a trusted partner to work with, especially on a mission like this. At the start, I'd had John, and Vern was with Rob; I saw how well that had worked so I endeavoured to continue this as I was bringing more people in. Harry and Craig. Jason and Chris. Gary and Mike. It just helped having somebody by your side to talk things through with.

Somehow, it was all put in place within an hour. Harry and Craig would be coming to Thailand.

When Jason and Chris arrived at Tham Luang on Thursday afternoon, John and I went to greet them at the police cordon, where we found them looking around the scene in a bit of a daze. I'm sure the incredulity on their faces mirrored the looks that had been on John's and mine when we'd first arrived. Was that only a week ago? In the eight days that had passed, I'd grown accustomed to the crowds and chaos on the mountainside – in fact, we had become a part of it – but they were seeing it all for the first time.

The latest addition to the commotion was the newest scheme of running a hose all the way back to Chamber 9, with the intent of piping oxygen directly to the boys. 'If their air quality is suffering back there, let's get them more oxygen,' was the rationale. We saw thousands of metres of hose being unpacked from a truck, along with hundreds of 50-litre industrial cylinders containing oxygen. A huge, choreographed pantomime was being staged – conveniently in front of the press pack. A great snake of people had formed, with 2.5 kilometres of hose being passed person-to-person, to get it to Chamber 3. It was Crisis 101: give everybody a job to do and keep them busy.

But if it takes all night and hundreds of personnel to weave it 800 metres through the largest section of cave . . .

I had no concept of how they were planning to get it beyond that, through the underwater portion. It had taken us only a second to realize the impossibility of leading a hose through 1,500 metres of winding, ragged cave – within 10 metres it would get snagged. Even if the hose was laid out perfectly, there'd be no way that oxygen could flow such a great distance through a hose of such a small diameter.[14] There'd been no joined-up thinking behind it.

Jason and I stopped into the SEALs' area to ask for something we needed; there were fifty SEALs there, yet not one of them could help. They began giving me the usual run-around, each one telling me to go and see a different person. Pretty much everything the SEALs did proved to be counterproductive. They'd attempt to help us, but nothing ever worked out quite the way they intended it.

'Everything they do is sabotage,' I had complained to John a few days earlier, and he'd corrected me. 'It isn't sabotage because it's not intentional,' he'd reasoned. 'It's just interference. They interfere with things they know nothing about and they always get it wrong.' Some of that had to be levelled to us, though, as we found it hard to grasp if they had fully understood things that we were explaining to them. I believe there were cultural issues as well; they didn't seem to ask for help or further clarification when it was needed. But I'd had enough.

'For fuck's sake!' I said, loudly enough for all of them to hear me. 'You're utterly incompetent.' Jason, of all people, was horrified by my behaviour.

'Mind what you're saying,' he hushed me. 'You're surrounded by the people you're insulting.' He hadn't had to deal with seven days of this madness, though.

I had last dived with Jason three years earlier, at Cogol dei Veci. In the preceding years, he had settled down with his partner Emma Heron, who is also a cave diver; in 2015, they learned they were expecting. Because Jason was well known among cavers for his direct and autocratic manner, many had expressed their surprise that he was becoming a father, and he'd been apprehensive about my response to his impending fatherhood. He'd put off telling me for some time, until one night when he happened to be in Coventry and he came to my house. We'd gone to the pub, as usual, and he'd waited until he'd had a good few pints before he was comfortable sharing his news. I wasn't as shocked as many people had been.

'I think you'll be a great dad,' I'd told him simply.

'Yeah, but you know me more than most.' I nodded, knowing the opposite was also true.

Eventually, Jason and I gave up on the SEALs and left their area, joining Chris and John in our gear room. With John and I not doing as much exploration in recent years, our withdrawal from the fore-front of the cave-diving scene had left a noticeable void, particularly when the question arose of a possible rescue. I'd been asked more than once, 'If you aren't diving any more, who will be called for a rescue?' With Jason as a given, Chris Jewell's had been the first name I'd offered. Although he'd never participated in a rescue, he had done some significant exploration,[15] he was very active in the CDG and he participated in many rescue training drills run by local caving groups. Chris is the youngest of us all, and I'd often described him as being the leader of the 'next generation' of divers in the CDG who would be coming up behind me and John and Jason. The Tham Luang rescue operation – one of the most difficult I'd been called for – would be his first test.

Standing at Tham Luang with John, Chris and Jason in the sec-ond (cleaner) room we had been given to use,[16] I considered the years of experience that was shared among us. We'd need all of it, for what we were planning. Although each of us had worked with oth-ers at various times on projects, this would be the first time the four of us were all working together, side-by-side. (The following day, when Harry arrived and was met by the four of us working together, he began calling us the Awesome Foursome.)

'The plan is set in stone,' I told the gathered team 'The boys are going to be fully sedated, and you are going to be carrying them out, individually, one-on-one . . . Your boy could drown in your arms, and you'll have no way of saving him.' I knew that the first day would be the learning curve. If there were any casualties on the first day, we'd re-evaluate and possibly revise the plan, but I wanted them to fully understand what they were agreeing to do.

'You can dive tomorrow, to become familiar with the cave,' I told them. 'The current has completely dropped; you shouldn't find the dive to Chamber 9 too difficult. You'll meet the kids there.' I gave Chris and Jason the same warning I'd given to Harry: 'Just remember, when the rain starts and the water rises again, we won't be able to get back to them. You could be the last people to see them alive. You need to steel yourself for that.' I paused, then offered a way out. 'You don't have to do this,' I told them. 'Go away and think about this overnight. Give me your answer in the morning.'

I knew Jason wouldn't be one to shy away from any challenge he was presented with, and that he would approach the rescue as unflinchingly as John and I were doing. I wasn't as confident with Chris, because I wasn't sure he had fully engaged with all of the implications. He'd never encountered a dead body before, and this would be a hell of a start. I was hoping he'd come through. They went back to their rooms and discussed the plan with each other, and with their partners at home. When Jason and Chris returned to the cave on Friday morning, they were both on board to move forwards with the plan.

Over the course of the night, while we were all asleep, a retired Navy SEAL named Saman Gunan went into the cave. The tragic result of Saman's dive would have a profound effect on the remainder of the rescue.

Nightly Correspondence:
Thursday, 5 July 2018

From: John Garvin
To: Rick Stanton

We met at Oztek. I'm the British diver who heads up the diving on
James Cameron's underwater projects (Sanctum, Deepsea
Challenge). I'm currently in the US working with Jim on the Avatar
sequels.
You clearly have a million stressful things to deal with at the
moment.
But I wanted you to know that James Cameron and Steven
Spielberg have been anxiously following the unfolding story and
have asked me to convey their personal gratitude and support to
you and the diving team for your extraordinary efforts.
Jim and Steven would also like to pass their well wishes onto the
families of the boys involved.

I read this message aloud to everybody the next day.

Friday, 6 July 2018

When we arrived at the cave on Friday morning, there was a solemn
mood, and we soon learned about Saman's death. Saman – a thirty-
eight-year-old husband, father and retired Navy SEAL – had come
to Tham Luang as a volunteer, intent on helping to save the boys in
the cave. I had seen him around the cave a few times that week.
Although we hadn't worked together directly, he was often nearby

and keen to see what we were doing. After working a full shift on Thursday, he'd stayed on for a double shift and had dived into the cave in the early hours of Friday morning. A few hours later, his drowned body had been discovered. The official report was that he had been taking in cylinders to be used during the rescue and he had run out of air himself during his dive out, just before reaching the rescue base. With Saman's death, a new sense of urgency arose. The operation now had a death count; the time for weighing options and playing things safely had ended.

Admiral Arpakorn came to see us. Making a last-ditch effort to save his zero-risk plan of letting the Boars wait in the cave, he asked if we'd assist with laying the oxygen hose through the sumps beyond Chamber 3. 'No,' we told him. 'We're not going to waste diving resources on that. Anyway, it won't work.'

'Would you dive in three months' worth of food?' Arpakorn asked us next.

'Absolutely not.' We wanted no part of it, and refused to provide the means of prolonging their deaths.

A few hours later, the four of us went to Chamber 3. The SEALs who had recovered (and attempted to revive) Saman's body earlier in the morning were still there. They were clearly traumatized, exhausted and emotional, and the mood in the cave was even more sombre than the one outside. Chris and Jason dived back to Chamber 9, to see the cave and meet the boys. They took in more food, along with wetsuits to be worn by the boys during their rescue. Jason, who'd had the brilliant idea to take in notes for the team that had been written by their families, also carried a waterproof pad and pencil for the boys to write their own messages in return. For the first time, the boys and the families would be communicating with each other directly.

John and I had initially planned to dive as well, but in the end we left it with them, realizing that we finally had an opportunity to sit without interruption and put together a rescue plan. Jason and Chris were diving, Gary Mitchell[17] was meeting with the officials, and Mike Clayton was with us to take notes and organize things. We spent the remainder of the afternoon planning the details and logistics of what the rescue dives might look like. Between the two of us, we had amassed a growing pile of lists and checklists. Mike Clayton was furiously writing notes and transcribing our plan as John and I talked.

For us, this was the fun part. John and I enjoy the challenge of solving complex logistical problems nearly as much as we love being underwater. There are very few activities, I've found, that equally require physical and mental engagement. Our extreme level of cave diving naturally combines these two things, as both elements have to work in partnership to achieve success. Tham Luang had provided both of these elements in extremis, and we relished being able to overcome them. This felt like an Olympic event we'd spent our lives training for.

After we talked at length about the best way to prepare the boys to be dived through the sumps, we focused on how to move them through the dry areas and canal passages. Ironically, the lack of rain – combined with the success of Thanet's water diversion – had created an additional problem. The passage between 7 and 8 had combined into one 150-metre-long walking stretch, which now required the victim being carried over boulders. We'd need to have two divers stationed in that chamber, with a stretcher.

We'd already begun counting on the help of the Euro Divers to provide support during the dive and to help move the boys through the drier chambers, but there were still some stations that needed to be filled. As we choreographed each step of each dive, working through each problem, it became apparent that we would need even more support from divers that we could trust. A few days earlier, when John and I had begun discussing our ideas with Derek, he had asked us, 'Who do you trust?' Only a few names had come to mind. In the whole world, I knew of only a handful of divers who would be comfortable and confident doing what was required for this operation. I had told him Jason's and Chris's names initially, but now we needed more. Next on the list was Connor Roe.

As the son of Ian Rolland and the adopted son of John Roe, Connor had truly been born and raised to be a cave diver. I knew him only casually but had been following his progression as he rose through the ranks in the diving community. Duncan Price had been mentoring him as a cave diver (only after being presented with a letter of permission from Erica, his mother). He'd sponsored Connor's admission into the CDG, and they had done a lot of diving together in Wookey Hole. I was confident that Connor would serve well on the team, and we requested that he be brought over, along with his diving partner, Josh Bratchley, and Jim Warny, a diver from Ireland. The three divers were soon being flown to Thailand. (Connor and Jim would arrive on Saturday; Josh, who was on holiday,[18] arrived on Sunday.)

We were devising a plan and assembling a team but still had not been given an official go-ahead to move forward with our plan to dive them out. John and I were growing increasingly frustrated and had been going around camp saying, 'If we don't fucking do something soon, they're all going to die.' On the mountainside, Josh Morris and Thanet Natisri had been hearing Vern speak of our frustration and they wanted to hear our thoughts for the rescue first hand. Vern brought them to us on Friday afternoon. This was the first time I'd met with Thanet and I learned details of the operation he was running in the mountain.

When Thanet first arrived, he had unintentionally left his GoPro camera running. John immediately spotted the camera's light and pointed it out. 'You've got your camera on. Turn it off.' Thanet obliged, and Josh looked a bit embarrassed. John and I had made the conscious decision to avoid all cameras and not to film anything ourselves, despite the fact that people might be expecting us to. We didn't think it was appropriate, we didn't want to be bothered, and we wanted to focus on the task ahead.

Josh Morris, an American living in Thailand with his wife and kids, is a member of the Chiang Rai rock-climbing club, many of whose members were searching the mountainside. (The first diver inside Tham Luang was also a member of this club.) After greeting us, Josh asked what we thought about the Thais' plan of letting them wait.

'It's not an option,' John told him, repeating what we had been trying to tell people for days. 'We have to dive them out.' Josh seemed to be one of the few there who understood that a decision needed to be made quickly. If we kept waiting, the decision would be made for us by the approaching monsoon.

He thought for a moment, then asked, 'OK, John, what will happen if we don't dive them out?' John looked Josh in the eye and said, 'All of them will die.' Just like that. He let his words sink in for a second before continuing. 'If we leave them there, all of them will die. If we dive them out, some of them might get a chance to survive.'

'What is "getting a chance"?' Josh asked.

John answered honestly, 'I couldn't say.'

On Friday, a so-called 'decision-making' meeting was held, with the Minister of the Interior present. This was meant to be the crucial meeting where something was decided, but (unsurprisingly) nothing was.

In the meantime, John and I were in our gear room planning the rescue, Jason and Chris were inside the cave taking in food and messages for the boys, and Harry and Craig were arriving in Thailand. We were tired of waiting, and we couldn't afford to lose more time, so we just kept going about with our plan. We didn't try to hide what we were doing, or what we were planning, and nobody bothered us. As John has pointed out, 'We kept moving forwards, and nobody told us to stop.'

10.
Mind What You're Doing

'Death must not play a part in the diver's thoughts,
since otherwise it would indicate that all necessary
precautions had not been taken.'

Jochen Hasenmayer

'How can a cave stop so suddenly?'

I was listening to a friend describing his recent dive in Saint Sauveur, another cave in the Lot region of France. I had first dived there
during that seminal 1991 trip with Steve and Dani and was aware
that it had been explored to a boulder choke at a depth of –87 metres.
A fair share of divers had since inspected that boulder choke, looking for a way on and unable to find one. My friend was one of those
divers, and, listening to his description, I agreed that it didn't sound
right. I'd been in the cave many times – it was one I liked diving –
but I hadn't seen any point in going to the end until he asked the
question. 'What do you think happened?'

'I won't know 'til I've been there,' I told him. There had to be a
reason for its end. I wanted to know what it was, and there was only
one way to find out.

I first returned to the cave in 2001, intent on understanding the
mechanism behind its apparent termination. That was my first trip
to France with a rebreather. (Coincidentally, I had bought a KISS

rebreather just weeks earlier, after seeing its ad in a magazine article. I knew that – for the first time – there was a rebreather that would be perfect for me. It was fully manual and did what it said. KISS = Keep It Simple Stupid.)

At Saint Sauveur's 'terminal' boulder choke, I saw clearly what had happened: the ceiling had collapsed, and the fallen boulders had filled the passage. It was indeed unpassable.

Inspecting the cave as I retreated, I'd spotted a ledge on the wall, which wasn't very obvious. When I got up close, I saw a shaft on the floor of that ledge; it was maybe a metre wide. You wouldn't spot it unless you were right on top of it, so others had gone right past. It instantly reminded me of an unusual feature in a Yorkshire cave.[1]

I descended into this fissure and when I re-emerged into the main tunnel, I found that I had bypassed the boulder choke.

For various reasons I was unable to return for several years and didn't get back until late 2005, when I followed the newfound passage to a depth of –120 metres. Continuing along the passage, I unexpectedly found myself at the top of a large vertical shaft. The space that suddenly opened below me was deep, unmeasurable. The light from my powerful torches was absorbed into the blackness below me, with no bottom in sight. It was at this point that I tore a massive hole in the glove of my drysuit, which completely flooded my suit with water.

I had to endure six hours of desperately cold decompression in this state. I was inverted from the ceiling like a bat – positioning my hand to maintain the hole at the lowest point to keep as much water out of my suit as possible. I was struggling for survival, while I watched other divers below me having a jolly nice time on their recreational dives, unaware that I was above them. I found this juxtaposition ironic, and it perfectly encapsulated the extreme nature of cave diving. There I was in a desperate situation while the novices, just metres below me, were having a great experience.

On a subsequent dive, I reached its bottom at −190 metres and found another huge tunnel leading off. I would have to explore it. Most deep cave diving around the world had all been vertical – people going down to these depths and then going straight back up – but there'd been hardly any instances of people descending to such a great depth and then continuing into new horizontal passage. I suspected this was the new frontier and I began focusing my efforts on making deep dives and increasing the time I was spending at depth. I was working up to the dive I'd be making in Saint Sauveur.

In the meantime, Jason and I were called out to recover the body of Norwegian diver Ståle Tveitane from Plura cave, the deepest cave in Norway, which was still being explored.[2] Always ones to do things the hard way, we headed straight for the bar on the overnight ferry to Bergen, a mistake that was paid for the following morning, when we spent three hours at 3,700 metres in a tiny, non-pressurized plane. By the time we disembarked in Rana, Norway, we were both looking and feeling pretty grim.[3] We were scheduled to begin searching for Ståle the next morning. Knowing that the cave reached a depth of −110 metres, we were prepared for a deep dive – with an ensuing long decompression – in the 6° C water.

Feeling as awful as you'd expect, Jason and I woke early to initiate the search.

Ståle's dive partner had last seen him 1,200 metres into the cave, at a depth of −75 metres; I was fairly confident that we would find him close to there, and I was correct. I found Ståle's body in a clean, roomy passage not far from where he had last been seen.

When we returned the following day for the recovery, I had with me Mark's sleeping bag stuff sack. This was Jason's first time dealing with a dead body and he had seemed uncomfortable with the thought of seeing Ståle's face up close, so when we reached the body, I slipped the sack over its head. Moving the body through the cave went as smoothly as could be expected. We had to use some trial and error to figure out ways to adjust and manage his buoyancy as we ascended, but we made it work. We strapped lead around his neck to keep him in trim and prevent him from floating into a vertical position, then snipped holes in the feet of his drysuit to vent air, and found creative ways to negate the expansion of internal air as we ascended through the cave.

I was alone with the body at my last deco stop – Jason's dive had been shorter, and he'd had less deco time. To keep from getting cold, I began swimming in circles while I waited for the fire service recovery divers to take the body away. There I was, −9 metres deep in a Norwegian cave, swimming circles around a dead body.

On the surface, Ståle's body had been laid on the ground, with policemen gathered and Jason in the water. One policeman began firing off questions about the lead necklace that was still circling Ståle's neck. (I understand why this would make him suspicious.) Another policeman began rinsing out the bag that had been used to cover the body's face. I watched as white flecks drifted away from the bag and headed straight towards Jason, who was mouth-deep in water.

'Get that fucking thing away from me!' Jason yelled.

This had certainly been an unusual, but educational, experience. Our first major, deep-cave body recovery. It wouldn't be our last.

⊕   ⊕   ⊕

The Pearse Resurgence in the South Island of New Zealand had been Oceana's prime deep-caving exploration site in recent years. I'd been asked to present at OZTek 2007, a technical diving conference that is held biennually in Australia, and I'd already learned to take advantage of these international dive conferences as a means of securing free airfare to visit caves around the world. I reached out to Dave Apperley, the expedition leader at Pearse, and told him I'd like to dive there, and he was agreeable.

I'd never met Dave before he came to collect me at the backpacker's hostel where I was staying. After he drove up in his van, we introduced ourselves, went to the supermarket and bought three weeks' worth of food, then drove into the middle of nowhere. When we arrived at the camp, I met Richard Harris and the other team members. Those who were going deep were all using complicated double rebreathers, and there I was wearing my homemade harness, with my small BOTS rebreather, and mismatched torches strapped to my helmet. I had designed my equipment for tight squeezes in Wookey, but didn't see why it wouldn't work equally well in this massive cave. I compared their equipment to my own.

'I seem to be using small-cave equipment in a big cave,' I laughed. Harry was beside himself at the state of my kit. When I had to ask to borrow his primary torch for my final dive, I was expecting him to make a comment about how I would probably benefit from replacing everything I was using.

Over the course of two dives, I extended the cave from its previous depth of −125 metres. On the second dive, I came upon a hole in the floor that looked like it was going deeper; I went down it and reached a depth of −177 metres. I could see that the cave continued descending and I was going to go further, but then my light imploded from the pressure.[4] There was a massive boom on my wrist, where the light head had been resting; it felt like my hand had

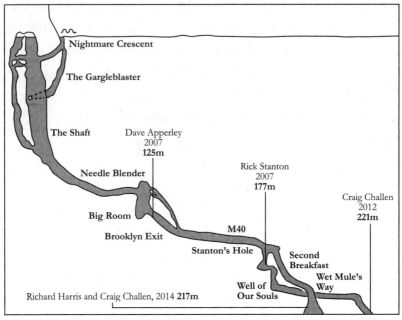

The Pearse Resurgence, New Zealand

imploded. While I was dealing with that, I dropped my reel down into the hole.

I knew that one of the Aussies would have the pleasure of continuing deeper into this cave, and I was happy to leave it for them.[5] As I was decompressing from that dive, Dave came down to meet me. I indicated with my fingers how deep I'd gone and his eyes widened as he looked at the ridiculous homemade rebreather I was wearing on my side.

'Well, that works, then,' he said.

I returned to Saint Sauveur on 19 September 2007, with John and Rupert Skorupka along as support divers, for a dive that none of us would forget anytime soon.

We knew this dive was going to be deep. I was using two rebreathers, with open-circuit cylinders stashed in the habitat to be used for the final, lengthy decompression stages. (I'd found I was able to switch off during these deco times, some of which lasted for numerous hours. Some people keep magazines or books to read at their deco stops – people these days even leave an electronic device waiting, so they can listen to music or watch a movie – but I've always preferred to spend these hours in silence, not thinking about anything.)

The plan for this dive was to descend the vertical shaft to −190 metres and then proceed horizontally as far as I could. I didn't want to be held back by the decompression time I'd be accumulating, so I was prepared with multiple rebreathers, the habitat and big batteries for my heated undersuit. We were so over-confident with our dual rebreathers – especially considering that John and I could swap rebreathers if we needed – that we didn't feel like we'd need a load of cylinders additionally staged for decompression. If things went as planned, I knew I'd be able to sustain myself underwater for twenty-four hours if I had to, with all of the rebreathers we had between us.

Things didn't go quite as planned.

When I got to the bottom of the shaft, my line reel wasn't where it should be. Reaching for it, my fingers encountered an empty D-ring instead. Fuck. It could have come unclipped anywhere in the cave. I should have turned the dive, but I didn't. We'd driven all the way to France for this, gone through all the trouble of mixing gases and setting everything up and getting everything ready. I wanted to keep going and I trusted my navigational skills.

Anyway, I've always said that a true cave diver follows the cave, not the line.

So, in spite of the lost reel and in spite of the tremor in my hands that was a sure sign that I was beginning to experience High Pressure Neurological Syndrome (HPNS), I set off into the unknown without a line. I still felt in control of the dive and I was committed to go onwards. The passage was ahead of me, open and clear, and I couldn't see any danger. Promising myself that I would stay in this passage, at this depth, without making any more turns, I made the mistake of pressing on.

After I'd travelled approximately 100 metres along the horizontal passage, there was still no end in sight. I was in a massive borehole whose clean, sculpted walls were layered with brown, yellow and black rock. I felt like I was inside an open artery deep inside the planet's crust. Not only was I travelling without a line, but the minutes spent at this depth were adding hours onto the time I would need to spend decompressing. With regret, I turned around and headed back for the vertical shaft I had descended through. I aimed straight for the place where I had emerged from my descent, and when I reached that spot, I looked up in preparation for my ascent.

Instead of seeing the vertical shaft above me, I found myself under a solid roof, with a blank wall of rock in front of me. Fuck. Deep inside a cave that had not been fully explored and mapped is not a place to become lost. Yet, there I was.

Don't panic. I had learned the importance of this early on in my diving. When something unexpected happens, stay calm and consider the options before making a decision. Act, don't react.

Breathing slowly, moving carefully, I began searching the rock around me. Minutes ticked by, and I was aware that each minute was loosening the grip of the guillotine that was suspended above me. I was carrying with me the realization that I had probably already killed myself. *I've been down here too long.* Even so, I couldn't just stop.

I had to find the way out.

I'd resigned myself to the fact that I wasn't getting out of the cave alive but I had to satisfy my curiosity and find the right way. I was annoyed that I had got it wrong. *This would be the one time I'm not able to find the way on, when I'm −190 metres deep. Typical.*

I kept looking, systematically searching the cave for a clue. In my imagination, the tunnel I was in should have led straight to the upward shaft, but I hadn't taken a complete picture of where I was. Actually, the base of the shaft was on a cross rift that intersected the tunnel; I had to go up and down the passage a few times to work it out. Finally, I saw the alcove in the side wall that I had passed by before. I dashed into it and found the shaft, open and soaring high above me.

Relief.

As soon as I located the route, I knew I'd be OK. I'd have to spend extra time decompressing, but I thought we had prepared for that. I began my exit. At my first stop, at −156 metres, when I checked my wrist-mounted dive computer to learn my deco obligation, I stared at the screen in disbelief.

Fifteen hundred minutes. Twenty-five hours. Shit.

John and Rupert aren't going to be very happy.

For various procedural and technical reasons not crucial to the story, after a while the computer settled on a new and revised time of fifteen hours. I've never been so grateful for a decompression obligation of fifteen hours.

Meanwhile, John had kept making dives down to −40 metres, expecting to find me decompressing. I had planned to only stay in the deep zone for a couple of hours, so when I failed to reappear in the shallower parts of the cave near the entrance, he began to assume the worst.

I finally appeared, a few hours later than expected, much to John's relief. Better late than never. We swam to each other, and I extended my arm to show the display on my dive computer.

His eyes widened as he read the computer. There were still at least twelve hours of deco time remaining, and my rebreathers were pretty much spent.

'I need your rebreather now,' I spoke to John through my mouthpiece, surprised by how calm my voice sounded.

'It's not working properly,' he told me in reply.

'I need it whatever,' I told him. This wasn't really up for debate. Without further discussion, we each removed our rebreathers and made the swap. As John swam towards the entrance with my rebreather, I looked at his electronically controlled Inspiration rebreather. 'I don't actually know how to use this,' I realized as I began fiddling around with the handset. While I tried to figure out how it worked, I noticed Rupert in the passage above me, staring with wide eyes.

John's rebreather was soon running low on its sodalime scrubber material, so it was about to become useless. My BOTS didn't have much either. By then, John had come back down with his side-mount rebreather, and I thought I was safe – a rebreather that was packed with fresh scrubber would last far longer than I needed – but when I tried to breathe from it, it wasn't working. John had always said that it was a bit temperamental, and I found myself unable to breathe through the mouthpiece without allowing water into the breathing loop.

When we had planned this dive, I'd decided to just go and do the dive I wanted to do and then worry about the decompression when it came. I was now realizing the flaw in that plan, as none of the rebreathers were behaving as they should.

After leaving me with his temperamental side-mount rebreather, John took my BOTS and his Inspiration back to the surface to refill them, so that they could get me through the decompression. Proving that we had failed to fully plan for everything that could go wrong on this dive, we hadn't brought enough CO_2 scrubber with us. He remembered the previous evening, after our set-up dive, when I had emptied and repacked my rebreathers. Desperate, he thought of the partially used scrubber material that I had thrown into the dustbin the night before. *It will have to do.*

John left Rupert with one clear instruction – 'Make sure he has something to breathe' – and drove to the campsite. I was powerless to do anything but stay where I was and keep breathing. My life was in John's hands at that moment. I was confident he'd figure something out, and there is probably no other person I would have had such faith in. He told me later that, while driving down the wooded road in the dark of the night, he kept his eyes focused intently on the road. 'I've never been so worried about getting into an accident,' he told me. 'I knew that if anything happened to me on that drive, you'd be dead in the cave.'

After John's side-mount rebreather had become unusable, I'd switched to the only open-circuit cylinder I had with me, even though it was filled with a mixed gas that was wildly inappropriate for decompression at that depth. There was a stash of cylinders in the habitat – a mere 15 metres above me – but I wouldn't be able to reach it safely for many hours.[6] Rupert kept pointing in alarm at the contents gauge on the cylinder I was breathing from, as its needle approached zero, while John was back at the campsite digging through rubbish bins.

Needless to say, this dive wasn't occurring quite as I'd planned.

I'd experienced decompression sickness once before, resulting from a dive in Elm Hole in 1990 – our original back door into Pwll-y-Cwm – during which I'd headed in the wrong direction for quite a distance before realizing my mistake and correcting myself. I used more gas than intended and, as it was quite early in my diving career, I was feeling a bit flustered by the time I got back to the bottom of the narrow entrance rift. I ascended more quickly than I should have. (I'm convinced I'd stayed within safe limits, but the added stress from the dive likely contributed to what happened next.)

Later that night, my hand began to feel numb, and I knew what was happening. The next day, I was driven to the hyperbaric chamber at Stoney Cove, where I spent six hours inside the pressurized recompression chamber. Two days later, I still felt something was wrong and was taken to see a specialist at a Royal Navy medical facility in Portsmouth. Back into another chamber for more decompression, then an overnight stay at the military hospital. My symptoms did not vanish for months, and to this day, I still have residual effects of that incident – from a dive that had never been deeper than –20 metres.

I later gained access to the doctor's notes from that visit in Portsmouth, which had been written by the Surgeon Commander of the Royal Navy: 'Mr Stanton engages in the highly dangerous pastime of exploring underwater caves. Not only am I concerned that he may not be temperamentally suited for this, he is planning further dives which sound particularly hazardous. If he should have further trouble with decompression sickness, we would be pleased to see him, and then it may be appropriate to try and dissuade him from continuing to dive in caves.'

I wonder what he'd think if I came back to him with this story, I thought idly as I hovered inside Saint Sauveur, breathing an inappropriate gas blend[7] from a nearly empty cylinder.

I stayed calm as I waited for John to return, which he did, just in time. He dived down to me with the freshly packed rebreathers, which got me through decompression until I could ascend to the habitat and switch to open-circuit oxygen. I emerged from the pool at 4 a.m., with no trace of decompression sickness. At 9 a.m. we had to dive again to clear all the cylinders out before rushing across France to catch the ferry.

Amidst the chaos of the morning, Rupert reflected on the events.

'That was a great dive,' he said drily. 'It felt like eight hours of spinning plates to keep you alive.'

The following year, John and I were back in France, but this time we were pushing the Goul de la Tannerie cave, in the Ardèche. I reached a depth of −222 metres on one dive, marking the deepest I would go in a cave. John came down to meet me as I ascended from that dive. This time, thankfully, I arrived on time.

'Thank fuck for that,' I heard him say into his rebreather mouthpiece.

I had panicked on that very early dive in the Dudley Mines with Steve, when I'd bolted for the surface after my demand valve had frozen. Since then, as the difficulty of my dives steadily increased, so had my tolerance for the dangers that are attached to them. Staying calm in the face of danger has been practised countless times over the years, as the dangers have increased. Assess the environment, consider the options, keep moving forwards one step at a time, find the way on.

By the time I was diving in Saint Sauveur, this calm response in the face of danger had been strengthened to the point where it had come effortlessly when it was needed. Even when that dive seemed to have gone horribly wrong and the consequences seemed final, I'd never lost control. *One breath after another, find the way on.*

This ability paid off for me again the following year, in the Resurgence de Marchepied, a cave not far from the Ressel. In 2008, it was a newer cave that was just being explored. The high CO_2 levels between the sumps left it unappealing to most, but I wanted to see what was in there. On my first dive, I reached the line's end at a depth of −50 metres in the third sump. Beyond that, the cave continued to descend towards a gravel squeeze.

Of course, a gravel squeeze.

I knew there was an element of risk, but I felt confident it would be one I could manage as I'd had success in gravel squeezes before. The roof was very low, and I used my method of sweeping the gravel away from me to set off avalanches that I could ride down, as I had done in Wookey. I had my side-mounted rebreather clipped to my harness and a back-up cylinder strapped to my chest. Things went well to a depth of −65 metres, as I carried on riding the mini-avalanches I was creating in the gravel. Then, at an awkward low spot, the gravel began to back up on either side of me, and I became effectively buried. The belt of my harness had become caught on a rocky projection hanging from the roof; I was stuck in place, unable to move forwards. The cylinder on my chest had become buried into the gravel beneath me and was acting like an anchor; I was wedged in.

I remembered the question I was always asked at dive shows, after talking about gravel squeezes: 'What happens if you get stuck?'

I would always give the same answer, perhaps a bit smugly: 'Don't get stuck.'

I guess it was inevitable that one day I would get stuck, and of course it would happen when I was three sumps into a cave, −65 metres underwater and underground. After a decades-long love–hate relationship with gravel squeezes, that relationship seemed to have reached its climax here, inside a cave in France.

I lay at a steep downward incline in the gravel-filled passage. I couldn't move forwards or backwards. Despite my well-honed calm response, I felt my heartrate begin to quicken, and I had to fight to control it. *Don't panic.*

I considered my resources. Thanks to my rebreather, the one thing I had in my favour was time. I could last here for ages.

I considered the environment. The passage was low, but it was also wide.

I considered my options. I couldn't move forwards or backwards, but I might be able to rotate. Inch by inch, degree by degree, I began to turn around.

Keep moving onwards, one step at a time. Soon enough I was able to unclip the bottle on my front, freeing myself from the anchor that had kept me wedged. Further rotation freed my belt from the roof's projection. Eventually I was perpendicular to the passage, lying across it; then I was fully turned around, facing up the slope and towards the exit. This was by far the better direction to be facing.

I began clearing the gravel in front of me more easily, excavating a small channel and moving back up the slope until the passage opened up again and I moved out of the squeeze. The process of freeing myself probably took only ten minutes, although it felt much longer while it was happening. I retreated through the sump and made my way out of the cave safely.

Not to be deterred from finishing a project I'd started, I returned a few days later. Back to the third sump, back to the gravel squeeze, but this time I'd come prepared. I'd purchased a garden hoe at a nearby hardware store and shortened its handle to make it more cave-friendly. At the squeeze, I used the hoe to clear a path in the gravel ahead of me and passed through without incident. *There's my gardening for the year.*

The cave beyond didn't go much further, as I quickly met with a boulder choke that looked loose and unstable. I wasn't tempted by anything I saw there, so I turned and made my way out through the gravel squeeze to exit the cave.

I left the hoe tied to the diving line at the start of the gravel squeeze. *Somebody else may need this one day.*

Looking back, I can see quite clearly that my ability to stay calm and think rationally in these seemingly dire situations are likely what kept me alive. Although these skills have certainly been strengthened over the years, I do attribute some of it to my upbringing. Although I was shy, it was never because I lacked confidence. Even as a child, I never became frightened or upset very easily. When something went wrong, my interest increased as I set to figuring out what had gone wrong, and how to make it right.

The very teachers at school who'd criticized me for laziness and excessive daydreaming had also credited this aspect of my personality. One year, my form teacher, Mr Boreham – the one who'd described my 'near comatose condition' and 'economy of effort' – had written: '[Richard] will need to show greater urgency and determination. But his unruffled nature should stand him in good stead.'

This unruffled nature held me in good stead during my speaking presentations, as well as in cave diving. Many people will list public speaking as one of their greatest fears, and it took me a long time to pluck up the courage for it. Once I'd taken the plunge, though, I found I wasn't fazed or shy – not even when things went wrong.

During one particularly high-profile engagement, I was on stage and had just begun speaking when the IT failed, and I found myself standing in front of a 700-strong audience with nothing to show. Terence Stamp had presented before me – I like to say he was my warm-up act – and was seated in the front row, watching me.

I froze, to consider my options – *Right. What am I going to do?* – and quickly came out with a joke to fill the dead air. 'Oh no, I'm scared of the dark.' Just then Terence jumped in to back me up, asking me a question from the audience, which further set me at ease. After that, I was going again and finished the talk.

Frank Gardner, the BBC's security correspondent, went on to present after me. 'I can't follow that . . .' he'd said when he took to the stage, then went on to graciously describe me as being 'casually confident'.

'We devised a simple plan on the premise that simpler is safer.'

Friday, 6 July 2018, Thailand

Harry and Craig arrived at Tham Luang on Friday in the early evening, after being confined to their hotel room in Mae Sai as they waited for Harry's local medical registration to come through. Now with six divers, two members of the BCRC providing surface support and a growing number of allies who were advocating for our plan to dive the boys out, John and I were no longer feeling like we were alone in a hostile environment.

As we were showing the Australians around the rescue area, Jason and Chris returned from their dive to Chamber 9. Jason had brought back handwritten messages from the boys to their families. These personal communications to their parents reminded everyone once again that there were thirteen lives depending on us.

Titan: 'Mum, Dad, Don't worry, I'm OK, please tell Yod to prepare to take me to eat fried chicken, Love you.'

Adul: 'I miss everybody. I really need to go back home.'

Coach Ek: 'All the kids are fine. There are people taking really good care of them. I promise I will take care of the children the best I can. Thank you for your support. I'm really sorry to the parents.'

In addition to allowing them to learn the cave and meet the boys, the dive had also given Jason and Chris a first hand look at the capabilities of the people who were supposed to be the ones in control.

'You do know that the SEALs used up most of their air diving in?' Jason asked me, soon after returning from his dive with Chris.

'I checked the contents of their cylinders, and they're all pretty much empty.' John and I looked at each other and shook our heads. *They don't have air to get themselves out. Unbelievable.* At least that explained why they had stayed in the cave, but I couldn't believe that nobody had bothered telling us that the men were trapped in there without air. On Wednesday's food run, the SEALs had asked us to bring in two masks for them – because somehow they'd lost the ones they'd worn – but they never thought to ask for cylinders of air to get out. I couldn't imagine what they thought was going to happen but I didn't have time to worry about it.

At a meeting in our room, with everyone present, we began reviewing the various components of the plan we had put together, while trying to conceal the most crucial part. Because the Americans were present, we didn't want to voice the 'one-diver/one-boy' component that we'd agreed was the only way to proceed. We weren't sure what Derek's and Hodges' stance on this was, and we couldn't be bothered trying to convince them. ('No one is going to know what we're doing in the sumps, are they?' Jason had pointed out, to settle the debate.)

This initially led to a bit of confusion at the meeting with Harry and Craig, as I hadn't had time to explain that side of things to them yet, but after the Americans left we got everyone on the same page.

The four core divers – John, Jason, Chris and I – would each dive one boy out per day. That person would be solely responsible for the boy, all the way through the cave. The support divers – Euro Divers Claus Rasmussen, Mikko Paasi, Erik Brown and Ivan Karadzic, plus Josh Bratchley, Connor Roe and Jim Warny – would be stationed in chambers throughout the cave, where they would provide support for the core diver and help to move the boys along. At Chamber 3, we'd hand our boy over to the Americans and the SEALs who'd be waiting there to check the boy over.

The next component of the plan: how to best configure the boys so that they would be easily transportable. John and I described the plan we had cemented the day before. The boys would be brought out face-down, to keep their airways clear since they couldn't be intubated. The cylinder would hang below them as we dived, secured with bungee at their chest and thighs. We would have to bind their arms and legs together – to form them into streamlined packages that would not catch on rocks or become entangled in the line, while also keeping them (and us) safe in case they came round. Jason quickly came up with a quick-release handcuff system, using cable ties and a carabiner. (Don't ask me how – or why – this was second nature to him.)

I quite like the fact that our plan hinged on cable ties and bungees; they were really the unsung heroes of this rescue.[8] It was all very much in line with my propensity for finding low-tech solutions for problems – like my wing. Because of its simplicity, I felt confident of its success.

The boys would be wearing a lifejacket-style buoyancy device, which Jamie Brisbin had already modified by adding a nylon-tape crotch strap to keep it from riding up. They'd also reduced the existing nylon harness – to better fit the boys' smaller frames – which had then created a carrying handle in the centre of the back. The idea was to package the boy up so that he could be handled like a shopping bag, to carry along with us on our dive. After I'd referred to the boys several times as an 'inert package', Harry jokingly began calling the rescue plan 'Stanton's Inert Package Plan'.

The face masks were probably the single most important thing (aside from Harry's sedation) that would allow this plan to be successful. We would be using full-face positive pressure masks.[9] The mask would cover the boy's entire face, with gas being constantly supplied from a cylinder, meaning that the boys would not need to hold the regulator in their mouth; they would just need to keep breathing. With a positive pressure mask, the pressure inside the mask is greater than the surrounding atmosphere – so any leak would be air going out, rather than water going in. Some protection was provided, but it wasn't risk-free. A faulty seal would drain the cylinder more quickly, for example.[10]

During a previous discussion of the masks, Mitch Torrel posited the idea of having the boys breathe 100 per cent oxygen, and we all immediately agreed that this was sound. Saturating their body tissue with oxygen could sustain them for a few minutes without breathing – if needed – and there were certainly enough cylinders of oxygen on site. Anything that we could do to increase the odds would be worthwhile.

Next, Harry began discussing his part – the sedation process.

He had consulted with colleagues – including anaesthetists and doctors specializing in underwater/diving medicine – and had settled on a plan to use ketamine, but he still couldn't commit to it. In all the history of medical journals around the world, he had been unable to find any empirical evidence of a human ever being sedated underwater. That didn't even bring in the main complication facing our boys: we were most worried by the fact that they would not be intubated. Intubation is a standard protocol for sedation, and for a reason.

The only bit of anecdotal evidence he had found that might be useful came from research on using ketamine with seals – the marine animal, not the Navy version. Researchers for the Australian Antarctic Division[11] reported on seals that had escaped after receiving sedation with ketamine. When the seals were later found floating in the sea, they were fully sedated yet with their noses in the air and breathing safely. Their airways had been maintained. One anecdote on marine mammals was hardly convincing, but that was all Harry had found.

The whole proposition now largely hinged on that anecdote. We were asking Harry to do something that went right out beyond any medical knowledge, to help us with a plan that he was convinced would kill some, or all, of the boys. It was unthinkable to anaesthetize somebody, without having the patient intubated and actively monitored. No doctor would ever agree to do that. And then to dive them through a cave? It was ludicrous. The only reason he was even considering it was because he knew this was more humane than any alternative.

'Will you do this, Harry?' I asked him. There was a long pause before he answered.

'I can't agree to anything until I dive in the cave. I have to see the place where I'm going to be sedating them.' I understood his need to see what his impromptu operating theatre would look like, so he could begin to plan the best way to work in such unusual conditions.

'I'll need to see the boys, to know their size and weight for correct dosages. I have to work out whether it's even possible.' This was his answer, but I suspected there was more. I had a feeling that Harry wanted to connect with them on a human level before showing up with syringes. It would make things easier for all of them, I suspected, if they had already met before the day of the rescue. I understood all of that, but the last thing he said took me by surprise.

'I'll have to tell them what we're going to do,' he said decisively.

To satisfy these conditions, we decided that Harry and Craig would dive to Chamber 9 the following morning, Saturday. I told Harry that Dr Pak was back there with the boys. The doctor is fluent in both English and Thai, so Harry would be able to speak with the boys through him. I began imagining the conversation that would have to be held, and I was grateful that Harry was the one who would be holding it.

For one final piece of business, Harry dropped the bombshell: although he'd administer the initial dosage, ketamine wears off quickly and would need to be topped up with booster shots during the rescue. Those booster shots would have to be administered by us, in the cave.

'The safest injection site will be the boy's thigh, through his wetsuit,' Harry told us. He gave a brief lesson on how to provide injections, then we all spent a few minutes practising our technique on plastic water bottles.

'Harry went to university for nine years to become an anaesthetist; we were given a five-minute course,' I said to Jason. 'What could possibly go wrong?'

While we were all doing our own thing, practising with the water bottles, Harry came over to talk to me. He sat down in the chair beside me before I realized what he was doing and – crack! – he sat right onto my reading glasses. Across the room, John's head snapped up at the sound. He looked at the broken glasses in Harry's hand, then he looked at me. *Oh, no.*

Harry started to apologize, but then stopped when he remembered that I'd broken – and never replaced – his dive light years earlier in the Pearse Resurgence. 'I guess this makes us even,' he said with a smile.

I was laughing. Now I had a perfect excuse to use my pinhole lens technique.

After we adjourned our meeting, Harry and Craig were called to the first in a series of meetings with Thai medical authorities, where they were interviewed at length about their medical experience and about the sedation techniques being used. The Thais, understandably, wanted to ensure that I had called in somebody who knew what he was doing, and not just any old quack.

Saturday, 7 July 2018

For half that week – since John and I had begun putting together the plan – I'd been walking around muttering, 'What we need is boys to practise this with, in a swimming pool.' I didn't realize that people had actually been listening, but when we arrived at Tham Luang early on Saturday morning, I was told that it had been arranged. Our team began filing back into Tom's and Bas' van, to be driven to the swimming pool of a nearby elementary school. But first –

'John, look at this. Is this legitimate?'

I'd just received an email asking me to phone Elon Musk, the South African billionaire and inventor. At first, I thought it was a ploy by a clever journalist who was fishing for information. *As if Elon would be wanting to speak to me.*

John looked at the email I'd received. 'That looks like it could be his email address,' he said. 'I think it's real.' I rang the number I'd been given and was immediately connected to Elon.

The chief designer of SpaceX and founder of The Boring Company was known to be a philanthropist, and he had recognized that his skills and resources might be of assistance to us in Thailand. On the phone, he told me his engineers were designing a tube that we could use to carry the boys during the rescue. An escape pod, if you will. He needed specifics about the cave now, to inform the designing process. I talked to him briefly, aware that the others were loaded onto the van and waiting to go to the swimming pool.

Finally, after trying to bring the conversation to a natural end, I was forced to cut the call short. 'I really must go,' I told Elon. I hoped that his team might come up with something that we could work with. (We'd continue the conversation later in the day via email messages.)

We all knew that the integrity of the face mask's seal would likely be the failure point, and we were open to hearing options to address this risk. We didn't have a Plan B. I hadn't been able to think of another plan with any of the materials that were available to us, but maybe if something useful could be created by a team of engineers . . . John and I agreed that if anybody could help us, it was Elon Musk. Because John and I are both engineers (he with a degree, me without), we were interested in seeing what Elon's team would come up with. Even if it wasn't something we could use for this rescue, it could be useful in a future rescue. It's never too early to begin planning.

While I'd been speaking with Elon, John had fielded a phone call from his brother, who'd left John with some troubling news.

'Rick, there's a problem,' he said after I'd finished talking with Elon. 'My mum's agreed to go on the telly!' He looked absolutely horrified at the thought and I laughed at his predicament. They'd already reached out to my sister Jane, who had refused an interview. John's mum had been more willing to talk, and she was set to appear on live TV on Monday morning. As we walked out to meet the others in the van, I tried to console John. 'It'll be all right. I'm sure she won't tell any of the really embarrassing stories . . .'

Four volunteer boys from a swimming club in Mae Sai were waiting for us at the swimming pool of the local secondary school,[12] along with a bunch of cylinders, small-sized wetsuits and the four positive pressure full-face masks. We were being given the opportunity to stage a full-dress rehearsal, with the hope of identifying any element of the plan that wouldn't work. Jamie Brisbin and Mitch Torrel were there at the pool with us, along with members of the Thai medical corps, Jay (the SEAL in Chamber 3) and several senior government officials. We knew the Americans were there to help us, and I figured the members of the medical corps were there to oversee the sedation, but I wasn't sure about the others. I guess they just wanted to watch.

John and I began preparing the first boy, going through the steps as we'd planned.

Put him in a wetsuit.

Put a hood on him.

Bungees under the arms and around the thighs.

Put the buoyancy jacket on.

Put a 6-pound block of lead in the jacket.

Fit the crotch strap. We got into waist-deep water.

Put the mask on.

Then he was submerged, to test the mask for leaks. After securing the straps tightly, we lowered the boy further. Breathing from his mask, face down, we watched closely for a leak and saw none. It worked. No water was entering the mask, and when asked if he was OK, we were given a thumbs-up sign.

Once we knew the seal was good, the cylinder was put in place. We pulled the upper bungee out through the neck hole of his jacket and slipped it over the valve at the top of the cylinder. The lower bungee was stretched around the bottom of the cylinder. The lead and the cylinder acted in conjunction as a sort of ballast and as the keel of a ship, weighting the boy down, holding him face-down and steady in the water. The cylinder would also act as a buffer during the rescue, to ride over protrusions on the floor.

Jason and Chris, kitted up in their diving gear and waiting in the pool, began diving with the boy. I watched as they took turns moving him around underwater. Keeping the boys' airway open was always our biggest concern. With the boy in the pool, we were pleased to note that the extra buoyancy created by the full-face mask had the added benefit of keeping his head lifted up and back, so the airway wouldn't be compromised. They weren't going to be intubated, but this performed a similar function. I was pleased to see that Stanton's Inert Package Plan was working exactly as we'd hoped it would. We'd thought of everything.

After a while John caught my attention.

'Nobody's interested any more,' he said, gesturing to the men by the pool, who had been watching over us intently when we'd started. 'They've seen it works and they're all on their phones.' I looked over at the distracted men and laughed. They seemed to be convinced that we knew what we were doing. I called Amp over to the side of the pool.

'I don't know if we've got permission to sedate the boys?' I asked her. Her eyebrows rose in surprise.

'These boys here? You want to sedate them?' she asked.

'Isn't that why the medics are here? To watch over the boys while they're unconscious?'

'I don't know why they're here,' she said. 'Do you really want to sedate them?'

'We'd like to see how the boys will fare breathing underwater while unconscious,' I told her. Because this had never been done before, nobody had any clue if their airway would be maintained and if they would keep breathing. All of our careful planning couldn't really control that. 'It would be a very beneficial morale-boost if we can see it all works.' Amp went over to speak to the medics. I saw them going back and forth for a few minutes before they got on their phones and began making phone calls. She walked back over to me.

'They refused,' she told me. 'That had never been part of their plan. It's completely unethical, and they're not going to do it.' She paused, and I suspected there was something she wasn't telling me.

'Who are they calling now?' I asked her.

'I convinced them to let you sedate me instead,' she said. 'They're finding some ketamine to use.'

I looked at her, aghast. *Why the fuck would you offer that without speaking to me first?*

'I'm not going to sedate you,' I told her.

'Why not? It will be helpful, like you said. This way, you can finish the test.'

She couldn't be dissuaded. The more I argued against the idea, the more passionately she insisted on going through with it. Finally, I appealed to her desire to help.

'Amp, the rescue could be starting tomorrow. We're going to need you to be conscious. I haven't got any extra capacity to be looking after an unconscious you today, while I'm preparing myself for the rescue.' I wasn't the only one she had been looking after; in the past few days, all of us had come to appreciate the things she was doing behind the scenes, to keep things running smoothly for us all.

She finally relented, and the search for ketamine was halted. I watched her sit down on the side of the pool, disappointment written clearly across her face.

She's so stubborn.

By the time we arrived back at Tham Luang in the early afternoon, things were beginning to change on site. Green mesh privacy screens were being put up in certain areas. The whole mood had shifted. We were met immediately by the Americans, who wanted to stage a Rehearsal of Concept drill. Similar to the dress rehearsal we had just held at the pool, the ROC drill is like a tech run-through before a stage performance, making sure that everybody knows where they need to be, and what they need to be doing, through every part of the performance.

As the Americans finished setting up, I stopped at our gear room to drop off my bag. I was amused – and disappointed – to see a brand-new pair of reading glasses sitting for me on a chair. I couldn't imagine when Harry would have had time to go somewhere to buy them. 'I guess this puts me back into his debt,' I thought ruefully and tucked the glasses into my pocket as I went out to join the ROC.

Traffic tape had been laid out on the ground to mark the line of the cave, with plastic chairs set to represent each chamber. Scores of water bottles had been wrapped with different-coloured tape to represent air or oxygen; they were also used to represent the thirteen boys. We played ourselves, with two Americans standing in for Harry and Craig, and we walked through each step of the rescue. Starting from Chamber 3, we moved between the chairs and placed ourselves in the correct order as we would be during the rescue, swapping cylinders as planned. We timed our departures, so we all ended up at the right place at the right time and didn't bump into each other.

Governor Narongsak and all the top military brass were watching closely. Aware of this, we started the ROC by showing them the way we assumed they still wanted the rescue to be conducted: two divers with each boy. I didn't want them to refuse the plan on this technicality, at this stage.

As expected, it was clunky and convoluted, with divers either clashing with others or effectively doing nothing for long stretches of time. The process was grossly inefficient, each diver had to do two journeys, and the second diver didn't add anything whatsoever. Because it hadn't looked smooth and they weren't convinced, we were asked to run through it again.

'Right. We're going to do it one-on-one this time.' One diver with one boy, all the way from Chamber 9 to Chamber 3. As expected, this method was much more streamlined and efficient, with much less confusion, and this run-through ended in half the time. I'm not sure if the officials even appreciated the difference – they didn't know what they were looking at – but we knew. There was no further mention of attempting two divers with one boy.

The dual successes of the day were leading to our growing confidence for the next day's rescue. We were still waiting on Harry's go/no-go decision, though. Soon after we finished clearing up the water bottles and garden chairs, the Aussies returned from their dive. I could see from the looks on their faces that everything had gone well, and Harry confirmed it. He had seen the boys, seen the chamber and had explained everything he'd be doing. The boys had agreed to the process, and now Harry was ready to proceed with the plan for sedation. Aware that his involvement carried both professional as well as emotional risks (his wife, Fiona, had pointed out that if things went wrong, it could be the end of his career), we knew that Harry needed additional protection. Before long, the Australian consulate and Thai government came to an agreement that would provide him with diplomatic immunity. We didn't want him ending up in a Thai prison if something went wrong, and the boys died.

The British embassy had a less diplomatic strategy in mind and had devised an escape plan for us. Should things go wrong, we would be put into an unmarked minibus and driven through back roads to the British embassy in Bangkok, where we would be held until we could be extricated. It would all be very James Bond.[13]

We were ready. We knew we were as prepared as we could be, so we retired to our rooms to unwind a bit after the very hectic and productive day. Everything was ready to go, but we were still hanging in limbo, waiting for the official approval. I didn't understand what they were still waiting for, or what they were uncertain of. I didn't know how else to convince them, if nothing else had done so.

Immediately after finding the boys, we'd been forbidden from diving and placed into advisory roles, yet all week we'd kept moving forwards, without consent. Diving food to the boys, bringing nine people in from abroad, holding the rehearsal at the swimming pool and then the ROC on site. Nobody had stopped us from doing anything. The Minister of Tourism had even been arranging the flights for the people we'd called over.

As the days had dragged on with no progress being made, I knew many people were losing hope that things were going to end well. I also knew that some of our friends back home were trying to reassure the people who had become sceptical. 'The boys will be fine . . . Rick and John can do this.' When no move had been made by the end of the week, one friend had been asked directly if she still thought I'd get them out. 'Yeah, of course,' she'd answered confidently. 'Rick wouldn't still be there if he didn't know he could do it. He's not one to take on jobs he can't finish.'

I appreciated their support but I didn't have their confidence, not this time. Although I was never afraid for myself or John – I knew we could handle ourselves in the cave – the ceaseless weight of responsibility for the boys' lives was draining, and this wasn't helped by the frustrations we'd been facing with the other teams at the site. I wish we could have just got on with the rescue we'd wanted to do.

I always felt the rescue was within the range of what we could do. Yet I acknowledged that this rescue would be unlike any of the other rescues I'd ever done in caves and floods or with the fire service. Typically, a rescue involves taking somebody from a place of danger and moving them to a place of safety. What we were going to do here was hugely unique. We'd be taking the boys from somewhere that had relative short-term safety, then moving them through an exceptionally hazardous environment to get them to a place where – if they survived the journey – they would be permanently safe.

'The probability of success was about as low as you can get,' Major Charles Hodges has said. 'I was fully expecting that we would accept casualties. Maybe three, four, possibly five would die.'

Harry was even less optimistic, predicting a 'zero per cent chance of success'. I didn't accept that assessment, and he probably didn't really think that; I don't know if he was just trying to cover himself.

There were too many risks that couldn't be properly controlled for. We had all accepted the possibility of boys dying during the rescue; we had even discussed what we would do with the bodies when that happened.

'Once you set off with that kid, it's a one-way journey,' I had told Jason and Chris when I'd explained the plan to them. 'The boy will be coming out, dead or alive.' We wouldn't be leaving any inside.

We had managed the risks as much as we could, and now we had to make a choice. Are we going to accept the risks, or are we going to walk away? For us, walking away was never a valid option. We'd come this far, it was time to finish.

My thoughts didn't keep me awake for long. Soon, I was fast asleep, still having no clue what we would be doing the next day. Whatever it was, I knew we were as prepared as we could be.

After the discussion with Thanet, John, and me the previous afternoon, Josh Morris had had a chance encounter with General Buncha Duriyaphan. Josh and the general were already acquainted through Josh's wife, a competitive Thai climber, so Josh felt comfortable approaching him and speaking candidly. 'Do you know what the divers are saying? If you don't do something soon, they're all going to die.'

This was overheard by a gentleman wearing a blue shirt and yellow bandana. Unbeknownst to me, these men that I had been seeing around Tham Luang were members of the Royal Guard, political figures with high-level connections. They were always present at the meetings, and they'd report things back to the King. They were on top of things, more than most people there, and they were powerful.

After hearing Josh's warning, it was the King's Guard who finally got things going.

'We need to organize a meeting.'

After getting the ball rolling Friday evening, a second meeting was held late on Saturday. Josh Morris, Gary Mitchell, several of the Americans and Thanet Natisri were all passionately and rationally arguing why we had to begin our planned rescue the following morning. Minister of the Interior Anupong Paochinda, General Duriyaphan, Rear-Admiral Arpakorn, and members of the Royal Guard were listening. Finally, Hodges stepped forward and laid it on the line. 'Sir. There is no zero-risk option. We have the option of saving some, maybe all of them, or we have the option of letting them sit there for the next four or five months, and I can pretty much tell you they're all going to die.'

The Minister of the Interior stepped away to consult on the phone with someone 'in higher authority'. When he returned, he nodded. With that nod, the approval was given for us to begin our rescue the next day. I'll never know for certain, but my instinct tells me that, in the end, our permission came from His Majesty himself. Who else would the Minister of the Interior have talked to, if not the King?

While I was lying awake in my room, mentally walking through the steps of our plan, a shield was erected around the Rescuers' Area, and all media were cleared from the mountainside. After three or four days during which myths and rumours had begun spreading through the international media, there was a new buzz – *something is happening* – and then silence.

PART FOUR
Perform

11.
Bunch of Baldy Boffins

'Experience is everything at this level, but after
40 years activity in this sphere I struggle to contemplate
what these guys are about to do.'

Martyn Farr, in his write-up of the 2010
Pozo Azul expedition[1]

I love my Land Rover Defender. It's a simply engineered British off-road vehicle that could take me anywhere. One of their mottos is, fittingly, 'Don't follow me; you won't make it' – something that has been said in regard to me more than once, and usually by Duncan. (*'Don't try to emulate anything Rick does . . .'*) It's big enough to fill with all the gear I would need, and it makes a comfortable-enough bedroom when needed. Like all of my favourite things, it's simple and robust, rugged and versatile. However, it does have the annoying habit of failing me at the most crucial times. A friend has said that my Land Rover fulfils the role of a demanding and temperamental mistress.

In 2009, I was days behind schedule due to work and already in a bad mood. Then, at the ticketing office at the Dover ferry port, my beloved Land Rover – fully loaded with cylinders and equipment – broke down with a catastrophic clutch failure. Bollocks. (The irony is that I had been expecting trouble with the Landy – I was carrying a spare gear box with me, knowing it was on its way out. I just had predicted the wrong problem.)

John, Jason and René Houben were at the cave in Spain and setting up for our big dive; I was already running late. Thinking fast, I was relayed to a car compound, hired a rental car and drove to Coventry with some of my equipment. A friend agreed to lend me her van, so I got a train down to London, picked up her van and drove back to Coventry. After packing the equipment into the van, I drove down to Dover, picked up the stuff that was still in the Land Rover, took the ferry and then drove to Spain. I was hugely motivated for this project. Nothing was going to keep me from getting to Spain.

Pozo Azul had first been explored in 1979 by Spanish cave divers who had dived 700 metres through its first sump and then travelled across 300 metres of dry tunnel to reach a second sump. In 1991, a different team of divers reached 780 metres into the second sump.

Those divers had hardly touched the surface – it was vastly lagging behind the limits of exploration that had been accomplished in other European caves – when Rupert suggested it as a next project. I didn't have the time or bandwidth to take it on as a project, but Jason immediately set to work. Returning to the cave year after year – sometimes alone, sometimes with Rupert or René – Jason kept inching the line forwards. By 2008, he'd gone over 3.5 kilometres – nearly twice the length of the Ressel – and the sump still showed no sign of ending.

There was a setback in 2008, when Jason fell ill and was unable to complete his dive. A German team led by our old friend Reinhard Buchaly mounted its own exploration in the cave and extended Jason's line in the second sump. Reinhard – perhaps thinking he could exact revenge for our success in the Ressel – had broken cave-diving etiquette by barging in while Jason was actively exploring the cave.

Jason was furious. Realizing that working alone left him vulnerable, he was spurred to organize an expedition team to support his efforts. Jason brought in me, John and René to formally join his team, and we all accepted. (Although they had dived together previously, I believe this was the first time that John and Jason worked together on a project.)

I'd stayed abreast of the work Jason was doing in Pozo and I knew he'd found a good cave. Pozo was similar to the Ressel in many ways – the imposing sump, the potential for massive exploration, the use of advanced equipment that suited both dry and wet caving, the need to camp beyond the sump. Yet Pozo took everything a bit further, with more challenges involved – for one, the massive dives were in the second sump, which meant that setting up for the dives occurred 1,000 metres into the cave, between sumps.

We'd be deep in our element with this project.

I'd phoned Reinhard to learn about his dives, but he was reticent about giving information that would help us to progress. I went to his website and easily found a computer dive profile that Reinhard had posted. Where Jason had last been, the cave was still deep at –60 metres, but on Reinhard's dive profile we saw that he'd ascended to –40 metres. This indicated he'd passed the sump's elbow, and it was now rising. Reinhard must have caught his mistake, because the post was soon taken down, but I had already learned everything I needed. If this trend was to continue and it was to surface, we would be in our exploration element – and Reinhard, we had observed, would not be.

Energized by the new project, we'd planned our 2009 dive with intensity . . . and with a lot of equipment. Four underwater habitats would be used – one wheelie bin like the one in the Ressel, and three Industrial Bulk Containers (IBCs), which the support divers had the job of towing in. I'd be diving with my KISS and BOTS rebreathers, two huge 20-litre cylinders and three scooters. I'd be riding atop my main one, which had previously been owned by Olivier Isler, while the two smaller scooters would be clipped to my harness and towed behind me. Isler had heavily modified the scooter for his dives in the Doux du Coly and it was massive – over 2 metres long and weighing almost 100 kilos.[2]

For this dive, we would be using everything – all of the knowledge, skills and equipment that we had spent years accumulating. Everything we each had done over the course of our caving and diving careers had been preparation for this, and we knew this would likely be the apex of our learning curve. As we would be travelling further into an underwater cave than we had ever been, this wouldn't be the place for anything to go wrong.

While I was held up by my broken-down Land Rover in England, Jason, René and John had set off on their dive together. Jason had an equipment failure and had to turn around, leaving John and René to extend the line. When I still hadn't arrived, Jason dived on his own, doing an impressive dive that ended 5,020 metres into the sump, at a depth of just –6 metres.[3] This was important.

When I finally arrived at Pozo, Jason greeted me with facts. 'We're over 5 kilometres in. It's going to surface. We'll put all our efforts into getting you there.'

'This is your project,' I pointed out. 'Why don't we support you?' It would have been a colossal undertaking getting all his equipment turned around for him to dive again, but it seemed fair. Competition exists between teams, but never within them.

He laughed. 'Right. I've done my big dive. It's yours.' People don't realize how exhausting these dives are, both mentally and physically. I had just turned up fresh (theoretically), and it was my turn.

This was my first major dive in the cave. I'd mentally prepared for surfacing on the far side but was also prepared for coming back. I reached the end of Jason's line, tied my line onto his and kept going. The sump continued at the shallow depth for some time, and I moved forwards slowly, allowing my body to decompress as I went. I'd find a bit where there was an undercut, go underneath that, inflate my suit (for both buoyancy and warmth) and then jam myself in so that I was secure. I'd stay in one place for a while, and my bubbles would dislodge the silt; the cave there was all quite murky. When I was fed up with the view where I was, I'd move forwards.

I had become accustomed to the sound of my bubbles running along the ceiling as I was doing this. When I progressed into a narrower tunnel, suddenly I didn't hear that any more. I looked up and saw the bubbles breaking into air on the surface ahead of me, but my dive computer indicated that I wasn't ready to ascend any further. There was some air – whether it was a small alcove or air bell, or the end of the sump, remained to be seen. The minutes of decompression ticked by, and I lay there, staring at the mirrored surface ahead of me, waiting impatiently to be free to explore. Finally, I was able to move on.

I lifted my head out of the water to find myself in a passage of pale-brown rock. The space extended ahead of me. I'd done it. I was on the other side. When the four of us had talked about this moment, one of us had commented that the dry cave found beyond this sump would have to be named Tipperary – after the First World War marching song 'It's a Long Way to Tipperary', and also as another dig at Reinhard. (. . . *And that's how we won the war.*)

I began walking through Tipperary for the first time, and after about 40 metres I reached the cave's third sump. I dipped in briefly, going far enough to see that it continued. The black void ahead of me promised more cave for future dives, but it would have to wait. Instead of rushing out, I waited for an arbitrary amount of time, allowing for some off-gassing, assuming it would be beneficial. (A lot of our dives would be classed as 'repetitive', and we were way beyond the guidelines of what was considered acceptable at the time. We excelled at this and were confident that the strategy we'd developed was safe.)

Nearly twenty hours[4] after setting off, I resurfaced outside Pozo Azul and proudly gave my report to the team waiting on the surface. The end of one sump and the start of another. The cave continued.

Our record-breaking sump dive drew attention to the project. People marvelled at the depth, the penetration distance, the hours of decompression, the time spent inside the cave, the massive amount of equipment and preparation required. People wanted to know how we were doing these seemingly impossible dives. We agreed to let Martyn Farr join the support team the following year, knowing he would also be photographing[5] the project and writing it up for magazines and future editions of his book.

Olivier Isler said something like, 'Hats off to the fighting spirit of the English divers.' He called us 'craftsmen' for devising the strategy of taking turns, with each successive dive providing information that was fed back to plan the next. We appreciated his sentiment, but we were hardly 'craftsmen' because, in reality, that aspect had not been planned. The diving-in-turn strategy had happened naturally, as a result of our buffoonery – Jason's equipment failure and my car breaking down, then Jason's dive ending when it did – but we had always appreciated the benefit of this approach, which also fed into our preference for diving solo.

⊕　⊕　⊕

I'd known John for years before I realized that his degree was in electrical engineering. I'd never talked to him about that. By the time we gathered in Spain in 2010, he'd put together this electronic

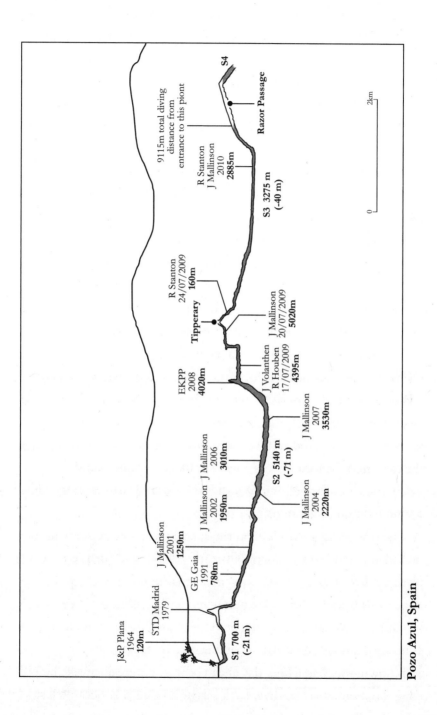

Pozo Azul, Spain

mapping device that would be amazingly useful. Due to the nature of European caves, surveying always lagged way behind the exploration. Nobody wanted to spend hours in cold water, taking compass readings and depth measurements. The sump in Pozo would have taken months to survey. John knew this, and he'd come up with the Lazy Boy Mapper, which sort of resolved the whole issue. It was quite innovative, and it paved the way for the survey of the 5-kilometre second sump.

Just getting through that sump would be a daunting challenge for many.[6] For us in 2010, that would be just the starting point. We'd be setting up camp inside Tipperary, which would allow us to be thoroughly decompressed and with freshly packed rebreathers before setting off into Sump 3, which was presumed to be equally as long – possibly even longer. We had to plan for diving enormous distances beyond Tipperary. The amount of planning involved was tremendous. It was great, a real logistical challenge.

Jason, who had been visiting the cave for a decade at this point, had developed a harmonious relationship with the locals, and he did an excellent job of keeping Spaniards involved in the project. There was always a balanced split of Spanish-to-English divers working at the cave, and the local divers never felt like they were being overrun. Their trade-off for helping was that they were learning long-range diving techniques from us.

The four of us spent days on the surface with our equipment. We had all experienced the disappointment of having to turn or cancel a planned dive because of an equipment malfunction in the past, and none of us wanted that to happen here. Fettling with gear seemed to be taking up a disproportionate amount of my time in those days, and although I always enjoyed it, it had become quite consuming.

Knowing we had a long day ahead of us, we were all awake before dawn on the day of the dive. I felt serene and quickly became lost in my thoughts as I visualized everything that was about to happen. We set off on our dives at intervals – spacing ourselves out as we dived through the sump – then we gathered again at Tipperary, where we'd be spending the night. We'd each carried our camping supplies in long, pressure-proof dry tubes – sleeping bags, sleeping mat or hammock, camp stove, food, dry clothes. I carried in a CO_2 monitor.

Of the many dangers involved in this year's dive, the one that we had been least able to plan for was the risk of camping in Tipperary. With four men spending two nights (or more) breathing the air in this closed space, we worried that the CO_2 levels would rise to a dangerous level. There was nothing we could do to prepare for this; we'd just have to be aware of the danger and see what happened. I could only hope that the air in Pozo wouldn't be as bad as it had become in the Ressel.

Whereas I had a CO_2 monitor – to at least give an initial indication of air quality – Jason had his own method for gauging his safety. As I laid out my sleeping mat and he set up his hammock, he explained to me that he would use his lofty perch to take advantage of an early warning of bad air. He reasoned that, since CO_2 is heavier than breathing air, I'd be overcome before he would. If I suddenly stopped snoring in the night, he'd have enough time to pack his gear, kit up and dive out. *Thanks, Jason. You're a pal.* Thinking of canaries in coalmines, I tried not to take it personally that he was using me as his personal CO_2 monitor.

Before we set up camp, René wanted to have a quick look into the third sump. If he'd discovered a better dry area within striking distance, we'd go ahead and set our camp there instead. We were expecting him to dive in no more than 500 metres, but when he returned, he had a huge grin on his face and held up an empty reel. 'One thousand metres,' he told us proudly. But then he described his dive – 'I went in, came to a junction and turned right, went to another junction and turned right, went to another junction and turned right . . .' By the third right, the three of us were looking at each other. *That doesn't sound right.*

In the morning, John dived first. As predicted, the route upstream – where we wanted to go – was to the left of René's last right. John tied on there and continued down the main passage, not turning back until he'd reached the end of his kilometre-long reel. Jason and I dived next, together. First, Jason went ahead, shooting his scooter straight into the blackness, and I followed behind him, placing the line; then we swapped roles. The cave was just there, waiting to be taken. Like kids let loose on a playground, we surged onwards as far as our lines would take us, only turning back when we had both emptied our reels.

We were now strategically using the 'multiple successive dives' technique that Olivier had commended us for the year before, and it paid off. We had reached a remarkable distance inside the cave, between us laying 3.6 kilometres of line during that year's dives. It was pretty impressive, and nearly unheard of. People had questioned the excessive amount of line we had taken in, thinking we were being presumptuous and overly optimistic.

We'd used it all.

The project was bringing us a lot of attention. It's not often that you hear good news coming from caves, and people were interested when they heard what we were doing. We were even scheduled to appear on *The One Show*, the popular UK evening television programme that covers topical news items. We were to be the novelty item at the end – 'British cave divers done good', or what have you. Jason had been the most motivated to appear on the show and had gone to the most effort – bringing his gear and setting up props as a background for our appearance.

In rehearsals, everything was always running over into our time and, as anyone could have predicted, this happened for the live airing as well. Dennis Waterman was the big name on ahead of us, and he went on talking about what he was up to. His time ran over, and then the whole show was behind schedule. We were brought out at the end and only asked one question, then the hosts wrapped it up.

When our time was cut, Jason was apoplectic. I knew to stay away from him, but the stage manager had no clue. She came over and started apologizing to him. 'I'm really, really sorry about that . . .' Her voice trailed off as he kept staring at her, his face frozen. She didn't know what to do.

'Is your friend all right?' she asked me nervously.

'He will be in a minute,' I assured her.

Of course, all of our friends had tuned in to see cave diving enjoy its fifteen seconds of fame. When seeing the three of us sitting on the sofa across from the person who had been given the unenviable job of interviewing us, one friend commented, 'Jesus wept! She's got her work cut out.' Another had burst out laughing, 'You all look like a bunch of baldy boffins!' I think it was their effort to keep the media attention from going to our heads.

None of us were ever seeking fame, of course, but it was fun to be caught up in the excitement.

Over the years, we had become known in the small and friendly village of Covanera, where Pozo Azul's entrance lay. We had our regular campsite behind Bar Muñecas, whose owners (Carlos and Tere Rodrigues) welcomed us warmly. While we were setting up for the dive in 2011, Chris Jewell and Artur Kozlowski – who were in Spain working on a different project – stopped by to visit us. In addition, my girlfriend – whom I had met in Australia at OZTek in March – was there with me that year. (I'm not going to use her real name, as she now serves as an advisor to the UN and she might not want to be defined by her relationship with me. Let's call her Anne.)

These projects are usually very intense, where we're all focused on the exploration and preparing for the dive. There's very little fun involved, and I realized it might have been a bad idea to take a girlfriend who was a non-caver on such a highly intensive trip. I didn't have much spare energy for her, and I felt like it was wearing on her. I made a mental note to not repeat this mistake.

It worked out, though, because Anne ended up feeding Artur and Chris while they were at the camp. Initially she'd felt sorry for them because they had no proper food with them, but Artur was quite charismatic, and she'd enjoyed his company. I was glad to see that they were all getting on well as I set up the dive.

Jason was forced to turn back when the tube he was using to carry his camping supplies was crushed from the pressure at 70 metres; John, René and I carried on without him and set up camp in Tipperary again. Again, we had excessive amounts of line, scooter batteries, gas reserves – we were prepared to dive another 5 or 6 kilometres. What I really wanted to do was break the 10-kilometre mark inside a cave.

Caves never do what you want, though, and the sump surfaced quickly, which was a nightmare. It would have been much easier to continue underwater; dry caving beyond long technical sumps added tiers of complexity.

René extended our line for less than 300 metres before surfacing. He de-kitted and began exploring. John and I had followed behind René, and we surfaced just as René was returning from his explorations. I looked around, taking in a chamber that was unlike anything else we'd seen inside this cave. Spray and droplets hung in the air, blown about by a breeze. From somewhere nearby came the rumble of falling water. Beyond the longest sumps in the world, Pozo had suddenly turned into a British-style cave.

'It's treacherous back there,' René warned us. John and I walked on through a short section of canal, and then a tremendous lofty corridor with sweeping bends and a staircase of twenty-seven small cascades, all of which we climbed. The virgin rock was jagged and sharp, and with each step I wished I was wearing my wetsuit and wellies. A torn and leaking drysuit would have been an absolute epic to deal with in a place this remote, with kilometres of sumped cave lying between us and safety. I wouldn't even let myself entertain the idea of what might happen if one of us fell and broke a bone so far back. I imagined Anne would be upset if I came out of the cave broken.

I was relieved to reach a pool of water, the next sump. We wouldn't be diving it this year. We turned and made our way back through Razor Passage – as it would come to be known – and then began the day-long process of diving out. I was still chasing my 10-kilometre goal.

Outside the cave, the owner of the Bar Muñecas surprised us with T-shirts that she'd had made, to celebrate our work in the cave. 'It's a long way after Tipperary' was printed in red across the shirt's front, around our penetration distance to date: 9,195 metres.

Unbeknownst to me at the time, 2011 would be the last year that I completed exploration inside Pozo Azul.

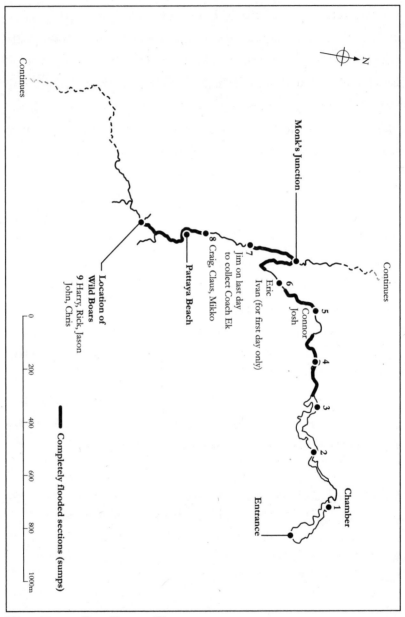

Tham Luang Cave Rescue Plan

'We tried to focus on what we knew was important and
what our role was because that was
all that we could cope with.'

John Volanthen

Sunday, 8 July 2018, Thailand
The Extrication Phase

This was the Rescue Plan.

Harry would be the first to arrive in Chamber 9 and the last to leave each day, staying there to administer the sedation. Craig would be in Chamber 7–8,[7] waiting for each boy to arrive with his diver. Being the only other medical professional on the team – and the only one of us who had prior experience using ketamine – Harry insisted that Craig be there to check over each boy after his first dive. Claus and Mikko would also be in Chamber 7–8, waiting with a stretcher to carry the boy across that dry stretch. Erik and Ivan would be stationed in Chamber 6, with Connor and Jim in Chamber 5. Working in pairs, as always. The divers in these canal sections would be acting as support, swimming the boy through while the rescue diver had a chance to recover and prepare for the next dive.

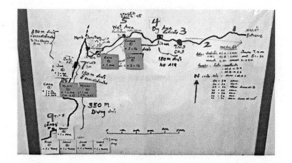

The map I drew, which became the crucial planning tool.

The four core divers – the Awesome Foursome – would all begin in Chamber 9, each waiting for their turn to set off with a boy. The process of dressing, packaging and sedating each boy took more than thirty minutes – from the time they dressed into their wetsuit to the time they were unconscious and in the hands of their diver. This worked out that the divers should be leaving Chamber 9 at approximately half-hour intervals, which created a natural staggering that avoided any congestion on the way out. Jason would go first, then John, then Chris, and then me. One diver for one boy, all the way through to Chamber 3, in a journey that was estimated to take three hours.

The first day would be a bit different, as I was going to stay behind in Chamber 8, waiting with Craig for the first boy to arrive with Jason. That first boy's dive would tell us if the ketamine plan was successful, or if it needed modification. (We wouldn't have many options to choose from, other than to modify the initial ketamine dose.) After Craig looked the boy over and gave his report to me, I'd dive back to Harry, who would be waiting for my report before sedating the second boy. This was our feedback loop.

The boys had been unlucky to be caught in the cave, but everything that had happened to them since seemed to be downright

After a week of intense planning . . . will the plan work?

charmed. We were all hoping that the boys' luck held out through the next three days.

There was no Plan B.

The drive to Tham Luang in Tom's and Bas' minibus was largely silent, as we visualized each step of what we would be doing during the rescue. My mental rehearsal of concept was interrupted when my phone pinged to announce an incoming message. Withdrawn from my reverie, I glanced at the screen to see the name: Elon Musk.

He was sending pictures of his team's ideas for an escape pod that could be used to enclose the boys during the rescue. I examined his design carefully and dismissed it with disappointment. The thing I was looking at was essentially a dry tube, nearly identical to the ones we already had. Elon and his team of rocket scientists had failed to consider that the pod would be used to transport a human being for three hours, and would require suitable life support. Those were the important parts that we had needed his help with.

Aggravated that my concentration had been broken for this, I replied to him tersely in an email. 'With respect, all I see is a tube, albeit made of fancy materials.' While there were cylinders and a gas-feed pipe to the pod, I didn't consider it a fully functioning and reliable system. We needed something that would be immediately ready to go in the cave without further fettling. 'The devil is in the detail. Breathing systems, off-board gas-venting systems, ballast and trimming arrangements, etc.' *Why hadn't they thought of this?*

Perhaps he wasn't accustomed to having his ideas criticized. 'With respect, I am trying to be helpful. Please do not be rude.'

The conversation was over as far as I was concerned, and I read the messages aloud to the team in the minibus. Jason seemed bothered by what I had written and he told me that I should apologize. I balked at first, and then relented. Slightly. I'd apologize for the tone, but not the content.

'Apologies, as the tone of that didn't come across well.' I went on to encourage them to keep working. Our biggest concern was the youngest lad, Titan, as it seemed unlikely that the face mask would seal tightly on his tiny, narrow face.

'Understandable.' He seemed to accept my apology. 'I have one of the world's best engineering teams who normally design spaceships and spacesuits working on this thing twenty-four hours a day.'

I told Elon to keep working because it couldn't hurt (and because I was still thinking ahead, for possible use in future rescues), but I wasn't relying on his team to provide us with anything useful. We were about to start and would continue as planned.

We arrived at Tham Luang a few minutes later to find the mountainside almost eerily calm. For the first time since I had arrived, there was no commotion and no press milling about. The governor had cleared everyone from the mountain, announcing, 'This is D-Day.'[8] In spite of the press being absent, we'd all been explicitly restricted from speaking to the press ourselves, which was not something that most of us needed to be told. Those of us actively completing the rescue didn't have the energy left to be negotiating our image in the media; we had other things to focus on. John and I often say that if somebody is at a rescue and talking to the press instead of participating in the mission, there's usually a reason.

Before we went into the cave, we were due to have a morning meeting. I had come to dread those meetings before any rescue, as they inevitably dragged on for ages – reviewing plans that had already been decided, people giving motivational speeches, telling us to be safe or whatever. I was pleasantly surprised that this meeting did have a purpose, though, as this is where we were given our pouches of ketamine. The rest of the meeting was over in minutes, and from my point of view I took that as a good omen for the task ahead.

Each diver entered the cave carrying what was required to deliver the boys: a positive-pressure full-face mask, a full wetsuit, zip-ties and bungees, extra lead, and a buoyancy jacket. This was all bundled up into two sausage-like rolls, which could be bungeed onto the cylinders. Finally, each rescue diver carried with him the pouch filled with syringes. Each syringe held 50 mg of ketamine, which we would use during the dive when the boy showed signs of stirring.

We each needed to begin our dive with five 11-litre cylinders: three for ourselves (containing standard breathing air) and two for the boys (containing 75 per cent O_2).[9] On our way to Chamber 9, we would leave an O_2 bottle at Chamber 6, to be swapped out during the rescue. We'd breathe off one of our bottles on the way in and then leave that used one in Chamber 9. That way, we could start our journey out with two full ones, without being encumbered by the empty one. This was my Throwaway Cylinder Plan: we'd just leave the used bottle behind in the cave, which we obviously would never do if we were using our own, but there were loads of cylinders there, and the SEALs had lots of regulators, so I didn't mind abandoning them.

We entered the cave together, ready to start the rescue. We'd had a short meeting, we had our ketamine, everything was in place. Things were moving smoothly. Then we got to Chamber 3, where all of the cylinders were stored, and everything completely ground to a halt.

All week, I'd been asking the SEALs to do useful tasks; somehow, they never quite managed to do them correctly. The previous day, I'd kept saying, 'Make sure you get the oxygen cylinders into Chamber 3. Whatever you do, they have to be there on Sunday morning.' To my pleasant surprise, this was done as asked, but when we arrived in Chamber 3, I was devastated to find that the cylinders all had the wrong fittings on them; they were incompatible with the regulators that we were using for the full-face masks. We weren't able to swap the regulators, and this could have been a total show-stopper if it weren't for the fact that some – maybe one in twenty of the massive stockpiles of cylinders that were in Chamber 3 – had a screw-plug adapter that could be used to resolve this situation.

Since I was only going to Chamber 8 for the first stage of the process, I stayed back to hunt down the adapters. Harry had to go in to start setting up, and Jason was champing at the bit as usual, impatient to get started, so he followed next. As each of the rescue divers was given the adapters they needed for their bottles, they dived on.

After being delayed with the search for adapters, I then spent nearly two hours getting back to Chamber 8. I had a hell of a struggle diving with all of the extra cylinders and equipment for the boys during that dive. It was my turn to struggle, as John had done when we'd gone back on Wednesday's food run. I finally arrived in Chamber 8 just as Chris disappeared towards Chamber 9, leaving Craig and me alone. The tension in the chamber was palpable, and neither Craig nor I spoke much. I couldn't remember the last time I had felt so tense.

Craig finally broke the silence with a question. 'Where the fuck are Claus and Mikko?'

They were our support in Chamber 8, there to carry the stretcher with the boy across the 150 metres of dry cave. I was a bit annoyed, but not worried about them. They hadn't previously been this far inside; I'd assumed they'd know to keep going until they reached the long dry chamber, but now I suspected they had stopped in the wrong place. I hoped they sorted themselves out and got themselves where they were supposed to be before the first boy arrived.

Unbelievably – I don't know if it was nerves or what – Craig went off to find them, leaving me alone in the chamber. I sat there, with my eyes fixed on the cave line that was running to Chamber 9, waiting for Jason to appear with the first boy.

A lot of people ask us how we selected the order we used to rescue the boys. In truth, we didn't choose. When Harry had been in Chamber 9 with Dr Pak the previous day, he'd left three criteria: he wanted to start with the four strongest ones (to improve our odds), save the smallest ones for last (because we were still mulling over the issue of sealing their masks), and obviously Coach Ek would be in the last batch. Beyond that, he left them to make the decision for themselves.

When Jason went up the ramp, the boy who was going out first (Note) stepped forward. Jason began the process by handing him a Xanax pill and getting him into the wetsuit; he then began packaging him up with the bungees and cable ties. Note walked himself to the water's edge, where Harry was waiting for him with two syringes. The first syringe contained atropine (used to counter the increased saliva secretions that were a side effect of ketamine) and the second syringe held the ketamine. Harry received his patient, sitting him gently on his knee and talking calmly to him for a moment before beginning the injections.

In Chamber 8, I saw the line beginning to twitch. I had my breath held as I watched the line tremble. Jason might be about to surface with a dead child. I didn't know what to think and I was sort of expecting the worst.

The last section of the sump Jason was diving through is quite low. I watched Jason crawl out, and then his right hand appeared, holding a boy. He stretched his arm as far ahead of him as he could and laid the boy down on his side, half in the water and half on the gravel bank. The boy was lying motionless in the shallow pool of water. I couldn't see any sign of breathing.

I was standing there, staring at the boy. I hadn't seen any bubbles. I felt frozen in place.

Oh no.

'He is alive,' Jason said, addressing the doubt he saw on my face. Craig came up beside me then; we crouched in the low passage to pull the boy over the gravel and out of the water.

Craig had Note on his side in the recovery position and was taking off his mask. I stood by to hear the outcome of Craig's examination while Jason carried his cylinders to the next sump. This took about twenty minutes, and there was still no sign of Claus and Mikko with the stretcher. We couldn't interrupt the process, so we'd have to carry Note through the chamber ourselves. I picked up his legs while Craig and Jason each took an arm and supported his head. Together, we carried Note across the gravel and sand banks, then through shallow water to a boulder area. Beyond this was the next sump.

Jason kitted up again while Craig and I laid Note down and carefully put the mask back on, tightening the five straps and spending an inordinate amount of time making sure that the mask was sealed properly. We pulled the bungees over the cylinder and handed him off to Jason. I watched Jason hold Note tightly against his chest as they disappeared into the murk and continued their journey. They quickly faded out of view, moving on towards Chamber 6, where Erik and Ivan were waiting for them.

But first, he came upon Claus and Mikko, who had stopped in a relatively small air pocket and were waiting there. Jason barked at them, 'Swim in! Swim in! You need to be back further!'[10]

After Jason left, I returned to the other end of Chamber 8, where I donned my gear and prepared to dive to Chamber 9 to close the 'feedback loop' by letting Harry know that there were no adjustments needed. The first of the boys had survived the first of his five dives.

We still had a long way to go, but at least we were starting with a success.

I was beginning my dive through the sump when I felt the line begin to twitch against my fingers. I moved to the side as John passed by, with Tern in his arm. The boy passed by very close to me – his shoulder brushed against mine – but I couldn't see if he was breathing. I worked on the assumption that if anything had been wrong, John would have done something to alert me. Trusting that John had everything under control, I continued on to Chamber 9.

When I saw Harry, my report was simple: 'All good.' The grin on my face said everything else. 'Did you forget that you were supposed to wait for me before sending John off?'

'I know. That was my fault.' He had been so tense after Jason left that he had immediately begun processing the next boy. After the second boy had been sedated, John realized the error and asked, 'Aren't we supposed to wait for Rick?' By then it was too late; the boy was unconscious, and there was no point in holding him there.

No harm done.

I got out of my kit, leaving it on the same sand bank where John and I had stopped the first time we'd arrived here – when we'd found the boys. I couldn't believe only six days had passed. As I sat there, eating another Snickers bar, I thought about everything that had occurred since my first time there. Two of them were on their way out, and two more would be following them, and then . . .

It was too soon to begin feeling victorious. There was still a lot that could go wrong.

Chris came down the ramp towards me, followed by his boy (Nick), and for the first time I was present for what I had been calling 'The Process'. Harry was standing on one leg in stomach-deep water; the knee of his other leg was braced against the same bank that the boys had been sitting on when John had captured that first video of the boys coming down to meet us. We sat Nick onto Harry's thigh, which was just below the water's surface. Dr Harry spoke to his patient in calm and reassuring tones, while Dr Pak translated his words. Chris and I stood on either side, ready to support Nick's weight as Harry made the injections. I could feel the boy shivering while he sat on Harry's knee.[11] Within minutes – much more quickly than I was expecting – the sedation kicked in, and Nick lost consciousness. He became floppy, as if he were dead, slumping to one side. Chris and I caught him before he fell into the water.

As Chris kitted up for the dive, Harry and I fitted the mask securely, then the cylinder. The final touches to secure the package was the binding. First we tied a bungee around his ankles, then used a carabiner to join the wrist loops behind his back. We did all of this in the water, out of sight from the rest of the boys, who were higher on the ledge and up the ramp. Harry told me that Jason had slipped the cable ties on to Note's wrists while he was still up the ramp, in full view of his teammates, causing the other boys to gasp audibly when they saw what was in store for their friend.

Harry had explained the process to them the previous day, and they had all agreed to it, nodding happily as Dr Pak had translated Harry's words, but perhaps something had been lost in translation. Watching Note's wrists being bound with cable ties seemed to be their first realization of what they had agreed to.

After Chris left with Nick, it was my turn. I would be taking Night – the one whose absence at his SpongeBob-themed birthday party had first set off the alarm bells – and I climbed up the ramp to where he was standing. He was waiting for me, having already donned his wetsuit and swallowed his Xanax. After watching the first three boys going through the process, he knew what was expected of him. His face was calm and stoic as he stood in front of me.

'My name's Rick.' I extended my hand awkwardly, as if I was collecting the next customer in a commercial adventure enterprise. ('Hello. I'm your guide out for the day.')

I motioned for him to raise his arms above his head and then I tied an elastic bungee around his chest. I put another one round his thighs, then lowered the buoyancy jacket over his head. I tied the crotch straps in place. I placed a 6-pound block of lead inside the jacket, then slipped on the hood. Barefoot, he followed me down the ramp to where Harry and I would sedate him, secure the mask, bind his limbs and attach his cylinder. Now it was just the two of us here – two pairs of hands to complete the process.

The journey started with a surface swim in a large passage before descending to the floor, where we would continue through an underwater tunnel. During the swim, it was evident that Night was barely breathing – maybe only three breaths per minute. It didn't feel right. Seeking some reassurance or guidance from Harry before taking the boy underwater, I shouted back to him. 'I'm a bit concerned. He's hardly breathing.'

His reply came back. 'There's nothing you can do. You just have to go.'

I had expected more concern from him and felt a bit frustrated, but knew he was correct. I couldn't hang around. With that, we descended and began the 300-metre dive to Chamber 8, one of the longer dives of the journey out. (This tunnel contains the area known as Pattaya Beach, the red herring in the initial search.) Jason had pointed out that the handles on the jacket weren't particularly useful, and I had watched him cradle the boy in his arm as he dived. I did this now and agreed that the cradling method was more effective.

As soon as I was underwater, I was relaxed and felt focused. I'd always said that I was most content and comfortable when I was underwater – this is why I call myself a water person. I typically fared better underwater than on the surface, and that was never more true than in Thailand. In spite of all of the pressure and stress of the rescue – the crowds on the mountain, the buffoonery, the press, everything – as soon as I was diving, I was calm.

Even so, the dive out of Tham Luang was not easy, as the ceiling was often low with countless projections. Typically, I'd dive through caves with my head up, looking forwards; even if I couldn't see anything, this was the most comfortable and natural position. To dive out of this cave, though, I was constantly braced for an impact on my head by tensing my neck and shoulders. Staying in this position was really tiring and uncomfortable, so occasionally – if I hadn't had any impacts for a while – I would stick my head up. Not that I could see anything, I just wanted to relax and stretch my muscles for a moment. Every time, within seconds, I was brutally reminded of this mistake when – *clunk!* – my head smacked into another projection and was whipped back with the collision. It was really jarring and painful on my neck, akin to whiplash. This wasn't just a simple swim; it was a punishing experience.

Knowing this, I held Night in such a way that his head was protected from impact by my own helmet-clad head and my shoulder hunched around him. With his body held tightly against my chest, Night's head was nestled against my neck, between my shoulder and ear. I had a flashing thought – *is this the first time I've ever held a child?* – before recalling that Ian had once given me his daughter Leonie to hold. All along, we'd been doing everything we could to turn them into packages and think of them as items, but this was where it became clear to me that this wasn't just an inert object. This one was breathing.

This one couldn't be abandoned.

On the inside of every bend, the passage became low, which forced us to manoeuvre back and forth across the line as we negotiated the twists and turns. This is easy enough to do when you're travelling alone, but another matter while keeping hold of a body. I was constantly having to swap hands and switch which side the boy was held on. I was so focused on the line, after a few minutes I realized that I hadn't been paying attention to Night's breathing. With his head so close to mine, I should have been able to hear and feel the bubbles of his expired breaths. I couldn't remember there being any in the past couple of minutes. I pressed the purge button on the mask, hoping that the increased oxygen being forced through the mask would trigger an inhalation or force oxygen into his lungs. If nothing else, I knew it wouldn't hurt, and it was reassurance for me. I pushed back the thought that I might be holding a dead boy against my chest.

I reached Chamber 8 and stretched the boy ahead of me as Jason had done. I expected Craig to be waiting to receive him, but he wasn't there. *Now, where is our reception party?* I dragged myself up the exit slope with Night in my arms, having difficulty gaining purchase as the gravel slumped away beneath me. I looked around but still didn't see Craig, or Claus, or Mikko. I laid Night on the gravel, removed my cylinders, then began removing his mask. A moment later, I was grateful to see Harry's head pop up out of the sump. He'd set off on his dive immediately behind me.

After hearing some chest congestion while sedating the boy in Chamber 9, Harry had become worried about a possible lung infection. Despite sounding dismissive when I'd told him of my concerns, Harry knows that I'm not one to worry or ask for help unnecessarily. He knew something was wrong, and he wanted to be there when we surfaced. Crawling out of the sump, he moved immediately to Night's side and began checking on him. When he saw me unfastening the mask straps, he stopped me. 'He's breathing, but just. Let's keep him on the oxygen for now.'

After a moment, I saw Night's muscles begin to twitch as he stirred from his sedation. 'You can give him your first injection,' Harry said. There was a time, a few years earlier, when a girlfriend had asked me for help injecting her contraceptive. I'd run out of the room, feigning horror, and could hear her laughing as she called after me: 'Some hero you are!'

There would be no running away now, and no better time to start than with Harry supervising. Drawing a deep breath, I reached into my pouch of syringes. With his watchful eyes on me, I pushed the syringe into Night's thigh as we'd practised on Friday, but maybe I was too keen. *Did I just hit the bone?* I shuddered as I pulled the needle out a fraction, before pressing the plunger all the way down.

At this time, Craig returned with Claus and the stretcher. Craig, Claus, and Mikko had just carried Nick through the chamber and had seen Chris off on his dive. Mikko had dived behind Chris, to provide support.[12] With Craig and Harry taking care of Night, I carried my gear through the chamber to the next sump. They'd told me they would bring my boy along in a bit, so I began kitting up.

I waited for what felt like ages, before they arrived carrying Night on the stretcher. Harry told me he had sat for nearly half an hour, cradling Night against him, waiting for the boy to warm up and begin breathing more strongly. At one point, Harry had thought he would need to begin CPR and when he'd taken off the mask, Night's lips had been blue.

'I think he's through the worst now,' Harry told me, not very convincingly.

We didn't know how the first three were faring on their rescue, but Craig had mentioned that they'd all seemed in much better shape than Night was looking now. My heart sank. We'd all accepted that there was bound to be one death today. Why had I drawn the short straw?

The next dive took us past Monk's Junction before turning south. There were a few low restrictions, and I needed to experiment to find the best way for carrying the boy, alternately cradling him against me and then holding him out to the side in the low parts. I inched along, focused on our passage through the cave instead of his breathing. I knew that I could only control one of those things, and I needed to focus my attention there. Once we were through the difficult parts, I pulled him close to me again and pressed the mask's purge button as a precaution.

Beyond Monk's inlet, there were some short canals in the southern-heading passage, where I floated Night on the surface as I swam beside him. Then a dive to the canal section known as Chamber 6, where the cave turns sharply to the east. I could see the orange hue of Erik's and Ivan's lights looking down on me as I ascended. They were sitting on a sand bank, waiting; when I surfaced, they sprang into action.

This is where I had staged the second O₂ cylinder for Night, and although it wasn't strictly necessary, I wanted to swap bottles as planned. Disconnecting the cylinder would have left him without any gas to breathe, so I removed the mask while the cylinders were being swapped. The process of securing the mask and seal again was a complete arse, and I instantly regretted having ever removed the mask.[13] Ivan and Erik helped me with all of this, and then Erik competently swam Night to the end of the canal. Opting to swap out one of my own cylinders, too, I looked around at the jumble that was strewn about the passage. I could see no way of discriminating the tanks that were new and full, from the ones that had already been used and discarded. Ivan pointed out a full one, but when I checked it, I found it was half empty.

'This needs to be better organized,' I told him.

From further down the passage, Erik called back to us that Night was starting to twitch and needed to be topped up. Ivan rushed down to Erik while I stayed back to sort out my cylinder. A moment later Ivan returned, mumbling that he'd forgotten to take the syringes with him. He grabbed his pouch and headed back to the far sump with the ketamine. He seemed very flustered.[14]

For fuck's sake, Ivan. Sort yourself out.

I arrived next in Chamber 5, where Connor Roe and Jim Warny were waiting for me. Before I knew it, Connor had taken control of the boy, powering along the surface of the canal like a human speedboat. I watched him charge ahead while I plodded along behind him, just as I had done while caving with his dad. I caught up with them at the far end of the canal, before the cave became sumped again, and I dived on with Night.

We went past a large area where there was an off-route dry sandy beach. This was Chamber 4, but it was never used during the Rescue Plan. The final leg of the journey to Chamber 3 was a complex dive, navigating along the roof of the tunnel with obstructions and protrusions that created the problematic line trap. This one was particularly challenging because the line here dropped vertically.

Descending here, I held Night below me with my right hand, using him to probe the darkness for the continuation, while my left hand was firmly encircling the line above my head. I was searching for the opening, a gap between stalactites and rock features. I would have to slide Night ahead of me, like dropping a letter into a letterbox. I was aware that I was banging his head lightly against the wall in the process, but it was unavoidable; it was the only way to find the way on. I made a note to provide more padding on the boys' heads in the following days.[15]

I located the opening after a few moments and passed Night through, then followed behind him, being careful not to lose grip on either him or the line. There was an unknown void beyond this slot, and it would be a challenge to locate him if I'd lost him. Aware of the danger in this section of the cave, I'd already clipped him onto my harness.

Soon, I heard the whirring of the water pumps and I saw the clutter of cables and hoses intensify as we approached the safety of Chamber 3. I surfaced to the welcome sight of Jamie and other Americans crouching at the water's edge, with a stretcher lying out in wait. I spat out my regulator and announced, 'He's still breathing.' They reached down and began pulling the boy onto the stretcher.

'Hang on!' I yelled. I was being dragged out of the sump along with Night. 'I'm still clipped to him.' I unclipped myself and asked, 'How are the others?'

'They're all alive,' one of the Americans assured me.

It was nice to hear those words again.

12.

Once in a Lifetime

'You don't start a cave dive with your fingers crossed.'

'Which end is the head?' the man asked us. Three of us were gathered in a damp moss-walled alcove at the entrance of Porth-yr-Ogof.

Fuck knows, I thought. *It's probably somewhere in the middle.*

I looked over to John for help.

I'd never forgotten about Paul Esser, the diver whose death I had learned about during my first South Wales trip with Steve Joyce, when I was eighteen years old and we camped outside Porth-yr-Ogof. I remembered how disturbed I had been then, knowing that his body was still inside the cave and so close to an entrance. In 2010, his brother approached South Wales Cave Rescue Team to revisit the idea of bringing out Paul's remains. When John and I were called, we didn't hesitate. I felt like I was closing doors that had been left open for decades.

I went there after work one morning in April and arrived at midday. John had arrived early, as is typical of him, and was already in the cave gathering the remains into a small body bag. Together, we looked around for any bits that were still lying around, then dived the bag to the beginning of the sump, close to the exit. We knew not to bring human remains to the surface until the appointed person was there to receive them.

After what seemed like ages, the undertaker finally arrived, telling us he'd gone to the wrong cave first. 'All these yr-Ogofs sound the same,' he'd muttered by way of apology.

John and I went back in for the bag, then laid it on the ground in the cave's entrance. Night was falling by then, so we arranged our dive lights to illuminate the alcove area. We didn't give our lighting arrangement much thought – we just put the torches onto the ground and pointed them upwards – but in the end, it looked quite atmospheric and ethereal, with beams of light piercing through the twilight and illuminating the sculptured rock walls. Paul's brother came in and knelt beside the metre-long bag, then looked up at us.

'Which end is the head?' he asked.

Like me, John is largely programmed to tell the truth, but because he runs a business, he's learned to have more tact. I didn't know what he was going to say, but I knew he was unlikely to be as blunt as I would be, and I was relieved when he came through with an appropriate answer.

'It's here,' he said, and pointed to one end of the bag. It was perfect. Paul's brother moved towards the bag's 'head' and spent a moment there, finally saying goodbye to his brother.

This was John's first recovery,[1] but I knew he'd had a previous job working in an operating theatre of a hospital, where he'd mended the machines that go beep. He had watched surgeries, seen people die, all that. I figured he had been desensitized to that kind of thing, and at Porth-yr-Ogof, I could see that he was as unbothered by it all as I was.

Six months later, in October 2010, I was at home in Coventry when I received a phone call from France. Olivier Lanet, the diving operations chief of the Spéléo Secours Français (SSF, the French cave rescue organization), was calling to tell me that a diver hadn't come back from a dive in the Dragonnière de Gaud, a cave in the Ardèche region. I was a bit surprised that I was the one being called to help, because there were some very capable divers there in France. Eric Establie – who was part of a group that were the French equivalent of me, Jason and John – had been working in Dragonnière, attempting to pass the cave's first sump. He would be the better choice, and I said as much to Olivier.

'What about Eric Establie? Why isn't he involved?'

There was a long silence.

'It's Eric who hasn't come back.'

Fuck. Hearing that it was Eric who was missing, I knew there had to be a very serious reason. He was someone who was able to get himself out of most situations. Something must have gone horribly wrong.

The following afternoon – thanks to the work of Bill Whitehouse and his contacts – John and I were boarding a naval helicopter from Bristol to cross the English Channel; with us was Charlie Reid-Henry, a British cave diver who speaks fluent French. We'd estimated that our equipment weighed 750 kilograms, so the pilots had lightened the helicopter by removing anything that wasn't needed. As the helicopter was still struggling to get in the air, the pilot spoke to us over the intercom. 'I think you've underestimated the weight of your equipment.'

In France, the fire service had been put in charge of overseeing the rescue operation and the local branch came out to receive us in Cherbourg, just as a forty-seater Civil Defence jet arrived to transport us the remainder of our journey. The jet's pilot balked when we told him that our cylinders were filled with compressed air, and he refused to load them. He had every right to do that, but it would have been a show-stopper for us, so the chief of the fire service turned to one of his men.

'You're going to have to drive these down to the Ardèche,' he told him, sending him on a 1,000-kilometre overnight errand. I smiled at the idea of that happening in the UK, where a firefighter would never be ordered to spend the night driving across the country and back; I commended their flexibility.

With our cylinders being chauffeured to the cave, the three of us boarded the jet, strapping our rebreathers and scooters into the empty seats. After making a hop to Switzerland to pick up three more divers, we landed on an airfield in southern France. As soon as we'd finished unloading our equipment, the jet's pilot turned around and took off again. The six of us were left standing there with our mountain of diving gear, at 3 a.m. on the side of the runway of a provincial airport, somewhere in France. When a security bloke came driving up to us a few minutes later, he was frantic with questions.

'Who are you? What's your plan? The airport is locked. Nobody can get to you!'

'I'm sure there's a plan,' I assured him, with uncharacteristic optimism. I trusted the French authorities must have some plan in place, even though I had no idea what it might be. 'By the way, where are we?'

Without answering me, he went off in a complete panic to work out what was going on. While he was gone, the local fire brigade arrived through the back gates, collected us and whisked us away. I can imagine the security guard's confusion when he came back after a few minutes, only to find we had disappeared as mysteriously as we'd arrived.

After driving to the Ardèche Gorge, we headed straight into a briefing with the SSF and local fire service. Eric had previously explored the sump to a distance of 1,040 metres, where the depth had been −42m and ascending. When he had left on his dive two days earlier, he'd been hoping to reach dry cave. After reviewing the basic details of the cave, the prefecture looked to the divers who were gathered.

'What are your thoughts? How should we proceed?'

There was a moment of silence. Nobody was prepared to put themselves forward, and then John spoke up. 'We've come prepared . . . We can dive first thing in the morning.'

John and I had a dry tube packed full of emergency supplies – spare diving equipment, tools, a Molephone[2] communications device, food and some basic medical equipment. We requested – and were given – controlled opiates and more significant medical supplies to take in.

We thought it likely that there had been a medical emergency or an equipment malfunction that had left Eric stranded in the cave beyond the sump, or perhaps in an air bell.

If Eric had passed the sump, he'd be able to survive for more than two weeks without food. However, if he were waiting in a smaller air bell, his time would be limited by the dwindling O_2 and rising CO_2 levels. We didn't have time to waste.

After getting a few hours of sleep, John and I spoke with Eric's diving partners on the bank of the River Ardèche. The divers briefed us on the conditions in the cave and the expected dive; they even showed us a video to familiarize us with the cave, which looked quite pleasant. Next, John and I set off in a fire service boat to cross the river. To make sure we were awake, the operator – probably a bloke who had been given a course but had no practical boat-handling experience – crashed into a rock before depositing us on the river's far bank.

The cave had looked quite nice in the video, but the moment we were inside, the water was thick and clouded with silt.[3] We couldn't see our hands in front of us, and at times we could hardly see our lights. It was a complete contrast to the video we'd been shown and the information we'd been given. I felt a sinking feeling in my gut. Something wasn't right. We had a slow journey in, methodically feeling our way along the line, with John in the lead. Suddenly I collided with a fin, and a leg that wasn't moving. I thought I'd found Eric at first, but then the leg did move, and I heard John speak to me through his mouthpiece.

'I can't go any further.'

I didn't understand what had happened. We had only gone 700 metres, and I knew the cave continued far ahead of us. We retreated up into an airspace, where the water was clearer and we were able to communicate better.

This section of cave was shaped like the top half of an hourglass that was leaning at a 45° angle. The floor was a slope of heavy clay with chunks of rock embedded in it, leading downwards to the 'neck' of the hourglass, which had been reduced to a small hole – maybe 50 cm in diameter. It would have been impossible for Eric to pass through, yet that is where his line went. I didn't understand it.

John and I dived down the slope towards the hole and as we were approaching, we simultaneously figured out what had happened. Something had triggered an avalanche. The sediment was unlike anything I'd encountered before. The steep slope, displaying jagged scars, looked treacherous and like it was poised for further collapse. It felt like a death zone. The debris from the avalanche had poured through the 'neck' of the hourglass, until only a small space along the top of the opening was clear. This was where Eric's line was passing through.[4]

I reached my arm through the hole to feel into the hourglass's bottom chamber, and my fingers hit metal. There was a scooter in the space beyond. Eric's scooter, but no Eric. I pulled it through the hole, then moved around to get a better sense of the slope. My stomach sank as I realized what had happened. Eric had likely set off the avalanche when he'd passed through, then found himself trapped when he'd returned. His exit had been closed off to this impassable hole.[5]

This was a nightmare. There was a huge probability that he had found an airspace beyond the sump. He'd be waiting there now, and we couldn't get to him. It was the worst situation ever. John and I were on the same page: we needed to get out of the cave and devise a plan. On the surface, one look at John's face told me he was feeling the same weight of dread and responsibility that I felt.

How on earth are we going to reach Eric without setting off another landslide and killing ourselves?

When we brought out Eric's scooter and reported what we'd found, the French thought that Eric must have pushed his scooter into the opening to leave a clue for his rescuers that he had survived the collapse. I was sceptical that this was what had happened, but it became the story shared in the media. The French authorities were clinging to any hope that Eric was alive, largely to maintain the momentum of the rescuers who had arrived to work on the surface.

Within hours, news of Eric's plight had spread across Europe. Eric was well respected and well liked, and there was a great outpouring of support for him. The next day, the SSF and teams of French cavers began digging on the hill above the cave, in an attempt to find a back entrance to the chamber where Eric might be waiting. Excavators had found a small cave in a vineyard, and they continued digging, hoping the cave would connect to Dragonnière de Gaud. The other option being considered involved boring down to the point where the avalanche had occurred and pumping out the debris. Mining engineers had already been brought in to begin developing this plan.

We could see that all ideas were being considered, with no expense spared, and for that we were grateful, but John and I knew that his only chance lay with us. Even the French cavers who were there digging had their hopes set with us. We went to see what they were up to one day when we weren't diving, and it was quite emotional. The French divers pleaded with us to help Eric. 'You're the only hope,' they told us. It was quite a lot of pressure, and we were reminded that his life was in our hands.

When John and I dived next, we again took our dry tube packed with supplies, this time to leave beyond the hole in case Eric returned. We'd also been given assignments. We had a radiolocation device, to pinpoint the exact location of the avalanche and facilitate the engineer's mining plan; a metal detector, to see if Eric was buried under the avalanche, which seemed unlikely; and I was asked to take sediment samples. I also took with me a cut-down garden hoe, which John and I had purchased from a nearby garden centre, to assist with these quests. If nothing else, we planned to leave it on the other side of the hole, in case Eric needed it.

When we reached the area of the avalanche, we were relieved to find that visibility inside had improved a bit, and I was able to inspect the cave around the collapse more thoroughly. While John was messing with the radiolocation device – it had to be perfectly vertical to get a precise reading – I investigated the area. I moved to the far end, above the hole where Eric's line was passing through, and I saw a narrow rift that looked like it could be a bypass. My immediate thought was that Eric, in desperation, would have ditched his equipment and attempted to get through, so at least his body could be retrieved. If he'd done that, he would be pinned, dead, on the ceiling of the chamber on this side. *Fuck, he'll have got through and then drowned here.* I ascended to examine every alcove in the ceiling, but he wasn't there.

The rift was very tight, even more technical than Wookey, and I wouldn't get through with the rebreather on my back. I'd need my BOTS. It would be a committing dive, probably not anything I would ever attempt to pass through for the sake of exploration, but I was convinced Eric was waiting for help on the other side and I didn't have any choice. At least the rift was above the avalanche cone, so safe from further collapse. After leaving the dry tube of supplies for Eric on his side of the hole, we again retreated through the cave. On our next dive, we would be attempting to pass the rift to reach the cave beyond.

Thinking that Eric was alive but not in a state to immediately dive out – and now knowing the difficulty of a rescue dive – it became clear that we needed at least one other person who could help us. Jason was the only diver I knew who was skilled enough to dive through the rift, and mad enough to do it voluntarily. I rang Jason at home, and he agreed to help without hesitating. I knew Chris Jewell was already on his way to Spain, where he was diving with his partner Artur Kozlowski. I phoned him next, to ask if he could divert to my house and then John's, to pick up our side-mount harnesses and drive them to us in the Ardèche, which was sort of on the way to Spain. The three men set off from the UK, driving over 1,000 kilometres through the night to reach us in the Ardèche the next evening.

After Jason, Pedro Balordi, and Luigi Casati staged the cave with open-circuit cylinders in preparation, John and I were ready to dive in for Eric on Monday morning, 11 October. A full week had passed since Eric had become trapped.

We dived back to the avalanche zone, and I went straight to the rift above it. John was laying the line, but I went in first. I could see that it was clear, but visibility was rapidly closing in. If I stopped and waited for John with the line, I'd lose my chance to clearly scan the scene, so I squeezed through on my side and went in. I had no clue where the rift would lead or even if it would rejoin the main passage, but I went on ahead, trusting that John would be behind me with the line. John watched me disappear into the narrow slit of rock.

'Oh shit, he's gone for it,' he thought and had no choice but to follow me.

Although only 5 metres long, it was a very tight and technical bit of cave to get through. It was very twisty and bendy; you had to be at just the right place to get through. I inched along on my side, pulling myself upwards or downwards as needed to find the way on. This was worse than any gravel squeeze I had been through – at least gravel gives beneath you and can be moved; this rock wall would have me pinned in place. I forged ahead on the hope that the rift would soon open into the main passage. I knew that getting back out was never going to be easy.

Thankfully, my head emerged through the far side and I was able to see down into the chamber beyond the collapse – the bottom half of the hourglass. It was a depressing scene of devastation. The tail cone of the avalanche had poured through the opening and quickly tapered off. The water was clearer on this side, with much of the silt behind me. Pieces of Eric's equipment were strewn about – some hardware, some cylinders, and there was line laid haphazardly. I followed Eric's line with my eyes, tracing its path, visualizing his desperate search for an escape.

John had followed me through the rift and joined me, where the visibility was already closing in. Together, we followed Eric's line as it continued upstream through the cave. Because he hadn't been at the avalanche area, we were certain that he'd found air and was still alive. We had no reason to suspect otherwise. After about 20 metres, the cave changed drastically and was more reminiscent of the familiarization video we'd been shown, with clean-washed walls and a nicely sculptured tunnel. We were going on a journey to find Eric where he'd been waiting in an airspace. Worried thoughts of getting back through the rift cleared my head, and I found myself enjoying this part of the cave. Then, just as we approached the deepest bit, we were brought to an abrupt halt.

Eric was on the floor, lying on his back, where the cave was −70 metres deep. His open eyes stared beyond his line to the roof of the cave above him. The emotional blow was like a kick in the stomach. As soon as I saw his body, everything changed. My thoughts returned to getting ourselves out of the cave safely.

I knelt on the floor of the cave beside Eric, grabbed him under the arms, and pulled his head up onto my lap. I looked over his equipment to find his dive computer, and clues as to what had happened. The information on the computer would tell us details of his dive, of what had gone on in his final moments. I searched his right arm first, then his left. No computer. I glanced up at John, to see him deftly slipping

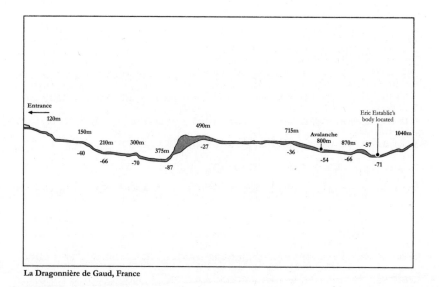

La Dragonnière de Gaud, France

the device into his pocket. 'I've already got it,' he said. If the IT business ever fails, he'd have a promising career as a pickpocket.

I looked down at Eric's lifeless body for a moment, before laying him to rest on the floor. He wouldn't be coming out of this cave.

John and I sombrely made our way towards the exit, both knowing we couldn't relax or begin thinking about anything until we'd got back through that rift. This time John went first; we dragged ourselves through sideways, wriggling around the bends, squeezing past the tightest sections. Knowing that Eric was dead – and probably had been this whole time – made me more acutely aware of the danger we'd placed ourselves in.

Having passed through, we continued up the incline beyond. During a decompression stop, one of the SSF divers came down to meet us, and John handed over Eric's dive computer. I took the diver's slate from him and scrawled the words 'Eric est décédé'.

When we finally surfaced, the gathered crowd rushed forward with questions. It was apparent that my message had not been passed on by the SSF divers, and I had to relay the devastating news.[6] As expected, the mood in the valley was distraught and mournful. I moved through the crowd, feeling a conflicting range of emotions. Knackered beyond belief. Relieved that we had made it back out through the cave. I looked at John's face, and saw my mood reflected.

The following afternoon – after John had spent the morning in a recompression chamber to treat mild symptoms of decompression sickness – we were asked to go to the police station to make a statement. With Charlie there to translate, I explained why a body recovery would not be taking place. We wouldn't do it, and I didn't know anybody else who could.

Cave diving contains a lot of risks, and the only way a cave diver stays alive is to become proficient at conducting constant risk-benefit analyses. Is this risk worth its consequence? I had accepted the risks of searching for Eric, and if we had found him alive, I would have accepted the risks that would come with rescuing him. For a mere body recovery, though, the risks were far too great. Nobody should risk their life for a dead body.

The police were clearly disappointed, and they made one final attempt, asking me to go back in to photograph Eric's body. I muttered something to let Charlie know what I thought of their request; I'm not sure how he translated it for them.

Before leaving, the police asked Charlie for his banking details. He was confused and asked why the information was needed. 'You're going to be paid for your translation services,' he was told, and we all laughed. After everything that John and I – not to mention the other divers and diggers – had done, Charlie was the only one of us who received any payment for their services.

I reflect on this incident quite a lot. The avalanche explains why he died, but I cannot answer the question of how Eric died. The avalanche provided the reason that he had been unable to leave the cave, but the exact cause of his death is unknown. Eric had probably set off the avalanche when he'd passed through on his way in. His dive profile tells us that he'd continued his exploration to a place where his computer registered a depth of zero metres. He'd turned around there and on his retreat had discovered his exit blocked. He'd stayed there for two hours, trying to find his way through the hole. It would have been absolutely pitch-black with the thick, suspended sediment; he wouldn't have even been able to see his lights.

Whenever I hear of a cave diver's death, I analyse the incident and try to learn from it. I imagine all cave divers do this. What went wrong? What would I have done differently? Do I think I could have got out? If I'd been in Eric's position, I'd like to think that I could have got out, but it's hard to say. It would have depended on me being able to find that rift, which would have been nearly impossible in the prevailing conditions. Even if Eric had found the rift, he'd have no way to get through it with his cumbersome dual rebreather unit – his life support and ballast and everything was in one huge package on his back – but my modular approach might have given me a chance.

I hope I never have to find out.

For our efforts, John and I were awarded a medal from the Royal Humane Society. I still maintain that what we did – diving through that rift – had been ludicrous. I hope to never have to do anything like that again. Eric's wife sent me heartfelt correspondence expressing her gratitude for what we did. Their son, Arthur, has since become a cave diver, and I speak with him occasionally.

Eric's rescue had been a major news event all around Europe – on the cover of every newspaper – but there was little media coverage of the story in the UK. This incident had occurred just as the entrapment of the Chilean miners was drawing to a close, and I've been told that the UK did not want to commit the media space to both stories. Hearing of two underground nightmares happening simultaneously would be too much.

⊕   ⊕   ⊕

Eleven months later, Anne and I were sitting in the living room, eating dinner and watching television, when the phone rang. I answered the call without taking my eyes off of *The Big Bang Theory*,[7] and found myself in a conversation with a member of the Irish Cave Rescue Organization. A minute later I hung up the phone and turned to Anne, who had already turned off the television and looked like she knew what was coming.

'What's happened?' she asked.

'A diver has died in a cave in Ireland.'

'They want you to go?' she asked, and I nodded. There was more.

'It's Artur,' I told her, and her eyes widened. Just two weeks earlier, she'd been feeding Artur and Chris when they'd visited us at Pozo Azul.

Artur had failed to return from his exploratory dive in a cave called Pollonara 10 on 5 September. On the following day, his body had been discovered about 800 metres into the cave, at a depth of – 52 metres, by his dive partner Jim Warny. Jim had felt uncomfortable swimming the body out, so I had been called.

I went through the round of phone calls, which were becoming all too familiar. First John and Jason, then Bill. Chris Jewell – Artur's friend and dive partner on several projects – was desperate to be involved in this recovery, but we didn't think it would be a good idea. Chris had never participated in a recovery before, and we thought he might have been too close to Artur. (In hindsight, it would have been a good idea to include him, so he could have gained relevant emotional experience before being called over to Tham Luang.)

Jason, John and I had just got back from Spain only days earlier. Pozo Azul is full on in every respect; we spend weeks preparing for the most difficult dives we plan to do all year, and it can be a little bit fraught. After Spain, the last thing I want to do for weeks – or months – is even think about diving again, much less working on a project with Jason and John. I knew the others would be feeling the same way, so I didn't know how we would do showing up in Ireland.

Jason drove the three of us to Pollonara 10, a cave in the Gort lowlands of County Galway in western Ireland, whose entrance lay on private land, behind a family's home. Artur had spent years diving there and had been welcomed by the family who owned the land. Indeed, all of the locals had come to know him well through the years, and there were already crowds gathered when we arrived.

The next morning, Jason went in first to get the body ready to be taken out by stripping the equipment off. Then John and I dived in together, to move the body out between us. The plan was to take an arm each. The visibility was horrendous, and there was a huge amount of confusion between us. Because we couldn't see each other, there was no coordination or communication, which resulted in us spinning around and travelling the wrong way. Both Artur and I became deeply entangled in the line, in absolute zero visibility. In the end, I was in a crucifix position against Artur's body, bumping faces with him. If I wasn't careful – if I cut the wrong line – I knew I wouldn't be getting out of there.

John eventually realized what was going on but was unable to help so he did the only thing that was available to him, which was to retreat until I could sort myself out. I freed myself from the line – and from Artur – and exited the cave. Tidy line management hadn't been my top priority while disentangling myself, and I wasn't sure what kind of mess I'd left behind. When John went back the next day to sort it out and resume the recovery, I'd warned him that the area could be full of line hazards, but he found that I'd left the scene safe. That was gratifying, knowing that muscle memory and instinct had come through when I'd needed them.

We'd proven that working together in this environment was unproductive, so the three of us took turns on the day's recovery. Finally, when Artur was near the surface, we turned him over to his friend and dive partner, Jim Warny, who gratefully accepted the responsibility of bringing Artur out of the cave for the last time.

With Artur's body being taken away, the three of us packed up our equipment and retreated from the scene, leaving the town to mourn the loss of the diver who had become their adopted son. As Jason drove the three of us back to the UK, we had no way of knowing that the next time the three of us would dive together again would be three years later, in Norway, on another recovery mission.

For that one, in 2014, two divers got into trouble and drowned in the Plura cave while attempting to make a traverse between two separate entrances. Typical of goal-oriented dives, they had only concentrated on the idea of success, without considering the possibility of failure. This had been the first step to it going badly wrong.

The original team had consisted of five Finnish divers, but the surviving three had (understandably) been forbidden from going back for the bodies. Norwegian authorities already trusted us because of our success with Ståle's recovery in 2006, so we were called in. John, Jason and I made our way to Arctic Norway, in the dead of winter (−10°C air temperature). *Whenever we get called for a rescue, it never seems to be at the time we'd want to be there.*[8]

The three of us dived in from the original team's exit location, which was closer to where the bodies were located. The first body we encountered, at −112 metres, was blocking the way through a restriction and was snared by something that was out of our reach. Heave as we might, we were unable to pull him forwards. The only way to guarantee success would be to repeat the dive the Finns had originally planned, counting on being able to free the first body by pulling him backwards. Recovering the two bodies would require a committing series of deep dives in 2° C water, where a suit flood (like the one I'd had in Saint Sauveur) would likely prove fatal. With all the best planning in the world, there was every chance that one of us could have succumbed to a decompression injury. The risks were way beyond anything we were prepared to take on to bring out the bodies of two divers we weren't emotionally connected to.

Unlike most of our diving, this was a rare occasion when other people (the police authorities) were responsible for us, and we could sense the weight of their unease. We all felt the original team had created the problem – by planning a dive that exceeded the experience of some of the team members – and we knew the survivors were capable and willing to sort it out themselves, with additional support.

The clandestine mission to recover the bodies was a bit controversial,[9] but I suspect the police knew what was happening and chose to turn a blind eye, happy to have the problem resolved. It ended up as a feelgood story; there was even a film of the event called *Into the Unknown*, which made them all out to be heroes. The drama of the emotive film disguised the fact that the incident should have never occurred in the first place.[10]

Leaving Norway, we all assumed this would be the last high-profile event we'd ever be called out to, and because we had left it unsettled, we had a bit of a sour taste in our mouths. It would have been nice to have finished with a success.

'I was confident of getting myself out, I was confident of not losing control of the line, I was confident of getting the kid out. I wasn't 100 per cent confident of getting him out alive.'

Jason Mallinson

Monday, 9 July 2018, Thailand

Some changes were made to the plan for the second day, as we learned from the mistakes that had been made on the first day. All of the boys were alive and safe in a nearby hospital, so we all considered the first day to have been an overwhelming success, but there was room for improvement.

The compressors had been running continuously and gone past the duty life of the filters, resulting in some cylinders containing oily, contaminated air that tasted disgusting and had been nauseating people. We hadn't had time on the first day to test them all, so it was a bit of a lottery. If a diver ended up with a bad cylinder – which I think all of us did, at some point – he'd just favour the other one. Claus volunteered to talk to the compressor operators, to get this sorted.

Jim Warny would be taking Ivan's place in Chamber 6. I wasn't the only one who had noticed how uncomfortable Ivan seemed, and how this had affected his performance during the rescue. In the evening, when he'd mumbled something about having the flu and not being able to continue, we all understood.[11] Josh Bratchley, Connor's dive partner from the UK, had just arrived and was ready to go straight in, so we weren't short-handed. For Day 2, Jim would join Erik in Chamber 6; Josh and Connor would work together in Chamber 5.

A criticism had come back from the hospital: the boys hadn't woken until the early hours, and the doctors had no way of knowing each boy's identity. We'd been a bit trigger-happy on the first day, topping up the sedation with a full dose at any indication of awakening. At the briefing, Harry told us, 'If you've got a smaller boy, don't give him all of it.' As we became more adept with administering doses, the boys were given just enough to keep them sedated during the dive, with many of them beginning to wake within an hour of leaving the cave.[12] For identification, we took in a permanent marker and wrote the nickname of each boy on the back of his hand.

We had thought that handing our boy over to thousands of rescuers would be safe, but in fact that was where everything had fallen apart. Everyone wanted to get their hands on a boy as he left the cave, wanting to play a role in the rescue, but nobody took care to notice what was happening with the boy himself. One of the boys – still wearing his face mask to receive the higher oxygen – had nearly breathed the tank down to zero. We'd managed to get the boy through the dangerous underwater sections, only to have him nearly suffocate in the hands of the rescuers? Fortuitously, Jason advised Derek to check the cylinder's gauge; when he did, Derek found it was nearly empty.

$$\oplus \quad \oplus \quad \oplus$$

The changes were all very minimal – just some tidying-up of loose ends – but the process was staying the same. Everything had worked, so we had no reason to mess with things too much. The first day's rescues had taken ten hours in full, and we were prepared for another long day inside the cave. I was a bit surprised to find myself more tense on this second day than I had been on the first. Instead of feeling relieved by the first day's success, I felt more pressure for this day to be equally successful. Knowing that the plan itself worked meant that any failure would likely be of our own making. With four healthy boys out of the cave, expectations had been raised, and we felt the pressure to meet them.

Because I began in Chamber 9 on this day and things were less hectic, I was able to watch Harry more closely, and I saw how well he interacted with the boys. As they were sitting on his knee, he chatted to them in his smooth, reassuring voice, making a little story about every diver who was leading the boys out. 'Ah, you've got Jason. He's the strongest swimmer. You'll be fine with him.' 'Ah, you've got John. He's the fittest. You're in really good hands here.' 'Ah, you've got Rick. He's got loads of experience.'

'Are you saying I'm old?' I kidded.

'Well . . .' he answered with a grin. Then he pointed something out to the boy sitting on his knee – 'Look up!' – and as the boy looked up, he jabbed the needle in his leg. 'I bet you didn't see that coming!' His confidence and almost carefree attitude helped to set the tone in the chamber.

I was diving last again, this time taking Dom with me. We'd been told that the boys in hospital had cuts and bruises on their feet from being dragged along the cave floor and I'd had the idea to tuck an empty water bottle into the bungee that bound Dom's ankles, to provide some buoyancy to his feet. This worked nicely as we moved through the cave, with the small improvement in trim making a world of difference.

Claus and Mikko were waiting for us with the stretcher in Chamber 8, along with Craig. I was impressed to hear the Euro Divers speaking calmly to Dom in Thai as they carried him through the chamber, mindful of the possibility that the sedated boys might be able to hear what was being said. I thought this was a nice personal touch, one I never would have thought of.

Erik and Jim were both present and calm in Chamber 6, where we swapped cylinders and moved along without any confusion.

Even before I'd surfaced in Chamber 5, I could hear Josh and Connor talking and laughing. They'd dug a platform out of the mud bank where they could rest out of the water, but when I surfaced, I found them standing in water up to their necks and grinning from ear to ear. I laughed and told them they looked like pigs in shit. They made a good team, working together to move Dom through the canal swiftly.

The dives all went smoothly, and by the end of the day, there were eight Wild Boars resting comfortably in hospital. All divers were out of the cave around 8 p.m., about eight hours after going in. 'You're not finished yet,' I reminded myself. Five were left inside: four boys and the coach. We still had one more day.

After we'd changed into dry clothes, we were told that Thailand's Prime Minister, Prayut Chan-o-Cha, was on site and coming to see us. I saw the look of horror on Amp's face when she heard this and realized he'd be coming to our room, which now contained seven piss-soaked wetsuits. The stench was overpowering in there. I reflected back to finding the boys, when I'd first removed my mask and been struck by how pungent that smell was. Now, an equally revolting smell was emanating from our gear room. Luckily we were outside when the Prime Minister arrived, so he didn't have to confront the smell too closely.[13]

We were all seated around a long table, eating our first real meal of the day, and none of us bothered standing to greet him. He took this in his stride, and it set the tone for what became a very informal and personal meeting. One of his men carried a box, out of which the PM began pulling small gifts – food treats – and handing them out to us like a children's entertainer. It was all a bit surreal. He spoke in English and spent a few moments chatting with us all light-heartedly before asking if anyone wanted to say anything.

'I'd like to say a word about these two,' John said, pointing to Tom and Bas, who had been indispensable to us throughout the rescue operation. I knew what John was about to say and was grateful that he had thought to do so. I glanced at the two men and saw them freeze in terror, afraid that their work was about to be criticized in front of their Prime Minister. On the contrary.

'They've done an amazing job looking after us,' John declared. 'They deserve a special commendation.' In addition to providing support directly to us, they had been tasked with looking after our welfare and making daily reports on us to the Minister of Tourism and Sport (who had called us in and may have felt directly responsible for us). I'm pretty sure that their respect for us was evident when giving these reports, and I believe this helped to persuade the minister that we were trustworthy. When we had proposed our plan – and especially when we began requesting foreigners to be flown in for the rescue – this would have proven pivotal, as he was the one who was arranging their flights.

Somebody spoke up next, on Vern and Tik's behalf. 'Vern needs a permanent Thai visa.' We all laughed as the PM grinned and punched Vern playfully on the shoulder.

'Just marry her,' he said. 'Then your visa will be no problem!'

After dinner, the divers' briefing was short and sweet. The only tweaks I'd thought of were adding a layer of foam beneath the boys' neoprene hoods to provide more padding for their heads and the bit about using an empty water bottle to lift their feet. The final issue involved the fact that the last day would involve five rescues instead of four, yet there were only four core divers. My preference would probably have been to have Harry bringing the last lad out with him when he exited Chamber

9 behind me, but on Saturday he and Craig had specifically said that they would not be transporting the boys because they weren't familiar enough with navigating the cave.

In typical fashion, Jason had already applied himself to this after he'd finished his rescue, and he presented the solution. 'I'll dive from Chamber 9 twice,' he volunteered. 'The first time, I'll hand the boy off to someone in Chamber 7, then go back for the last lad.' That was a good plan, requiring minimum modification from what we knew already worked. Who would we trust to take the first boy from Chamber 7 to 3? Jason suggested Jim Warny.

John and I hesitated, remembering how Jim had been reluctant to move Artur's body through Pollonara 10. Jason had to ask us three times before either of us answered. Finally, not able to think of a better solution, we agreed to give Jim the responsibility.

Tuesday, 10 July 2018

I awoke the next morning – the final day of the rescue – to the sound of frogs croaking outside. The forecasts in the preceding days had kept giving us a three-day window before the rain started. Clearly, our time was up; the window was closing. I stepped outside to see rain pouring down into standing puddles that were already several centimetres deep. *Had we waited too long? Would we be able to get the final five out?*

The group of us met at Tham Luang for our usual pre-dive meeting, and today's topic was the rain's implication for our dive.

Although the forecast showed the rain would be stopping, it was still raining during our meeting. Vern had been telling us about Thanet's diversion efforts in the mountains, where he'd been using kilometres of plastic pipe (and, when that ran out, split bamboo stalks) to prevent surface streams from entering Tham Luang. These diversions could be overwhelmed, but we hoped that the water from the surface would take hours to reach our location in the cave.

Only John and I had seen how ferocious the water could become when the cave was flooding; we felt like it was worth going ahead with the rescue, but with extreme caution. If we saw the water rising when we were inside, as it had done during our first days on site, then we would abort the mission, but we knew we would be efficient and thought we'd have enough time.

Hodges had been constantly reminding us not to be complacent, and this morning he reiterated that message. 'Just because you've had two successful days, doesn't mean you're certain to achieve a third.' We didn't need to be told that. Derek had originally argued that bringing one out alive would be considered a success. After eight successful rescues, the ethics tables had been turned: one death now would be viewed as a complete failure. People had high expectations.

We would have been more reassured if we'd seen the rain stop (as forecast), but when we entered the cave, rain was still falling. In spite of this, the water level in the cave was the lowest we had seen it since that first flood on our first night there, showing the effects of the targeted pumping, as well as the water diversion being done on the mountain. The water in the U-bend between Chambers 2 and 3 had lowered to the point where it was walkable, but just. (We still wore a single cylinder going through, as we didn't know what would happen, but I think we all free-dived the duck under the archway.)

In the canal passage beyond Chamber 6, John and I came upon an unwieldy-looking duffel bag that was floating off to the side. It was like a bloated doughnut, very much out of place. The thing had caught my eye on both of the previous days, but I hadn't engaged with it enough to consider what it was or why it was there. Today, spurred on by being together, our curiosity finally got the best of us.

'What do you think this is?' I asked John.

'I don't know. Let's investigate.' We started pulling off the wrapping and found it was full of wetsuits. A preposterous and buoyant bag, with no streamlining, it had been deposited here for reasons unknown, and by persons unknown. 'I don't know who brought this in,' I said to John. 'Whoever it was must have had a right epic.'

By the time I surfaced in Chamber 8, Jason had already arrived with the first evacuee of the day. As I made my way through the chamber, Claus and Mikko walked past me, carrying Coach Ek on a stretcher to where Jim was waiting to begin diving him out.[14] I was a bit surprised to see that Ek had elected to go out ahead of some of the younger boys – I think it caught us all out.

Inside the cave, we had no way of knowing if the rain had stopped or if it was worsening, but the stream in the 7–8 passage was negligible, and there was no sign of the flood pulse we had been fearing. I was fairly convinced that Thanet's water diversion was largely responsible for keeping the current rainfall from filling the cave, and I could only hope that it would be effective enough to last us through the day.

I dived to Chamber 9, where John was preparing to leave with his boy. After John had left, I processed and departed with Titan. Chris would be following behind me with Pong. The last boy out of the cave would be Mark, taken by Jason and followed out by Harry.

Processing Titan went smoothly. He's the youngest lad and we'd worried all along that we would have difficulty sealing the mask to his small face. After he'd been processed and we were fitting the mask, Harry said, 'OK, good to go.' I wasn't so convinced, and one last investigation revealed a tell-tale leak. 'Good spot,' Harry said as we further tightened the straps.

RICK STANTON

I set off and was happy to note that Titan was breathing like a train. The little guy was breathing maybe fifteen breaths per minute. They were small breaths, but steady. It was reassuring. At intervals, I held him to the side and rotated his body towards me, allowing me to look into the visor. I was checking to make sure there was no water in there, and I always took note of his face. He looked so calm, as peaceful as though he were asleep in bed. It was a bit surreal.

The dive out was uneventful until I reached the challenging line trap that lay beyond Chamber 4. We had all learned to negotiate the vertical letter box while carrying a boy on the first two days, but the guide line had shifted today. Something had caused the rope to be pulled more tightly into the trap, and manoeuvring the boy through it was even more difficult. I had to poke around for the correct part of the slot to descend through, moving Titan below me awkwardly until I had located the letter-box opening he was to be passed through. This one part of the line should have been tidied up before the rescue began, but none of us had had the opportunity to engage with it.

Breaking surface in Chamber 3 for the last time, I was blinded by the lamp of a Chinese volunteer who was lighting the scene. I cursed quietly as I shielded my eyes, then pulled myself from the water to stand in the chamber. The water level in the cave had receded so that the journey from Chamber 2 to 3 was now completely walkable. Volunteers had taken advantage of this newly dry passage to carry tubs of Thai noodles and KFC into Chamber 3, and I gratefully accepted some food, mingling with the others while we waited for the remaining divers.

While I had already begun celebrating, Jason was facing his own problems in the cave. After I'd left with Titan and Chris had left with Pong, Jason and Harry had prepared to process the final boy.

When Mark came down the ramp, Jason and Harry were horrified to see how small he was.

'Oh fuck,' they said in unison.

We'd been worried about Titan, the youngest lad, but there was Mark, and his face was much smaller and thinner. The positive pressure mask we'd intended to use for the fifth rescue was our reserve one, and it had an older-style inflexible rubber skirt, not the soft pliable silicone of the newer ones. We hadn't been convinced about it from the start – and we were right, it simply didn't fit. Thankfully, we'd also brought along a spare. This bright pink recreational mask was not positive pressure – but at least it was small and flexible.

'We put it on him, really strapped down tight so his nose was flattened against his face. We just couldn't get it to seal. We knew we didn't have any more time and we knew this was the last option,' Jason said later. The seal was clamped down on Mark's face, and Jason knew the mask would dislodge very easily if it was knocked. He'd have to swim even more cautiously, with most of his attention focused on keeping Mark's mask in place.

'Fish on!' I think it was Jamie calling out to the other Americans that the line was moving, signalling the impending arrival of a diver. Then nothing happened, and I thought it must have been a false call. Nearly thirty minutes later, when the line began moving again, I realized that quite a bit of time had passed while I'd been busy eating. *Somebody should have arrived by now. Something must be amiss.*

'Wouldn't it be funny if Jason turns up next?' I said to John, just as Jason's head broke the surface, carrying Mark.

'I found Chris in Chamber 4 with his boy,' he told us. 'I stayed with him there until Harry arrived.'

'Should we go back in?'

'No, I think Harry's got it under control.'

When the line began twitching a few minutes later, I kept my eyes on it until I saw Harry emerge with Pong. *Thank fuck for that.* The smile on Harry's face showed how happy he was, and I was glad that he'd been given the chance to participate in the delivery of the boys – bringing one boy out alive – instead of just being the one who'd sedated them in the cave. Now he was a deliverer, and not just the dispatcher. It gave him some closure and completed his journey.

Not much later, Chris surfaced and told us what had happened. While trying to negotiate the tricky line trap, he had let go of the line and become disoriented. Feeling around blindly, he'd located one of the many cables that were festooning the passage, but then he had followed it in the wrong direction. After surfacing to find himself back in Chamber 4, he had waited there, apprehensive about attempting the line trap again. He'd still been there twenty minutes later when Jason had been on his way through.

Within minutes, we were joined by all of our divers from the cave – Craig, Claus, Mikko, Erik, Connor, Josh. The three SEALs and Dr Pak had been strategically supplied with enough cylinders to dive out. They'd be moving more slowly through the cave, but they were on their way. Chamber 9 would be empty. The Wild Boars were safe.

When Erik produced a large bottle of Jack Daniels[15] and passed it around, the celebrations officially began. We all stood around for some time, chatting and laughing. For the first time in over two weeks, I could relax. There was a smile on everyone's face.

When enough time had passed that we knew the stretchers were out of the cave – an hour or so – the team of divers left the cave, with the Euro Divers and Americans staying in the cave to wait for the four Thais. On our way out, we passed through a massive crowd of greeters and well-wishers who were waiting to congratulate and thank us for our roles in the rescue. I don't think I've ever shaken so many hands in my life as I did on the walk out from Chamber 3.

After we'd left, the chamber was stripped clean of all its cylinders; almost immediately after this had been completed, a pump casing cracked in the archway between Chambers 2 and 3. The pump was still operating, and water dramatically began spraying everywhere. The power had to be cut while it was being fixed, which disabled the other pumps. With the chamber emptied of cylinders, those remaining would be trapped if the archway became sumped again, and it was already beginning to fill. Everybody scrambled to leave Chamber 3. Just in time, the four SEALs emerged and walked out with the Americans, leaving the cave at peace.

We'd always said, 'Keep expectations realistic, and then nobody's going to be disappointed.' Since arriving in Thailand, I'd been so busy managing everyone else's expectations that I hadn't allowed myself to consider the possibility of a successful rescue. A 100 per cent success rate had seemed impossible, unfathomable. Yet there we were.

Derek would later say, 'You under-promised and over-delivered.'

All the time we'd been there, we'd seen the boys' families watching us as we walked into the cave, but they'd never asked to speak with us, and we'd never engaged with them. I remembered the French cavers pleading with us outside La Dragonnière, as we were searching for Eric Establie's body. (*You have to find him. You're the only hope.*) The pressure from them had been immense; I didn't think I could cope if the parents of these children pleaded with me the same way.

After the rescue, when we were back in the gear room, we were told that the boys' families wanted to meet us. I was so exhausted, with my head still filled with thoughts of the rescue, that I didn't feel ready for this emotional scene, but now seemed like an appropriate time to finally meet them.

We ended up standing in two lines, facing each other. The divers stood side-by-side, across from the boys' mothers, with Josh Morris standing at the head of the line-out to do the translating. As we had become accustomed to, we were surrounded by a crowd, all filming the event. This time, we couldn't shy away from the cameras. It felt a bit awkward.

Not having any children of my own, I couldn't fathom what the previous eighteen days had been like for them, the torture they must have felt not knowing whether their sons would live or die. Before the extrication began, someone in the Thai authorities had asked that the parents give their consent to a form that said something like: 'There might be deaths, but the death of your child might lead to the life of others.' It was pretty blunt, and they didn't really have the option to refuse. As far as I know, that was the most information they had been given about the process. I had not considered the parents when I had been planning the rescue. I imagined Jason and John would have been more empathetic to their plight, but we'd never talked about it.

The woman I happened to be standing across from was very small – she didn't even come to my shoulders – and I suspected (correctly) that she was Titan's mother. She looked up at me as Josh spoke. Her eyes were fixated on me, and I noted that she wasn't crying, as other mothers were. I've never seen a purer look of happiness and gratitude. Josh gave a talk and when he was done, the mothers stepped in to hug us. Titan's mum squeezed her arms around my torso. We didn't share a common language, but her embrace let me know how she was feeling at that moment. I remembered earlier, in the cave, when I'd realized that I was able to relax for the first time in over two weeks and I was struck with the understanding that those two weeks had been infinitely harder for her – for all of them – than it had been for any of us. I couldn't imagine what they had been going through.

(*'You are very strong. Very strong.'*)

I put my arms around her and returned her embrace.

13.
Surface Reflections

'In the end, however, I have a feeling that Richard
might do quite well, giving us all a lesson in economy
of effort. But it is a dangerous game to play.'
My final school report from Mr Boreham

My relationship with Anne had ended just before Christmas 2011, when she'd moved out and gone to South Africa, where her family lived, before heading home to Australia. I hadn't treated her very fairly, she quickly grew tired of it, and she left. Her leaving was not unexpected, but I was surprised by how much I missed her – so much so that I chased her to South Africa in the new year.[1] We spent a couple of weeks together there – during which I had my first experience in a sea kayak and had immediately enjoyed it – but nothing was going to change the situation between us. When I left, I expected I wouldn't be seeing her again.

I had never figured out how to proportion my energy between cave diving and girlfriends (or anything else, really) in any way that even approached a fair distribution. It has been pointed out to me that, while I'm a complete natural underwater and in caves, I don't always do so well when I have to interact with people on the surface.

At this same time, I was also reaching the end of my patience as a firefighter. For my first fifteen years with the fire service, I'd been very conscientious. I was quiet and didn't speak out, and I was skilled at the job. After that, however, I began to switch off. I was present in body but not in spirit. By the final few years, I'd had enough. By then the work had changed, and we were constantly being sent on asinine assignments, like giving fire prevention lessons for kids in schools. It was horrible. I'd structured my life to avoid children as much as possible, and the last thing I wanted to be doing at work was putting on a show in a classroom. It's nothing personal against them, or any specific children; it just wasn't what I signed up for.[2]

The guys on my watch were the one good thing about work during this period. We were all competent workers who could think for ourselves but didn't take very kindly to authority. As a result of this shared mindset, we went through a lot of officers who didn't know what to do with us. Finally, they became determined to split us up, and I was the easy target, because I kept sticking my nose out. My final years with the fire service became a rollercoaster, alternately receiving awards and disciplinary actions. It was ridiculous.

In 2011, I was disciplined for reversing a fire engine over somebody's paving slabs and cracking some, then the following year I was nominated Fire Brigade Hero of the Year.

Then one day, first thing in the morning, I strode into the watch officer's office and announced, 'I'm sorry, but I think you're a total ****,' before spinning on my heel and leaving his office as abruptly as I had entered. I don't even remember what I was angry about, and it was probably nothing, but I was at my wits' end in those days. Meanwhile, Chief Officer Vij Randaniya – who was my greatest advocate[3] and had already chosen me to represent the West Midlands Fire Service at a royal garden party – put my name forward to receive a Member of the Order of the British Empire award (MBE), honouring my work with cave rescues.

Around this same time, in the summer of 2012, after spending a lazy Sunday at home enjoying one of the hottest days of the year, I arrived at the station in the evening to be told that a hot breathing apparatus drill was going to be run. I always liked those drills, but it seemed like a needless punishment to put men into a stifling room on a stifling day, just for the sake of running a drill that could be run any time.

'You're fucking joking,' I'd said. 'On a hot day like this?'

'Fires happen on hot days, too.'

'Yes, and we'll deal with them,' I told him. 'When we have to.'

The watch manager didn't appreciate my comments, he ran the drill, someone went down with heatstroke, and I was transferred for my insubordination. The transfer happened just as I went to Buckingham Palace, where Prince Charles presented me with the MBE. After being moved to a different station – which I referred to as Sleepy Hollow – I lost all interest in the work.

In hindsight, I do realize that my behaviour in those final years of work make me sound like a grumpy old man. The moment I was eligible for early retirement in 2014, I didn't hesitate. It came with a reduced pension, but I didn't mind. What I gained in freedom would be far greater than what I'd lose in my pension. I'd never been very concerned about money (which is good, because I've never had very much), and I was known for being extraordinarily frugal. As with everything, I always had enough money, but not plenty.

In fact, my habit of repurposing and reusing things extended beyond my diving equipment. A classic example of this is when a colleague was sent to collect a donated three-piece suite, meant to be set alight in a house-fire demonstration. He returned with it and said, 'I can guarantee this is better quality than anything that's in your house.' I looked at it, agreed with his statement, and we made the swap. Twenty years later, I still have one of those armchairs in my living room at home.

All along, although I'd done the job well, my career as a fire-fighter was never really a priority or a part of my identity. I'd always considered work (as a firefighter) to be a hobby, while my hobby (cave diving) was more like my job. All of my effort was given to cave diving – managing, planning, motivating, writing reports, researching, innovating – with no energy left for work. In addition, my tolerance for stress and frustration were certainly allotted exclu-sively to cave diving (hence my quick irritation with the officers). It's probably best that I took early retirement; I'm sure the fire station was a more pleasant place after I'd gone.

In spite of the way it ended, I am really grateful for the fire ser-vice. It was a secure form of employment, so I never had to worry about being out of work. My hours were set, and I didn't take any work home with me, so my mind was free to think about other things. Crucially, the schedule suited my lifestyle. I don't know another job that would have given me such flexibility and afforded me as much time away. If I hadn't spent ninety days abroad in any one year, taking full advantage of my holidays and four-day breaks, then that wasn't a very good year. Most importantly, it wasn't a 'bullshit job' that had been created to feed into the modern econ-omy. Instead of spending my life creating wealth for somebody else, I was doing something that needed to be done. I can't imagine any other job that I would have been able to stick with or been as well suited for.

I've heard that some people have a hard time letting go of their career and moving into retirement, but I didn't expect I'd have that problem. I was intent on leaving work behind me, opening space for other activities. True to this, within hours of my final day at the fire station, I boarded a plane for Florida. I'd been invited to speak at a diving convention, and then I'd be spending a week diving with Duncan. As I flew across the Atlantic, most of my stories and information from the fire service were jettisoned into the ocean, never to be retrieved.

At the conference, somebody asked me a question about work and I just looked at him blankly. I really couldn't recall any of it, nor did I want to try very hard.

⊕　　⊕　　⊕

I can't explain exactly what led to my withdrawal from cave diving; I don't even know if it was a conscious choice. The motivation just wasn't there any more, not in the way it had always been before. I'd always said that I was very selective with my diving projects; now I was joking that I had become so selective, that I wasn't really selecting anything.

I did some diving in Sardinia, where there were major caves waiting to be explored.

I returned to Pozo Azul in 2014, but an equipment failure during a set-up dive prevented me from participating in the exploration. When my Land Rover had broken down in 2009, I'd run back and forth across the UK like a madman, getting everything set up so that I'd make it to Spain. In 2014, I just couldn't be bothered getting things sorted out in time to join the dive, so Jason and René went in without me.[4]

I returned to Cogol dei Veci with Jason in 2015, in an attempt to find the continuation beyond Sump 2, but was unsuccessful.

They were all good dives, but nothing excited me the way previous projects had done. After Pozo, very little seemed worth pursuing. Maybe I was reaching the end of a line, but even now, I can't quite give up diving completely. There is one last project that I'm still inspired to complete – a cave in France, unsurprisingly. I won't be satisfied until I have a look in that cave . . . even if it kills me, which it might do if I went there now.

My last big exploration project was in Bel Torrente, one of the sea caves along the eastern coast of Sardinia, during the summer of 2015. The beautiful island has limestone mountains that are filled with dry caves and walls for climbing; the coastal cliffs plunge into the sea, and beneath the surface are major caves. I'd begun visiting in 2007, and in recent years, Sardinia had become my new playground. I'd been welcomed into the local caving community and had partnered with Thorsten Waelde (Toddy), the owner of a local dive facility, to explore Bel Torrente.

As I was preparing my equipment and filling my dry tube for the nights we were planning to spend in the cave, I began thinking about all of the countless hours I'd wasted over the years – fettling with equipment, hand-sewing harnesses, designing modifications, testing new gear, building new lights.

'This has been a fucking waste of my life,' I complained bitterly to Karen, who was sitting on the ground beside me as I packed my dry tube for the dive. 'So much time wasted, fettling with gear, packing equipment. What has it been for?'

I was really angry, and resentful, at the trap I had created for myself. I'd taken my diving to such a gear-intensive extent that that aspect of it had become everything. I used to enjoy it, but I'd come to loathe it. Unfortunately, I knew that if I wasn't willing to dedicate the time to fettling, any future projects would be impossible. No more exploration projects, no more big dives. I could leave it all behind, for the sake of things I enjoyed doing.

When I felt the same after the dive in Bel Torrente, I was convinced. The project had been successful – a really good trip and enjoyable – but I knew I was finished. The realization came as a relief.

A few weeks later as we drove back to the UK, the Talking Heads song 'Once in a Lifetime' came on the radio.

It was one of my favourite songs, from one of my favourite bands, and I felt like I was hearing it for the first time. 'That's been my life,' I said. 'My whole life has been about water flowing underground.'

The guys at the fire station used to tease me by saying, 'Only you would excel in a sport that has no practical purpose. You don't even get paid for it. If you were at this level as a footballer, you'd be earning a fortune.' And they were correct. I'd devoted my life to reaching the pinnacle in this one activity that was absolutely pointless, it brought nothing to anybody.[5]

In the meantime, if people – usually Jason or John – were going on a big project, I knew they were still putting my name down as the person to call if there was an emergency. That was pretty much the only time I seriously looked over my gear, and I did just enough diving to make sure that everything still worked. I knew I'd have to be ready if I was ever called.

When Jason dived alone inside Pozo Azul in 2015, John and I both promised that we'd be on standby in case something happened, and we were both counting on nothing going wrong. Neither of us wanted to have to go into Pozo Azul for a rescue. Jason made it into the sixth sump that year, then barely got out alive. On his exit, his rebreather flooded before he'd reached the elbow of the second sump, there were only just enough open-circuit cylinders staged, and he'd ended up skip-breathing to conserve air. John and I received a text message from his surface support, cryptically informing us that 'Jason just got out.' I didn't realize the full implications of those words until I later heard the story of the dive.

After a few years of not diving much, something changed, and I began to miss being underwater. I took a cave-diving trip to Greece in early May of 2018. A few weeks later, John and I planned a diving trip to France. This would be our first time diving together in a couple of years, and we wanted to make sure that nothing – including ourselves – had got rusty. We visited some of the classic sites, which I'd been keen to explore earlier, but now I had no motivation for going so far inside. Without the added stress of pushing limits and chasing exploration, we were able to relax and enjoy ourselves.[6]

One day, while in France, we were at the dive centre where divers tend to congregate, and somebody recognized me and John as we were getting our cylinders. As is typical, the stranger began asking us about our exploration plans. This is the expectation that people always have: they assume we're always diving to explore.

We just shrugged. 'Nothing planned,' John said.

I think it was clear that neither of us were very interested in even talking about future diving projects, much less pursuing one. He followed up with another question.

'If you were called to another cave rescue, would you still go?'

We both laughed. I was nearly sixty, John nearly fifty. The idea was ludicrous, and I told him as much.

'I can't imagine anybody's going to be needing us for a rescue.'

'The distance between insanity and genius
is measured only by success.'

Wednesday, 11 July 2018, Thailand

It was over. We had done it. The Wild Boars were out of the cave
and they were all alive. We spent the next day busily rinsing and
packing up from Tham Luang – the local fire service filled a tub
with water for washing our gear.[7]

That evening, a huge party was planned at the Meridien, the
super-posh hotel where the Americans had been staying.[8] It was
a really festive time, with food and drink. There were even some
of Elon Musk's representatives from SpaceX there, who spoke
with me and Jason. Elon had shown up at the cave himself on
Monday night, while we were all asleep after the second day of
the rescue. No one made an effort to have us look at the capsule,
which I didn't understand; I would've liked to see it. *Why would he
have made a nice shiny thing that he was proud of and then not seek out our
feedback?*

The party spread to a local bar and then a nightclub, and by the
end of the night, I was so drunk I was barely able to walk. I leaned
on Amp for support, and she kept me from falling over as I stum-
bled down the hotel corridor, bouncing from wall to wall. Possibly
as a result of this display, there was an online article in the UK's
Daily Mail the very next day, announcing our romance: 'Thai Hero
Finds Love with Local Nurse'. I found it all quite embarrassing, but
was very grateful that there weren't any photos of me from the
night before.

I might have never been in a place where so many people were so
happy, yet amid all of our celebrations and drunken revelry, a

tragedy sneaked in when Harry received a phone call with the news that his father had just passed away. He was clearly devastated and spoke stoically of the good life his father had led. 'He made me who I am,' Harry said, and I took a moment to silently thank Mr Harris Snr for whatever he'd done that had led to Harry becoming the person who had arrived in Thailand. I still maintain that Harry was the only person on the planet who'd have the courage to act on the audacious plan that I'd presented him with, and the rescue's success falls heavily onto his shoulders. In his own way, by moulding his son, Mr Harris had played a part in the rescue himself.

Thursday, 12 July 2018

The seven of us who were flying to the UK gathered our bags in the evening and headed for the airport in Chiang Rai. I couldn't help but remember the flight, sixteen days earlier, when I'd been travelling in the other direction. On that flight, I had been with John and Rob; now I was returning with Chris, Connor, Josh, Jim, Mike and Gary. (John and Jason had left the Meridien party early to fly home, missing out on the late-night drunken shenanigans.)

At Chiang Rai airport, we were treated like celebrities and were ceremoniously presented with a plethora of gifts. There were some nice things: a 3'x2' collage of photos with a glass frame; various framed pictures, illustrations and artwork; Thai trinkets; a delicately woven silver box from the King. I was amused to receive a hanging garment bag from ThaiAir, to be used when travelling with nice suits.

'What on earth am I going to need this for?' I whispered to Connor as we accepted the parcels graciously. 'I don't even own a suit.

I'll never use this.' I thought of the time, just after university, when I was out of money and applying for a civil service administration job in London. I didn't have a suit to wear, but a friend was going to the same interview on the same day, so I borrowed his suit. My interview was first, and when it was finished, we changed in the toilets before he went in for his.[9]

I'd managed to get by without owning a suit my entire life, but they clearly had a much better idea of what was going to be happening to me in the coming months and years . . .

The requests and invitations will begin pouring in immediately after I return to Coventry: speaking engagements, publicity events, awards presentations. I'll hire a suit for the first few occasions, but as the invitations continue, I'll finally come to realize that it's time to own one for myself. A friend will take me to Birmingham for an uncharacteristic shopping spree, during which I'll purchase my first (unbelievably expensive) three-piece suit plus accompanying shirts, socks, ties, and shoes. The whole lot. A few days after that, I'll be packing the suit into its garment bag and taking it on a speaking tour.

The Queen's New Year's Honours List is announced at the end of each year, and we will all be included on it in 2019. John and I will be awarded the George Medal, the second-highest civilian gallantry award, which we'll receive at Buckingham Palace from the Queen and Prince William (respectively) in the spring; Chris and Jason will be given the Queen's Gallantry Medal; Josh, Connor and Vernon will be appointed MBEs.

In the summer of 2019, I will be awarded an honorary doctorate in Technology (Hon. DTech.) from Coventry University. For this ceremony, I won't have to worry as much about the suit I'll be wearing, as I will be adorned in traditional academic dress: cap, gown, robe with sashes. My mate Dan – the same one who'd driven me to Heathrow dressed in his Morris Dancing regalia – is a PhD and lecturer at Coventry University so he will also be there, wearing similar garb. 'These days, you always seem to be in costume when I'm with you,' I'll say to him as we stroll the university in our 'wizard robes' as he calls them.

Aston University will award me an honorary doctorate of Science. Forty years after beginning my studies there – and thirty-eight years after dropping out – I will finally receive a degree, and a DSc at that. Not bad for two years of (non-)attendance.

There will be further local awards – the *Daily Mirror*'s Pride of Britain, Coventry's Award of Merit. At the Thai Embassy in London, I will be presented with a Knight Grand Cross (First Class) – the Royal Decoration of the Most Admirable Order of the Direkgunabhorn – which, I believe, is the Thai equivalent to our knighthood. I became adept at writing speeches at the last minute, sometimes on scraps of paper while on the train to an event.

To round off the year, the whole group of us will be awarded medals from the Royal Humane Society, presented to us by Princess Alexandra at the Royal Geographic Society. Because John and I had previously been given a bronze medal for Eric Establie's search, we will be given silver medals which will then be promoted to gold medals. Yes, my first suit will be put to exceptionally good use through it all, as will the garment bag I always use to carry it.

This new stage of my life will not be without its share of problems, though. For the first time in my life I will find myself confronted with new issues such as having to find a steam iron (in Lisbon) when the hotel doesn't have anything. I will be amused to find John having the same experiences, and by the year's end we will both be proud possessors of travel steam irons.

Friday, 13 July 2018, London's Heathrow airport

When the seven of us landed in London early on Friday morning, we were greeted by Dr Peter Dennis, chair of the British Cave Rescue Council, who shepherded us to an area that had been laid out for a press conference. We didn't know what had been released publicly about the rescue and the sedation. There were rumours that the Wild Boars had been given tranquillizers, but nobody really knew yet what had happened. The use of ketamine was bound to be a contentious issue – which we knew would come out in time and be properly dealt with – but none of us wanted to be dealing with it there and then.

We were seated at a long table, facing a crowd of journalists and cameras, as Peter made a brief speech. 'We are here to welcome back our BCRC team from their support to one of the most extraordinary cave rescues that we have seen, ever . . . The international collaboration has been an inspiration . . . The Thai authorities asked for assistance from our volunteer organization, formed from cavers and rescue teams who've had decades of experience. The skilled cave-diving team that you see before you are in a class of their own . . .'

I was next to Peter and I heard him speaking, but the words were running through me. I had been thinking about the rescue for so long, now that it was all over I felt like my brain was still running but without a point of convergence. There were no formed thoughts, and I was having trouble focusing on any one thing. Being jet-lagged and hungover certainly wasn't helping.

'Do you consider yourselves heroes?' a journalist asked me after Peter finished speaking and turned it over for questions. *I've saved twenty-seven lives now . . . only four of which were lives I'd put into danger in the first place. That's not a bad ratio.*

'No,' I answered honestly. 'We were just using a very, very unique skill set – which we normally use for our own interest – and [in Thailand], we were able to give something back to the community, so that's what we did.'

That was important, and I wish I had spoken a bit more on this point. I'd spent all of my life building this skill set – always learning, always holding myself to a high standard so that I would progress – and it had all pretty much been for my own benefit. I'd contributed to exploration, but that had never been my true motivation. The main reason I cave dived was always for personal fulfilment. Simply, it was what I enjoyed doing, and I think now you can say that I had a flair for it. We all did – me, Jason and John worked together in a way that not many people are able to. I'd first identified it while watching *The Underground Eiger* when I was still a teenager, and my life since then had confirmed it.

To now, finally, have used these skills in a way that helped others was surprising, unplanned and fulfilling. I began to feel that maybe I hadn't wasted my life. People from around the whole world had worked together on this rescue, and I was proud to have been a part of that. Having said that . . .

'Is this the rescue you dreamed of doing?' one reporter asked me.

'No. It's the one I dreaded doing.'

After the press conference, lots of television shows approached us. One lady came up to me and asked, 'Would you all be prepared to go on *The One Show*?'

I remembered the disastrous appearance the three of us had had on the show following our Pozo Azul dive – when Dennis Waterman had run over, causing our bit to be cut. I agreed, but with a condition.

'Only if we can have Dennis Waterman as the guest after us,' I told her, with complete seriousness, and left it at that.

It will be years before I'll be able to go back and watch some of those very early interviews, and when I do, I'll be appalled by how gaunt and shell-shocked I appeared. After coming home, we will all be offered trauma counselling, if we wish to avail ourselves of it. This would be proper counselling – not the nonsense that the WMFS had offered after a critical incident, for which some bloke had taken a day's course and then half-arsed it – but I will turn it down. I believe counselling isn't necessary unless one is still dealing with residual thoughts six months after an event; I'd rather just let the natural things take their course and work themselves out.

As it was, the first few months back home will be a bit rough. I'll often wake up in the night, after a non-specific dream about an overwhelming task that has yet to be completed, but which I don't know how to do. We just don't know how. It will not necessarily be related to the cave – it could be anything – but it will always be that feeling. It will feel like waking up on the day of an important exam that I hadn't prepared for, and thinking, 'Shit, I have a big test ahead. I'm not ready.' This will happen frequently in the beginning, and will fade after about three months or so.

I will feel like I'd used up all of my thinking power for the year, and for the next few months I will rely on others to make my decisions for me. It will be a busy year – with all of the flying around to events, giving speeches, returning to Thailand – but I will pretty much be going on auto-pilot for most of it. I won't be giving too much thought to anything.

Friday, 13 July 2018, Coventry

The BCRC's treasurer drove me from Heathrow to Coventry, leaving me in front of my house around midday. I was relieved to see the garden was empty, as I'd been warned that there might be reporters waiting there for me. I knew that journalists had begun talking to my neighbours as soon as my identity as one of the divers who'd found the boys had been released. The press was tracking all of us down, looking for any way in. The level of press intrusion was such that they'd even managed to reach Angela and Jane for interviews. Angela is an ex-partner, and we have no traceable connections; Jane doesn't have my surname and has no internet presence. They certainly had to delve to find their information. My immediate neighbour was also approached but declined any comments and wouldn't answer their questions. 'I couldn't even tell you if he's married,' was his reply. The best they got from another neighbour was the comment: 'He's a quiet, unassuming man, who keeps himself to himself.' It's the classic line you'll always hear people say, even about murderers.

I unlocked the front door to my house painfully, with stiff and swollen fingers. Our hands had become cut up in the cave during the search, and those cuts had quickly become infected from the extended time spent in the water that was badly polluted with diesel and shit. (Those festering cuts will take months to heal completely.)

Inside the house, I began walking through and opening windows, turning on the water and electricity, settling back in at home. While I'd been away, Angela had looked after it for me, something I always count on her for when I'm away on extended trips. I depend on her for a lot and I'm grateful that she and I have stayed close friends, even after so many years. I called her to check in and let her know I'd returned, and we chatted for a while.

As I was hanging up the phone, I heard a knock on the door, and when I peeked out through the living-room window, I saw a reporter standing there. He stayed outside for the rest of the afternoon – camped out front, waiting for me to either arrive or leave. I let him sit there. If I needed to, I could go out through the garage to the alley behind the house, but I had no reason for leaving. I sat on the sofa, flipped on the telly and didn't move for the rest of the day.

I'm really proud of the fact that I've never hung wallpaper in my life, and I've hardly done any painting either. I'd always said that my plan for the house was to never do any decorating or repair-work. 'If I do no maintenance, then maybe when I die it will fall down around me, and bury me,' I'd tell people who criticized the state of my home. 'I'm just hoping it holds out until I pass away.' As I was sitting there, utterly exhausted and with my mind reeling from the events of the past eighteen days, I thought this would be as good a time as any for the house to cave in.

In the next few days, weeks, and months, I will be continually surprised by how emotionally involved people had become over the events in Tham Luang. We hadn't been aware of any of that while we were over there. Although we knew it had become a big story, we hadn't quite appreciated how emotionally invested people around the world had become. Back at home, people will be thrilled to see me, eager to congratulate me for the successful mission . . . and inevitably, they will end up in tears, crying as they thank me.

Whenever caving is shown on the telly or in the news, it's never a good story; in fact, it's often people's worst nightmare. I guess the thought of children being trapped, helpless, in that environment made it all too much for a lot of people to cope with. They thought they'd known how the story was going to end – they'd braced themselves for a tragedy, and the happy ending had been a surprise. 'It was like watching the ultimate reality TV programme,' a friend will tell me. 'I would tune in every day – for two weeks – to follow what was happening in these boys' lives. But this was real. I knew it could go either way . . . and I wasn't expecting it to go the way it did. I don't think anyone was.'

Monday, 16 July 2018, Coventry

I've agreed to an on-camera interview, which is going to be held at my house this afternoon. I look around the mess of the living room, whose floor is now packed with the gifts from Thailand, in addition to the usual assortment of kayaks and scooters. *Right. We'll be going outside for the interview.* I have a nice fence with ivy back there, so it will make a more agreeable backdrop. I go into the back garden to begin setting up, while I consider what I might say to the reporter.

As information about the ketamine has been released, people (unsurprisingly) began criticizing our decision to sedate the boys. None of us were bothered by the criticism. People who understand the risks we were facing have affirmed our decision while applauding us for being able to come up with a sound plan that included elements from outside of our skill set, finding the people to make it work and then executing it successfully.

Many people – in Thailand and around the world – immediately began referring to the rescue's success as being a 'miracle'. The Thai SEALs even went so far as to post publicly – 'We don't know if this is a miracle, a science, or what.' While I appreciate the sentiment of the statement, I think that calling it a miracle is a disservice to the people who made it happen. It hadn't been a one-off event. The rescue plan had been carried out successfully thirteen consecutive times, which I feel is the mark of planning and competence[10] more than a miracle.

I've also heard Tham Luang compared to some of the great rescues on record, including Apollo 13 and Ernest Shackleton's Antarctic expedition. These comparisons, while humbling, do feel closer to the truth. I understand now that what may look like a miracle from the outside can be explained by thorough preparation, risk management, confidence and maybe a bit of good fortune. Like ours, those rescues involved a lot of pieces moving together precisely; things may have seemed tenuous from the outside, but everyone on the inside knew what they were doing and why they were doing it. Similarly, despite the expected clashes and buffoonery at Tham Luang,[11] the teamwork shown was remarkable and contributed to the operation's success. Every person there was given the specific task that they were best suited for, and everyone had stepped up.

John and I have always said that it's better to be operating under our capacity, with the full confidence of those in control, than to be on the edge of our capacity. Even in Thailand, when things were most stressful, neither of us were ever beyond the edge of our capacity. People kept referring to us as heroes, who had put our lives at risk for the sake of helping others, but we didn't deserve such credit. The rescue had combined my two favourite things: cave diving and problem-solving. In spite of the stress and the risk to the boys' lives, it had boiled down to being a great logistical challenge, which I enjoy and was probably better prepared for than anybody else. My life probably had been leading up to that moment. Why would I have turned away?

For years, John and I had spent a lot of time thinking and talking about cave-diving rescue – contriving scenarios, discussing techniques. We'd been practising creative problem-solving, but the problems had always been imagined. We'd done all that practice, and at times we'd wished there were some way for it to be put to the test, so we had a way of knowing if our solutions would work in reality. Sometimes you'd better be careful what you wish for.

I'm really pleased that we were given the chance to solve the 'impossible' problem, and I am very proud of my involvement. Having said that, I would never wish for it to be repeated.

Since returning from Thailand, John and I have been spending a lot of time debriefing. We always go through this process after a dive – discussing a completed dive is part of planning for the next one. The rescue plan had been a success, and there's hardly anything – pretty much nothing – we'd have done differently. The only true regret about the rescue is the senseless death of Saman Gunan.

'Whoever dived with this must have had a right epic,' I had said to John on the last day of the rescue, after inspecting that massive bag of wetsuits that we'd found floating near Chamber 6. It turns out that Saman had been diving with that bag the night he'd died. Regardless of what Saman had been planning, the outcome was clear. His struggles with the huge, buoyant bag would have caused him to deplete his air rapidly. Where we'd found his bag was presumably where he'd turned around after realizing that he was in trouble.[12]

When the reporter arrives at my front door, accompanied by a cameraman, I lead them quickly through the ground floor of the house, through the sliding glass door at the back and out onto the paved garden. I've placed two chairs in the empty space and as the cameraman sets up his tripod, I see the reporter looking around. Is this what a hero's home looks like?

I'm still uncomfortable with that word I have been hearing for days.

I'd always said that I became comfortable public speaking as an adult while presenting at dive conferences, but the next year will really have me finding comfort on the stage as I begin drawing crowds of thousands for presentations I'll give about the Thailand rescue. I'll even be asked to give corporate talks, travelling on an international tour with IBM for one of their conventions. One of the appearances for that tour will be in Thailand, unsurprisingly, a country I will become quite familiar with.[13]

During another trip to Thailand, in March of 2019, I'll ask if it would be possible to see the boys from the cave again, and the meeting will be arranged. Our reunion will be disconcerting, not at all what I am expecting. The boys will seem stiff and uncomfortable as they're shepherded between rooms by the abbot of the monastery where the meeting is held. Titan's mother, who hugged me warmly the day I'd brought out her son, won't make eye contact with me, nor will any of the boys. There will be one brief moment of levity, when I make the boys laugh by 'bringing to life' the big stuffed wild boar they'd given to me as a memento, but it will be fleeting. It will all be quite tense, with the boys not seeming to be acting freely.

I'll return to worrying about the boys, even going so far as to tell John, 'I don't think we've saved them.'

As the reporter speaks with the cameraman, I sit down on the garden chair and look around me. I've been home for a few days now, but everything still feels a bit unreal, and I wonder if things will ever go back to the way they'd been before the rescue. I remember the words Amp had spoken to me as she ended her visit in Coventry – *'I really like your life. No pressure. Calm and exciting.'* How quickly things had changed.

I think back to the last time that had been calm, free and without pressure: it had been the weekend before I'd left for Thailand. A bunch of friends had gathered at Steve Joyce's house on that eventful Saturday (23 June) to finish cutting down a tree. Some of my oldest friends had been there – Steve and his twin brother Andy, Chris Cooke, Philip Hall, Pete Wilkinson, Adam Sargeant – all friends I've known since the early 1980s. Then on Sunday, Phil and I had gone off on a whitewater kayaking trip. It had been a lovely weekend with great company – relaxed and carefree. Back home on Monday, everything had quite suddenly become serious and stressful.

(*'Please call me the moment you wake up.'*)

I'd been deeply satisfied with my decision to take an early retirement from the fire service. I had taken advantage of my newfound freedom and sworn to never spend another day of my life working for somebody else. There would be no more commitments; my time would be my own, to do with as I pleased. I'd enjoyed that life for four years before being called to Thailand. Now, even with the rescue finished – successfully – and everybody back home, the demands and commitments were still pouring in, and I've struggled to find a free moment since returning home. Books, films, awards and honours, interviews . . . it all sounds glamorous until it consumes your life.

I'd nearly got out, but now I'm trapped in a cave of my own making – and I'll never get out of this one.

'Hey, Rick, have you started working on your book yet?' Steve had asked me at his house on the Saturday, with all of the other guys around to egg him on. For years, my friends had been telling me I should write a book of my cave-diving stories. They mostly did it to wind me up, as I'd never really entertained the thought seriously. Although I knew I had a book's worth of stories, anyone familiar with me would know that I'd never get around to writing them down.

'That would be too much work,' I'd said dismissively, remembering how much time and effort Duncan had spent when he'd written his memoirs a few years earlier. 'I can't be arsed.'

('Richard continues to do just enough to get by satisfactorily without putting himself out . . . ')

'You don't have to actually do the writing,' Steve had said. 'That's what ghostwriters are for. They'll do the work for you.' I had laughed at the idea then, but maybe I should reconsider it now. Maybe now I have a story I need to tell, and maybe I've found my voice.

I thought back to the message I'd sent to Karen from my computer three weeks earlier, while I'd been waiting for Dan to drive me to Heathrow: *'I'm on my way to Thailand . . . to meet up with a football team.'* When I'd sent that message, I'd had no clue what I was about to walk into. How could I have? Even now, I'm still trying to process everything that happened.

'Are you ready to get started?' the reporter asks as he sits in the chair across from me, and the cameraman starts filming.

I nod to the reporter. 'I'm ready.'

Yes, I think it's time I started working on that book. I even think I know who can help me. Since we met, Karen has been telling me I should let her write my book; maybe I'll give her a chance.

What could possibly go wrong?

Receiving the George Medal at Buckingham Palace in May 2019.

Notes

Prologue: The End of the Line

1 More on that later.

1. Water Flowing Underground

1 For anyone not familiar with the O-level system of school
examinations in the United Kingdom: I was sixteen years old
and just about to take my final qualification exams.
2 The Church of the Brethren is notable for its strong stance of
non-resistance and pacificism, as illustrated in its phrase 'all war
is sin'. Members of the Brethren are encouraged (and in earlier
times were forced) to live simple, monastic lifestyles, eschewing
many modern conveniences and luxuries in order to be more
ecologically friendly and have less of an environmental impact.
Although I have not followed a religious life, it is clear to me
now that many of the Brethren's core values have been passed
on to me through my upbringing.
3 When the war broke out, Dad filed as a Conscientious
Objector and, instead of fighting in the military, he served as a
firefighter.
4 Hamleys toy shop, on Regent Street in London, is one of the
oldest and largest in the world.
5 *The Underground Eiger* is a made-for-television documentary by
Sid Perou, documenting the historic cave dive of Geoff Yeadon

and Oliver Statham. The title alludes to the mountain in the Bernese Alps, the north face of which is considered to be one of the most dangerous and challenging ascents for mountain climbers. Although 20 million people – one-third of the nation – were watching that night when it was first aired on prime time, I'm sure few remember it as clearly as I do; nor were as affected by it as I would be.

6 This was actually staged for the film; in reality, it had been held a week earlier.

7 Said by Geoff Yeadon in *The Darkness Beckons*, by Martyn Farr.

8 The Coventry Cathedrals are not to be missed. Neither is the Broomfield Tavern, which is the local pub I tend to frequent. We spent more time at the latter than the former, and I was once again pleased to see that Amp had no trouble keeping up.

9 *Moo Baa* in Thai.

10 Stateless people include indigenous hill-dwellers and children of migrants who were born in Thailand. They have limited work options and are barred from voting, travelling outside their province and buying land; as a result of these restrictions, they often fall prey to traffickers looking to pull children into the drug trade.

11 A cultural tradition in Thailand, short, easy-to-remember nicknames are assigned by parents soon after birth. An official name is given weeks later and is largely reserved to be used in formal situations.

12 An alternative name for the mountain range containing Tham Luang cave is Doi Sam Sao (Three Rocks Mountains).

13 I wish that the rangers had been empowered to use their discretion for closing the park sooner when the need arose, but (from my understanding) Thai culture doesn't permit such

freedom to make autonomous decisions. I know that hindsight is easy, and there's no use in placing blame once something is finished, but I wish that the boys and Ek had not been condemned for entering the cave that day. They aren't the ones who should have known better. The cave should have been closed immediately following that torrent of rain.

14 The group of park rangers now included Petch, his chief and Wakulla Sipun (a fellow ranger who was familiar with the cave).

15 A tributary named Monk's Series flows from the north and intersects the main tunnel at this junction; the waters from the north and the south converge, and the united streams flow outwards towards the entrance.

16 From Langcliffe Pot in Yorkshire, in the 1970s.

17 All credit should be given to the ministers for their forward-thinking actions here. They showed both courage and competence by recognizing that Vern – an ordinary guy whom they'd never met before – was making a credible suggestion.

18 I quickly chastised Rob for his continued employment when I saw him at Heathrow, especially after learning that he had already survived three life-threatening illnesses. 'What are you still working for, you silly old duffer?' I asked him, with the grin that tends to stretch across my face whenever I'm thinking about how much I truly enjoy being retired.

19 Thanks to the coordinating effort of the BCRC, all divers and equipment would arrive at Heathrow, from points across Great Britain, within a few hours of notification.

20 John, who was in a business meeting and could not be interrupted, was left with even less time.

2. First Things First

1 Not owning any specific caving garments, I just wore my everyday clothes.

2 From the cave guidebook *Mendip Underground*.

3 Domestos is the name of a popular toilet-cleaning product in Britain, and the bend was so named by Pete Rose and Nick Chipchase because, as described by Chipchase, it was 'a bit like a toilet trap'.

4 I wouldn't achieve this comfort for myself until I was in my forties and had been speaking publicly for some time.

5 A cave is termed *active* if there is still a river flowing through.

6 I don't recommend this practice to anybody. As friends of mine have often been warned: it's typically not safe to try to emulate the things that I do. Ask Duncan Price about this, or just read his book *Underwater Potholer*, which chronicles how he learned this lesson for himself.

7 This can be attested to by anybody who knows me and has seen the holes in my shoes, my steady rotation of two to three favourite T-shirts at any one time, the broken reading glasses I continue to wear, the empty cupboards in my kitchen . . .

8 Rubber Wellington rain boots, so named for being worn by the Duke of Wellington, are the footwear of choice for UK cavers. They're inexpensive and they're robust. They're made of rubber and moulded, without any stitching or welts to fall apart. They grip well on wet rocks and they protect your ankles and shins. They're perfect for the job.

9 I recognized the images as ones that had been taken just hours earlier, at Heathrow.

10 My luggage on the flight had consisted of: two empty 7-litre cylinders; a 17-litre dry tube which would be used for carrying

items through the cave to the boys; two tackle bags holding dive line, wetsuits, wellies and other pieces of soft equipment; a big barrel with torches and loose diving hardware; and a small waterproof rucksack carrying my clothes and personal items.

11 Specifically, he reminded me of a character from *The Simpsons* television show. Later, a friend showed me a side-by-side comparison of Governor Narongsak and Hans Moleman (the unluckiest man in Springfield), and I have to admit that the resemblance was uncanny. All due respect to the governor.

12 That's an understatement. Some would say that I've structured my whole life to avoid children.

13 This went out live on Thai TV, as a prime example of how *not* to behave in front of the press.

14 Larry is an expert in search and rescue, as well as thermal imaging. He had acquired his impeccable American accent while obtaining a doctorate degree in Criminology from Pennsylvania State University and he currently held the rank of deputy commissioner in the tourism branch of the Royal Thai Police.

15 Larry introduced this guy as being a caver, but I didn't trust him. After a few unsatisfactory answers to simple questions, I made a mental note not to be involved with him. In the cave, he was useless. He didn't carry anything and, at the first sign of flood, he wanted to flee.

16 During the first few days, we were walking through deep mud, until finally they put down road stone in critical areas.

17 It usually takes people much longer to realize they dislike me.

18 From that point on, when Thais were helping us to carry our gear to the cave, John and I strategically placed ourselves – one in front, one in back – to ensure that none of them wandered off.

19 We shared the bed, placing a pillow lengthwise between us to form a divide, because that's what men do.

3. Finding What Works

1 Dido's is a flooded mine level which in all contains twelve sumps. This would be the site of another amazing rescue, conducted by Geoff Crossley and Chris Rhodes.

2 A note about silt-outs: in British cave diving, stirring up silt is never a consideration because there is no functional visibility to begin with. These caves up north are also peat-stained, and you can't ever see very far because the tannins absorb much of your light. British cave divers have to be adept at finding their way around in the murk. I know that there are huge protocols about not disturbing silt in clearer caves, but that doesn't exist in Britain. In fact, there's almost a perverse sense of trying to make it bad for the guys behind you. Duncan Price is a nightmare, he's the best (worst?) at creating these silt-outs. If anyone cared about silt-outs, he wouldn't ever be allowed to dive. (He's also the fastest, so he's always ahead and everyone has to fumble through the silt clouds he's disturbed.)

3 Years later, another team found a second, more accessible entrance to this passage. At first, I was disappointed that the exclusivity had gone, but on the other hand I was quite pleased because it is one of the finer bits of streamway in Yorkshire, and I'm glad more people get to see it.

4 We later learned that they were providing direct updates of our activities to the Minister for Tourism.

5 The SEALs' area was comprised of multiple adjacent gazebos, located directly beside the path leading to the cave's entrance. We had to walk through their area to get to the cave.

6 Surapin had a somewhat different version of events, as he expressed later in an interview for a documentary on Thai PBS: 'I tried to pass him. I was on the surface above him. He tried to

pull me down, but I struggled. I didn't trust him, you know. I tried to go up. Then my neck got caught by some electric wires in the cave. He dragged me down and I pulled him up. My mouthpiece was gone. At that point, I was about to drown. I struggled to breathe. I was thinking, "I mustn't die here!" I let go of him, but he kept holding me . . . My hand and head went up first as I didn't trust him. I pushed myself right up and hit the cave ceiling, cracking my head and ear. He dragged me down again . . . I accidentally hit him a little on the way up and then I felt some fresh air above. Now I darted away.'

7 Like many involved with the rescue, Surapin had been determined he'd be the one to save the Wild Boars. He never lost sight of his reason for being there. 'I'm not going home until I find the boys,' he'd said on many occasions. Although he didn't participate in the boys' rescue directly, his own rescue did help to inform the techniques we used, so he did have a role. Clearly not in the way he'd intended.

8 Lalochezia (n.): the emotional relief gained by swearing or using vulgar language.

4. Teammates and Rivals

1 CRO is one of over a dozen rescue groups scattered across the UK, each one formed to watch over the caves of their area, and is noteworthy for being the first of its kind in the world.

2 The lost cavers were eventually found and brought out safely.

3 Despite our differences, I do have to give the Rock Steady Crew credit here, for having a much better strategy for long-term exploration. While Ian and I enjoyed the bleak sparseness of our existence, it wasn't sustainable. They absolutely had it right

for continued long-term success. Ian and I had mopped up all the open leads, but they went on to find much cave through sheer perseverance.

4 The 320th Special Tactics Squadron of the US Air Force 353rd Special Operations Group was based at La Shima airfield in Japan. In addition to being the Air Force's only special operations rescue in the Indo-Pacific region, the 320th had capabilities suited for rescues in extreme environments (including mountains, jungles and underwater) and were trained in combat diving skills. Their training is one of the longest and most comprehensive special ops training courses in the world.

5 Charles Hodges has since been promoted to the rank of Lieutenant-Colonel.

6 I noticed that Ben, on the other hand, appeared quite comfortable in front of the cameras; John and I commented to each other that he was overly concerned for the media.

7 We now all have high-vis jerkins to take with us on future events.

8 This technique had proven effective during a 2010 cave rescue in Bulgaria. A group of cavers had been neck-deep in rising water until the water was suddenly released when boulders had been removed from the cave's resurgence, allowing the water to drain out. This type of engineering does have a place if you understand how to use it correctly, but it would not have been useful at Tham Luang.

5. Making Progress

1 She later confirmed that she had been, telling me that I had looked 'quite sexy' in my tight caving suit that weekend.

2 Among them were Pete Riley, Paul Whybro, Martin Holroyd, Rupert Skorupka and Geoff Crossley.

3 I was especially familiar with the standard fire service footwear: wellies. It became a joke that I spent much of my adult life wearing them.

4 This was the incomplete recovery of Roger Solari, following his death in Agen Allwedd.

5 Ukrainian by birth, Maksym had served in the French Foreign Legion. Although we didn't converse much, he looked like a solid, stoic, no-nonsense individual. I'm convinced he would have provided immense support for Ben.

6 Although the water was warm (23°C), body heat is lost quickly while submerged in water.

7 In reality, Captain Anand was the superior officer in Chamber 3, but because Jay was more fluent in English, we interacted with him much more.

8 UK divers tend to use 5mm polypropylene, which the rest of the world considers to be overkill; it's nicknamed 'elephant rope' by divers in warmer caves, where 2–3mm nylon line is more standard.

9 John had brought thick rope with him to Thailand to be used in case we encountered anything vertical.

10 In hindsight, we should have taken the time to reroute the line when we had the chance.

11 I've never been interested with pictures or filming while I dive (or any other time). If we ever had to film, John would always be the one to do it.

12 A note about 'Pattaya Beach'. A few years earlier, a ranger had incorrectly told Vern that the passage that contained the raised section – where the boys were found – is named Pattaya Beach, when in fact it's this indistinguishable stretch that bore that name.

Although this inaccurate naming did not have any negative effect on the search, it did result in the common belief that Vern was mistaken in his claim that the boys would be found at Pattaya Beach. He had the right location but the wrong name for it. I feel like Vern has never been given the credit he deserved for immediately predicting the boys' exact location inside the cave.

6. A Force of Nature

1 From the article 'Journey Towards the Center of the Earth' by Anne Goodwin Sides and Hampton Sides, for the *Washington Post*, published 28 August 1994.

2 This was something I'd learned to endure early on during my schooldays; by now I've come to accept it, and even encourage it – in the right context. My favourite example occurred in Spain, when I was sitting round a table with a bunch of Spanish divers. When I turned my head from one side to the other, all of the divers sitting across from me ducked in turn as my head passed.

3 For a complete recount of our dives together, I highly recommend reading Duncan's detailed and humorous memoirs, *Underwater Potholer*. His memory is much better than mine.

4 For the next few years, I worked with Duncan on a few projects inside Pwll-y-Cwm, which led to Daren Cilau.

5 His one on Earth anyway. Stone had already begun setting his sights on the Moon for future exploration.

6 Rebreathers have existed since the late nineteenth century and were extensively used during the Second World War, before the invention of open-circuit (Cousteau's aqualung). UK cave divers used them after the war, as there was a surplus of

military equipment, but the newest generation have been developed to work with mixed gases, allowing the diver to deliver the correct gas blend needed for the depth during deep, technical dives. These are electronically monitored.

7 Ian had been diagnosed with diabetes in 1992 and was vigilant in managing the condition to keep it from interfering in his life. He had immediately reported the diagnosis to Bill, prepared to be removed from the project, but Bill had been convinced that it would not pose an unmanageable risk.

8 A week later when I was home in Coventry and washing out the suit, I found myself retching at the smell of it.

9 I'd meet up with him again twenty-two years later, during a sea kayaking trip round Tasmania.

10 Four of his five cylinders were still filled.

11 Dom was the football team's captain.

12 Later, when I heard that a retired SEAL had died, I was dreading that it was Chenyatta, as I'd come to like him.

13 The Australian team at Tham Luang was comprised of six police divers from a special response group, a liaison officer and an official from the Department of Foreign Affairs and Trade (DFAT).

7. Spirit of Adventure

1 Dave will go down in cave-diving history as the person who coined the term 'snoopy loops' to describe the elastic bands – typically made from the inner tubes of tyres – that are used to secure and stow gear.

2 Isler, who worked as a science teacher, also designed and pioneered the drysuit dorsal buoyancy bladder, the integrated

p-valve, the auto-hoistable mini deco habitat and underwater scooter couplers.

3 During a trip to Bavaria with Angela in February of 1996 – not long after first meeting Jason – I had met up with a group of Germans who were support divers for Markus and Philip. The Germans had invited me to join their dive in May.

4 Like Isler, they were wearing very long free-diving fins, which I emulated for a while before going back to my ordinary fins.

5 The current configuration had been heavily adapted from the US system by Duncan Price and myself, during our dives in Pwll-y-Cwm. and Daren, where it proved to be highly effective in our exploration beyond the Gloom Room sump.

6 Mine was an Oceanic Mako, smaller and with less capacity than the Aquazepp.

7 I've still got those somewhere.

8 Leigh Bishop, a good friend and a technical diver who is a renowned underwater photographer, got a photo of it, which he put on the cover of a magazine.

9 We had Alien, Richard Hudson, Ian Williams and Pete Mulholland as our support divers.

10 Cave diving becomes a competitive sport when there is exploration involved. Everybody wants to be the first in. The ethics of exploration dictate that once a project has been claimed by a team that is actively working on it, all other explorers back off.

11 A boulder choke is a collection of large rocks that obstructs a shaft or passage in a cave or mine.

12 There were five big J cylinders of gasses and two compressors, more than thirty diving cylinders and all of our personal diving kit.

13 Gas blend of nitrogen and oxygen, with a higher O_2 concentration than breathing air.

14 I was, by then, kindly sponsored by drysuit manufacturer O'Three, and we received modest grants from a caving expedition fund.

15 I was easy to find on Facebook.

16 This had led to another issue, when I had worn my gritty wellies without socks during a long walk to the truck after a day of diving. I'd deeply abraded the skin on one ankle, an injury that was painful, quickly became infected and needed to be dressed every morning by Amp.

17 Which they did, quite literally. John and I would have our morning meeting with the Americans and we would tell them how things were going. Then they would go for a meeting with the Thais and relay the exact information we had just told them, but in a military language.

8. In My Element

1 'He wastes nothing, and he still cave dives using a red canoe helmet that I'd given to him after its chin strap had worn out. I have since wised up to Rick's ability to make do and mend: if he offers to dispose of anything I've broken, I realise that it can probably be repaired' (Duncan Price, *Underwater Potholer*).

2 At Cogol dei Veci in 2004, we were both diving on closed-circuit systems. After passing through the sump, John and I found a big dry passage leading to another sump, which I dived but did not pass. Returning in 2005, we camped in the galleries beyond the first sump, with Italian diver Luigi Casati coming through to help. We had a staggered start, and I

passed the second sump, finding further large galleries that lay beyond.

3 His film, *Into the Darkness*, would depict all aspects of the project – from logistics planning to fettling with equipment to diving and discovery.

4 The team included Jon Beal, Charles Reid-Henry, Gary Jones, Duncan Price, Andy Chell, Nick Lewis, Laura Trowbridge, Gavin Newman, Vic Cooper, David Haselden and some others.

5 Knowing that he wouldn't be able to follow us or repeat our dives, Gavin tasked us with wearing a helmet-mounted camera on one of our dives – which is how I ended up with that video through the gravel squeeze that leaves audiences on the edge of their seats.

6 Pinyo, of all the SEALs I interacted with, was probably the one I got to know the most. He seemed more understanding of matters.

7 Meals Ready to Eat. Although the vacuum-packed rations (commonly used by military in the field) are more palatable when heated, they're equally as nutritious when eaten at room (cave?) temperature.

8 Although the trip felt like it had taken for ever, in reality the bags only added thirty minutes to our previous dive time.

9 I hadn't been wearing my glasses when I'd been given the device, and all I saw were the letters CO, but had missed that the 2 was absent. This device measured carbon monoxide, not carbon dioxide. Had I known this, I would have taken in my own gas analyser. Mine is non-electrical, is equipped to measure oxygen and carbon dioxide and would have been more reliable in this situation.

10 The analyser is meant to be calibrated to 21 per cent in a 'clean fresh air' environment before being taken into the test environment, and this was impossible to do in the cave.

11 People assumed that the water would instantly go down as soon as the monsoon stopped, but Vern clearly indicated that there would be another three months after the rain stopped before it was clear to walk back there. In fact, it wouldn't be until March 2019 that Vern was able to lead the first dry trip to Chamber 9. Nine months.

12 A reasonable cave survey still carries a small percentage of error; with a 2,300-metre distance between the entrance and Chamber 9, the margin of inaccuracy was in the order of tens of metres, for a passage that was 5 metres wide. We'd worked out that the boys were 900 metres directly beneath the surface, which is beyond the range of any known location equipment; there'd be no way to accurately pinpoint where to direct their drills.

13 This technique had been used successfully during a cave rescue in France, but the rock there had been soft, and they'd only had to bore 30 metres down.

14 On Monday, they'd told John and me that they'd been swimming into the deep water surrounding their ramp: upstream for drinking water and downstream to relieve themselves. I've never understood where the press had got the idea that the boys couldn't swim.

9. Calling Out the Cavalry

1 https://www.theguardian.com/news/2018/jul/07/thai-cave-rescue-how-survivors-deal-trauma-ordeal.

2 Somewhere along the line, the Army Caving Association had been renamed the Combined Services Caving Association, now including military personnel from the Royal Navy, British Army and Royal Air Force.

3 In fact, British cavers had previously been trapped in the cave for a twenty-four-hour period during a flood.

4 In 2003, Jason and I had been working on connecting Saint Georges to Padirac, which was an important bit of exploration for me. I'd brought my friend – Irish cave diver Natasha Mitchell – along with me to France, to do some diving with her while I was there. Jason had said I wasn't focused enough on the project and he'd left without diving. I'd ended up diving alone, finding the connection, and celebrating over drinks at 2 a.m. with Tash.

5 Vern had given this same instruction to the Thai SEALs on the first day of the Tham Luang search, when they had still been able to walk to Sam Yaek. The SEALs ignored Vern's requests, but Jonathan listened to mine.

6 The underground communications device is able to transmit signals through rock.

7 They were down to their final meal, which they saved to be consumed on the morning of the rescue.

8 In addition to our diving gear, we'd flown to Mexico with eight cylinders, and the embassy had acquired a compressor in Mexico City.

9 This natural, adaptive response is called the Mammalian Diving Reflex.

10 https://www.theguardian.com/news/2018/jul/07/thai-cave-rescue-how-survivors-deal-trauma-ordeal.

11 This is what Harry said that I told him, and in essence it is correct. I don't remember my exact words. The full account of Harry's and Craig's involvement in the rescue is told in their book, *Against All Odds*.

12 Mike Clayton is a friend of mine, and Emma Porter's partner. They live not far from me, and we see each other occasionally. Recently, we've been doing more kayaking together than caving, though, and Emma has dubbed our growing group 'Cavers Who Kayak'.

13 Having the word *controller* in their title caused some consternation, as people assumed that they were going to arrive and take over control. This is what they're called in UK rescue circles; in Thailand, their role was to provide logistical support. They freed us from having to manage the message-sending, note-taking, meetings, etc. Their presence gave us more freedom to concentrate.

14 I have since done the calculations to confirm my scepticism. It would never have worked.

15 Chris had led a very impressive and involved UK expedition to dive the sump at the bottom of San Agustín.

16 With the arrival of the others from the UK, we had been allocated a second, much-needed room; this was adjacent to our original one and would give us a clearer space to use for planning. Amp had happily helped me to move our map into the more palatable surroundings, relieved to no longer have to bear the stench of urine-soaked neoprene that had overpowered our gear room. (Divers piss in their wetsuits, and as this room doubled as our changing room, it had been holding our soiled wetsuits for days. The smell had become quite foul.)

17 Gary, Mike and Martin Ellis had all arrived at Tham Luang on Friday morning.

18 Josh had been on holiday in the Italian Dolomites. After receiving our call, he'd had to fly home, repack his bags for Tham Luang and fly right back out.

10. Mind What You're Doing

1 It was like an upside-down version of Poetic Justice in County Pot, of the Easegill System.

2 My friend Mark Dougherty, who had worked with me on Gingling Hole, was living in Sweden at the time and was appointed as surface team leader for the operation. Without any local divers who were qualified to search for the missing diver, Mark put forward my and Jason's names to the Norwegian authorities.

3 Note: Neither *flying at high altitude with decreased oxygen*, nor *diving deep in cold water* are ideal activities for nursing a hangover.

4 Harry will say that I broke his light, because it was in my hands when it stopped working, but I disagree. The light failed.

5 These divers and others would come back in later years to continue exploration.

6 The cylinders staged at the habitat contained breathing mixtures that were not safe to be breathed at greater depths; they were of no use to me where I was.

7 The gas was low-oxygen, high-helium, which was safe to breathe but was not contributing to my off-gassing and decompression.

8 The Americans went to local shops and bought up all the bungee luggage ties they could find.

9 Quite fortuitously, of the load of masks the Americans had with them, they had four that were positive pressure.

10 If the mask's seal did fail, all wasn't necessarily lost, as we would never be more than a seven-minute dive away from an airspace. We could all do CPR, with varying degrees of competence.

11 The Australian Antarctic Division – a subsection of the Department of Agriculture, Water and the Environment – leads the Australian government's scientific programme in Antarctica, researching such issues as climate change, conservation and sustainability.

12 Several of the Wild Boars in the cave attended this school, so they had happily opened the pool for us.

13 It seemed unlikely that we would need this, and I was genuinely not concerned. There is not a blame culture in Thailand, which was most evident when the parents showed genuine appreciation for how Coach Ek cared for the boys inside the cave, instead of seeing him as the villain who was at fault.

11. A Bunch of Baldy Boffins

1 http://archive.divernet.com/cave-diving/p302437-diving-everest-in-pozo-azul.html.

2 Following Isler's lead, Jason and I had both begun using ride-on scooters during the Ressel dives. We're pretty much the only group of divers that use ride-on scooters today. They're old-fashioned but much more comfortable and practical for our long dives, especially when we're heavily laden.

3 Jason had run out of line and had four more hours of decompression to complete so – not knowing when the sump would surface – he'd turned around.

4 Including the dive through the first sump, then setting up for the next dive, then a six-hour dive through the second sump, time spent in Tipperary and the third sump; then doing it all again. At least sixteen of those hours had been on my own.

5 The photograph on the cover of this book was taken by Martyn on that 2010 trip to Pozo Azul.

6 To date (2021), only seven have passed through.

7 Remember Chambers 7 and 8 have now been combined into one dry, walkable passage, as a result of the water diversion and pumping efforts.

8 After our initial briefing with the governor at the airport, we'd not had much interaction with him. His role seemed to be as a spokesperson, giving speeches for the press. He was good at it.

9 The industrial oxygen cylinders used to fill the diving cylinders were at a lower pressure than we were used to. To fill the diving cylinder, it had to be topped up with air; this is why we couldn't have pure 100 per cent O_2.

10 Claus and Mikko were both skilled divers, but with limited dry-caving – and no prior sump-diving – experience. In this case, they had difficulty recognizing one part of the cave from the one where they should have been. The Americans' ROC had not taken into account the cave's lack of defining features. We had placed number boards – laminated pieces of A4 paper – labelling Chamber 5 and Chamber 6, but we hadn't done this for the final chamber; maybe we should have.

11 The boys' loss of temperature once in the water was a concern, but as soon as they were sedated, the shivering stopped, and we

moved them as efficiently as possible. Even so, they all had significantly lowered body temperatures when they were checked in hospital. Most were around 33–34°C, and one was as low as 29°C; he required active rewarming.

12 Much after the event, it became clear that Chris was more uncomfortable with the responsibility than he had ever let on. He'd requested Mikko's support, and at one point asked Mikko to take over through the most challenging section (between Chambers 4 and 3). When Mikko couldn't do it himself, he handed the boy back to Chris.

13 For the future rescues, when I swapped the boy's cylinder, I kept the mask on and let him go without breath for the few seconds I needed for the swap. This was a much smaller risk than tampering with the mask's seal unnecessarily.

14 In the confusion brought about by trying to work as a pair in poor visibility, Erik and Ivan had immediately become separated during their dive to Chamber 6. This had caused tension, which Erik was able to recover from, but Ivan was badly affected by it.

15 Although we were all wearing helmets, we had elected not to put them on the boys for two main reasons: 1) to allow freer access to their masks, should we need to adjust/remove them, and 2) to eliminate the risk of the helmets dislodging their masks.

12. Once in a Lifetime

1 I probably wouldn't even consider this a recovery, as there was no body. It was more like retrieving remains.

2 So named because it is meant to be used underground.

3 This sediment became so deeply engrained into the fabric of my drysuit that it would take months of use for it to rinse out.

4 I'm only aware of a handful of underground avalanches. One was in Indian Springs, Florida. Two men were trapped, one dug himself out. The other was in Saint Sauveur. It occurred after my first dive there and was one of the reasons I wasn't able to go back for years – the cave was closed for approximately eighteen months. Miraculously, nobody was inside when it happened.

5 Another diver had been to this point on his previous dive with Eric, and I'm led to believe he'd recognized the risk of an avalanche, but we had never been told about it. I was furious that we hadn't been given the full picture of what we had been heading into.

6 The news had been restricted by the SSF divers, so it could be broken to his family by the appropriate channels.

7 This is a favourite programme of mine. Angela constantly compares me to Sheldon, but I don't see any similarities.

8 Same as Thailand – it's a lovely place to visit, but we were there at the start of the monsoon, when the tourists have the sense to stay away.

9 I'd had some discussions with Sami Paakkarinen, another Finnish diver who'd originally made the connection. With him competently leading the recovery team, I knew it was in good hands.

10 The Finnish diver who'd instigated that fateful Plura trip went on a dive in a deep French cave, which resulted in the death of another dive partner.

11 While we were in the cave continuing the rescues, Ivan spent the day in front of cameras speaking about how emotional the whole thing had been.

12 For the record, none of the boys remember anything of the journey. They have no memory between sitting on Harry's knee and waking up in hospital.

13 I noticed he didn't hover around the doorway or windows during his visit. Maybe that was deliberate.

14 Ek was the liveliest of all of the rescuees, struggling even while sedated. At one point, he managed to grab the hose of Jim's regulator with his bound hands. Jim was really put to the test by Ek, but he performed capably. Harry told me later he'd given Ek the choice of diving out without being sedated. Thankfully, Ek had chosen to be sedated. I think it was daft of Harry to have given him the choice; I wouldn't have dived out with him if he'd been conscious. I don't think any of us would have.

15 The park was dry, and this was the first time I'd seen alcohol on site.

13. Surface Reflections

1 Despite some close friends disagreeing with me, as they thought it would make me look weak.

2 It's especially ironic that, after everything, I would become most celebrated for my involvement with a group of children.

3 He was my greatest advocate. Partly because of the profile I was getting with my rescues, he began championing me. He respected what I'd made of myself, and we got on, which may have pissed off some of the mid-level officers.

4 In 2013, Jason and John had carried in wetsuits and wellies for Razor Passage, then dived through Sump 4 to reach Razor Passage 2. In 2014, Jason and René got to the end of Razor 2, and into the next sump.

5 The irony being, of course, that when I began sea kayaking, I essentially switched from one gear-intensive activity to another – 'Richard traded one obsession for another' – but at least

now, instead of going around to different parts of the world and sticking my head in a muddy puddle, I was going on a journey and seeing something. It felt more worthwhile.

6 This gave me two 'getting dived-up' trips in the month before we were called to Thailand. Did fate know where my destiny lay?

7 Jason and I each pocketed one of the life jackets that had been used; we figured we'd earned the memento for our troubles.

8 I remarked to the others that it was a good job we hadn't been staying in such opulent conditions, and with a 40-minute drive to the cave. It would have been harder to get our act together every morning.

9 We were both hired for the job, so it must have been a good suit.

10 Competence = a combination of: training, skills, experience, knowledge and the ability to successfully and consistently apply all of those things to complete a task, even while under pressure.

11 I've been critical of Thailand's response at some stages, but the truth is that no country would have been prepared for that. It had been a perfect storm – a sudden onslaught of natural disaster and personal tragedy, a high-risk rescue conducted in the glare of the global media.

12 By the time of Saman's death, the Euro Divers and Thai SEALs had already left bundles of air cylinders in that section of the cave, and he must have passed numerous full cylinders as he'd made his way to Chamber 3. Had he seen it as a loss of face to take one of those cylinders, which had been left for the rescue?

13 In the lobby of the Meriden hotel, there's now a statue of an elephant adorned with the faces of the rescuers. Harry was keen to point out that, for some reason, my face is on its ass.

Glossary

Aven: In a cave, a vertical space that usually requires climbing.

Buoyancy control: Control of vertical movement in a water column (i.e. ascending, hovering or descending with control). This is accomplished by managing the quantity of air in an air bladder (e.g. a buoyancy device or *wing* and/or *drysuit*).

Buoyancy device: See *wing*.

Closed-circuit: See *rebreather*.

Cockwomble: A foolish person, usually male, prone to making outrageously stupid statements and/or behaving inappropriately while generally having a very high opinion of himself. Can be used endearingly, as most British insults can and often are.

Counterlung: A gas-filled, flexible bladder for the *rebreather* user to inhale from and exhale into.

Death stare: I have been told that, when I am displeased with somebody's actions, I possess a certain look which perfectly conveys my thoughts, without using words.

Decompression injuries: The inert gases (e.g. helium, nitrogen) that are used to avoid oxygen toxicity or nitrogen narcosis become dissolved in the body's tissues. Following a *decompression schedule* during a slow, gradual ascent allows them to be released in a controlled manner. Failure to do this will result in decompression injuries (aka 'the bends') that are painful at best, lethal at worst. Jochen Hasenmayer, a pioneer of *trimix* diving, was himself the victim of one such injury. In 1989, after surfacing too quickly from a deep dive, he suffered a severe case of the bends and was left paralysed.

Decompression schedules: These are the guidelines that let a diver know how much time they need to spend at specific depths to release the inert gases before it is safe to ascend to a shallower depth. Today, these complex schedules are often generated by a wrist-worn computer.

Demand valve: See *regulator*.

Dive Propulsion Vehicle (DPV): Also known as a 'scooter', a propeller driven by a battery-powered motor, encased in a pressure-resistant watertight hull, used to pull a diver along more efficiently, thus conserving gas used during a dive.

Drysuit: As the name implies, a drysuit keeps the diver dry. By keeping water out and air in, a drysuit is important for thermal protection. By holding air inside, it is also used – sometimes in conjunction with a *wing* – to control a diver's buoyancy.

Fettle: To tinker with something in a purposeful way, usually with the aim of making it work or assembling it. It can also refer to concentrating on a task out of all proportion to its apparent consequence, like spending an hour to fit three small screws. (It does have a technical definition in metalworking, but it's been misappropriated by cave divers.)

Fiddle job: A second job. Many firefighters have a trade that they pursue on their days off. Mine was caving.

Flood pulse: The rapid transit of a deluge of water through a watercourse (above or below ground) following a period of rain. It appears as a wall of water rather than a gradual, steady increase in flow.

Free dive: One in which the diver holds their breath while underwater, without using any breathing apparatus.

Gravel slope: When a passage ascends and the river can't carry the heavier sediment load, it is deposited and forms an inclined slope of mobile gravel. In flood, the gravel is pushed further up the slope, making the passage larger for the increased flow; during normal flow, it then slumps back down again, coming to rest at the angle of repose. This slope remains unstable.

Habi-bin: A *habitat* made from an inverted garbage bin.

Habitat: An underwater structure where a diver can complete decompression without being fully submerged, so they can remove their *regulator* and breathe gas that is being pumped in from the surface.

Heyphone: Underground communication device.

High Pressure Nervous (or Neurological) Syndrome (HPNS): This can result from breathing helium at elevated partial pressures, a risk for dives below −150 metres depth. Its principal manifestation involves tremors and shakes.

JCB: A commercial brand of a backhoe excavator.

Lalochezia: The emotional relief gained by swearing or using vulgar language.

Land Rover Defender: A British off-road vehicle that spends much of its time off road in the garage. Capable of going anywhere, when it is working.

Master cave (or main drain): A main underground drainage pathway for a watershed. Streamways from all other caves collect into this one channel. Think of it as a street's drainage collection, where each house feeds into the main drain.

Nitrox: Enriched air nitrox (EAN) is a nitrogen/oxygen combination in which the oxygen is higher than the 21 per cent found in standard breathing air.

Open-circuit: The most commonly seen diving equipment, where gas is breathed from cylinders via a *regulator*, and each expired breath is released into the water as bubbles.

Perched: A caver's term to describe a cave in which the terminus is located at a significantly higher elevation than the water's *resurgence*. This indicates that dry passage exists between the two.

Pinhole lens technique: My *cockwomble* technique of using my fingers and thumb pinched together to aid with reading; useful when I've misplaced (forgotten) my reading glasses.

Pothole: A British term for a specific type of cave that contains tall vertical shafts; potholes are common in Yorkshire and Derbyshire.

Rebreather: Instead of breathing from an *open-circuit* system that releases wasteful bubbles, a rebreather is a closed system where the diver's exhaled breaths are recirculated, a soda lime *scrubber* material is used to remove exhaled carbon dioxide, and then oxygen is added (either manually or electronically) to fuel the diver's metabolism. No bubbles are released, so no oxygen is wasted, making the system more efficient.

Regulator, or reg: A diving regulator (frequently called a 'reg' or 'demand valve' in the UK) is used to regulate pressure, reducing it through two stages to allow the diver to breathe the compressed air in their cylinder at ambient air pressure.

Resurgence: A point at which an underground stream resurfaces; it often appears like a spring.

Scooter: See *Dive Propulsion Vehicle*.

Scrubber: A soda lime material used in closed breathing systems to remove excess carbon dioxide (CO_2) from expired gas. The soda lime essentially 'scrubs' the gas clean so it can be breathed again, hence the name. This is also the component name of the canister that holds the soda lime.

Siphon: See *sump*.

Snoopy loops: Elastic bands cut from inner tubes, which are used by cavers to hold their gear in place. The name was given by Dave

Morris when he made a new usage for the word 'snoop' to describe the motion of stretching the rubber band into place.

SRT: Single Rope Technique.

Stage cylinders, or staging a dive: Extra supplies of gas placed in strategic locations or carried on you, to ensure gas is where you (might) need it during a dive.

Sump: A portion of a cave that is filled completely with water with no airspace overhead. Continuing through a sump requires diving.

Trim: During a dive, *trim* refers to the horizontal positioning of a person or object.

Trimix gas blend: Combining oxygen, nitrogen and helium to increase a diver's depth capabilities and duration while avoiding oxygen toxicity, nitrogen narcosis and *decompression injuries*.

Wellies: Rubber Wellington rain boots, so named for being worn by the Duke of Wellington, are the footwear of choice for UK cavers, as well as firefighters. I feel like I've spent more of my life in wellies than any other form of footwear.

Wing or buoyancy device: An air bladder that is worn on the diver's harness to control buoyancy and vertical movement in the water.

Acknowledgements

The first thing I should probably acknowledge is that I have a 'selective' memory for people, places, dates, and details. Just about anything that happens outside of a cave is not guaranteed to be remembered accurately, if at all, which is one of the reasons I've put off writing this book for as long as I have. As such, this section will be briefer than it should be, and not as many people will be personally thanked as deserve to be. Please know that I appreciate every person I've met along the way who has provided support in so many ways, helping me to reach the ends I've been searching for.

Every caver who has lugged equipment and cylinders underground to help me set up for exploration, then spent time mapping the discovered sections when I couldn't be bothered.

Every person who has sat on the surface, waiting in support, while I was having 'fun' underground.

Every friend who has been ignored while I was focused on a project and who was still there waiting when the project was over.

I thank you all.

I wouldn't have got to the places I have if it hadn't been for each and every one of you.

Now, for the book.

As mentioned, people (predominantly Steve Joyce) had been telling me for years that I should write this book. After the events in Thailand, those suggestions became requests and then demands, but I wasn't convinced until one night in a pub, when journalist David Rose persuaded me that it was time I finally set my focus on something above the surface and away from the water's edge. I agreed – not for financial gain or acclaim, but because I realized I now had a story that needed to be told with worthwhile messages to share. What followed were many months of David listening to my endless stories, asking questions and taking notes that somehow managed to be assembled into a coherent report from which this book was eventually crafted.

Not only did David convince me to get started and work with me through the tedious beginning stages, but he also made the connection with Rowland White, Publishing Director at Penguin's Michael Joseph imprint. Agreeing to publish my book was the easy part for Rowland; what would follow were two years of trials and challenges that I'm sure he was not expecting. When David and I parted ways, I insisted that Karen be given the chance to work with me on the book's revised concept – despite her distinct lack of writing credentials. He agreed to this unusual request and then stood by for the next nine months, probably expecting very little to come of it, and when we handed him this manuscript, he sprang into action to ensure its speedy publication. The fact that you're now reading these words is a testament to the tenacity of everybody involved with this book.

If David started the process, and Rowland plus his team at Michael Joseph completed it, there were many others who helped along the way.

I should probably thank Karen for putting up with me whilst we were writing the book; most people were amazed we managed to work together for so long without falling out. Karen would like to thank the people who were always willing to help when she came up with a question that I couldn't answer. Duncan Price, Steve Joyce, Pete Riley, Dan Goldsmith, John Volanthen and Richard Harris were all turned to repeatedly, and they came through every time. She's grateful that their memory is stronger than mine.

Thanks also to those who generously provided time, information and interviews to David Rose: Steve Joyce, Jane, Sallie and Betty, amongst others. Thanks to Duncan, Linda Wilson, and Chris and Jacquie Danilewicz, who then provided input and comments.

Karen and I would like to thank the members of our own sounding board: Pete Riley and Linda Palmer, Angela Timms and Martin McCrystal. The valuable feedback you provided to us has helped to shape this story into its finished product.

I cannot fully express my gratitude to Linda Wilson for acting as an advisor and friend throughout this whole process. From reviewing early manuscripts to providing legal advice over contracts, your input and support have been invaluable to me along the way. I'm lucky to know somebody as knowledgeable and generous as you are. Thank you for sticking through this with me.

Finally, my heartfelt thanks to everyone who provided support during the Thailand rescue. From Bill Whitehouse, Emma Porter and the volunteers within the BCRC, to Vern and Rob, Amp, Derek, Tom and Bas, and the local residents who looked after us — there are too many of you to name here, but I hope this book has given everyone the credit they deserve.